CIPS Study Matters

Level 5

Advanced Diploma in Purchasing and Supply

COURSE BOOK

Management in the Purchasing Function

Printed and distributed by the Chartered Institute of Purchasing & Supply

Easton House, Easton on the Hill, Stamford, Lincolnshire PE9 3NZ

Tel: +44 (0) 1780 756 777

Fax: +44 (0) 1780 751 610

Email: info@cips.org

Website: www.cips.org

First edition August 2006
Second edition July 2007
Third edition April 2009
Reprinted with minor amendments October 2010

Contents

Preface

Welcome to your new Study Pack.

For each subject you have to study, your Study Pack consists of three elements.

- A **Course Book** (the current volume). This provides detailed coverage of all topics specified in the unit content.
- A small-format volume of **Passnotes**. For each learning objective, these highlight and summarise the key points of knowledge and understanding that should underpin an exam answer. Use your Passnotes in the days and weeks leading up to the exam.
- An extensive range of **online resources**. These include a **Quick Start Guide** (a rapid 40-page overview of the subject), practice questions of exam standard (with full suggested solutions), notes on recent technical developments in the subject area, and recent news items (ideal for enhancing your solutions in the exam). These can all be downloaded from the study resources area at www.cips.org. You will need to log in with your membership details to access this information.

For a full explanation of how to use your new Study Pack, turn now to page xv. And good luck in your exams!

A note on style

Throughout your Study Packs you will find that we use the masculine form of personal pronouns. This convention is adopted purely for the sake of stylistic convenience – we just don't like saying 'he/she' all the time. Please don't think this reflects any kind of bias or prejudice.

October 2010

The Exam

The format of the paper

The time allowed is three hours. The examination is in two sections.

Section A – case study scenario, with two application questions based on the case study, each worth 25 marks.

Section B – questions to test knowledge and understanding. Candidates will be required to answer two questions from a choice of four. As with Section A, questions will be worth 25 marks each.

The unit content

The unit content is reproduced below, together with reference to the chapter in this Course Book where each topic is covered.

Unit characteristics

This unit is designed to enable students to manage their own area of responsibility within an organisation's internal supply chain, in line with the overall strategic business plan and the operational plan for the purchasing function.

Students should be able to implement operational plans for their own area of responsibility to achieve objectives set out in their plan. In doing so they should be able to employ a range of resources, including human, physical and financial resources, and manage and delegate tasks effectively.

This unit is about managing the expectations of the stakeholders that are directly involved in the student's own area of responsibility and will provide them with management techniques to help them to involve others, be innovative, consultative, influential and persuasive in order to achieve targets effectively.

This unit at level 5 is concerned with the day to day management responsibilities within the purchasing function and wider organisation and appropriate links and understanding of the relevant theories.

Statements of practice

On completion of this unit, students will be able to:

- Evaluate the challenges facing managers in dynamic and changing organisations
- Analyse the characteristics of different organisational structures and cultures
- Use a range of techniques to support and implement justifiable management decisions
- Formulate plans to effectively manage work groups and teams
- Propose processes and systems to enable the successful implementation of change programmes to maximise purchasing efficiency and effectiveness
- Assess the impact of current legislation relating to employment and equality upon purchasing and supply activities

Learning objectives and indicative content

1.0 The challenges of management
(Weighting 20%)

		Chapter
1.1	Define the term management and differentiate management from leadership	
	• Definitions of management: Fayol, Mintzberg, Drucker, Brech and Cole	1
	• Management: planning, coordinating, controlling and motivating staff	1
	• Management styles	1
	• Leadership perspectives and styles: Hersey and Blanchard, Tannenbaum and Schmidt, Kotter, Lewin	1
1.2	Identify the key stakeholder groups who impact directly on the purchasing function, analyse their potential impact and explain how to manage their expectations effectively.	
	• Stakeholders: employees, customers, shareholders, suppliers, government, lenders, trustees, elected members	2
	• Identifying and fulfilling stakeholder/customer needs: good products and service, return on investment, quality, price and measurable outcomes	2
	• Working within ethical codes of conduct and practice	2
	• Expectations: on time, within budget, meeting terms and conditions	2
1.3	Evaluate the key roles and functions of managers in the purchasing and supply function	
	• Ensuring value for money/quality at the lowest price (purchaser)	2
	• Advising and recommending suitable purchasing and supply systems	2
	• Building good relationships within the purchasing and supply chain	2
	• Management of resources (human, financial, materials, equipment) to be effective in the role	2
	• Policy development	2
1.4	Compare and contrast the diverse purchasing management practices of the private and public sectors	
	• Tendering	2
	• Recommended suppliers	2
	• E-commerce: internet, e-auctions, e-catalogues, electronic data interchange (EDI)	2
	• Outsourcing	2
	• Authority levels (ie purchase orders)	2
	• Relationship building	2
	• Payment terms and other contracting arrangements	2

		Chapter
2.4	Define the term culture and assess different models of culture which may exist within organisations	
	• Definitions and terms associated with culture	6
	• How organisational culture impacts on behaviour, values and assumptions	6
	• Organisational influences of company politics, power, bureaucracy, rules and standards of behaviour	6
	• Models of cultural strength, masculine/feminine societies, cultural values and individualism/collectivism	6
2.5	Evaluate methods and formulate plans for managing effectively in international or cross-cultural organisations	
	• Stages of planning	6
	• Methods: managerial and leadership styles, approaches, communication and media channels	6
	• Evaluation process of research (primary and secondary), conducting pilot schemes, gathering feedback from staff and choosing most successful option	6
	• Considerations: cultural diversity, existing structures, codes of conduct, differing goals and expectations	6
3.0	**Management decision making** (Weighting 15%)	
3.1	Evaluate and apply a range of tools to make effective management choices and decisions	
	• Problem solving and decision making process	7
	• Pareto analysis, Ishikawa (fishbone) diagram, strengths, weaknesses, opportunities, threats (SWOT), decision making trees, cost/benefit analysis, risk evaluation, paired comparison analysis	7
	• Balanced scorecard (BBS)	7
3.2	Explain how to formulate, implement and monitor operational plans for the purchasing and supply function to achieve organisational objectives	
	• Aligning plans with strategic objectives/direction of organisation	8
	• Agreeing objectives and targets: reducing defects, improving lead times, reducing costs	8
	• SMART principles	8
	• Importance of and ways to involve the team in the planning process	8
	• Monitoring systems and processes including annual and periodic reviews	8
	• Reporting structures	8

		Chapter
3.3	Evaluate the resource requirements for the implementation of operational plans for the purchasing function	
	• People as a resource	8
	• Financial resources	8
	• Physical resources	8
	• Time	8
4.0	**Managing work groups and teams** (Weighting 25%)	
4.1	Evaluate the concept of authority, delegation and accountability when managing the purchasing function	
	• Understanding of key concepts: taking ownership, decision making, empowerment and responsibility	9
	• Reasons: workload, prioritising, developing individuals and the team, minimising blame and achieving results	9
	• Good time management	9
	• The delegation process	9
4.2	Apply techniques for building, motivating and managing successful teams within the purchasing and supply function	
	• What is a team/group?	10
	• Stages of team development: Tuckman and Jensen	10
	• Team roles: Belbin, Schutz, Holland, Cattell	10
	• Building a balanced team	10
	• Motivational determinants: innate drive, desire, fulfilling need	10
	• Satisfying individual and team needs: praise, rewards, recognition, responsibility, promotion, pay	10
	• Building relationships through leadership, with trust, fairness, equal opportunities, ethics and respect	10
4.3	Assess the sources of conflict which may arise within the purchasing function	
	• Disagreement about needs, goals, values, priorities and interests	11
	• Poor communication	11
	• Lack of trust in leadership	11
	• Lack of direction	11
	• Lack of clarity in role	11
	• Scarcity of resources	11
	• Interpersonal and hygiene issues	11

		Chapter
4.4	Explain how to build relationships and encourage integration with other parts of the business.	
	• Changing perceptions of purchasing (from process to advisory)	11
	• Advocates for the profession/business	11
	• Consultancy	11
	• Adding value	11
4.5	Evaluate techniques to deal with conflict within teams and between individuals in the purchasing and supply functions	
	• Consultation	11
	• Mediation	11
	• Negotiation	11
	• Arbitration	11
	• Dispute resolution (including discipline and grievance)	11
4.6	Assess the benefits of a systematic approach to recruitment, appraisal, training and development	
	• High calibre of staff	12
	• Recognition of achievement	12
	• Conducting appraisals/personal development reviews (PDRs)	11
	• Identification of development needs	12
	• Providing appropriate training to meet individuals' role needs	12
	• Retention	12
	• Contented workforce	12
	• Maintaining high levels of performance	12
5.0	**Managing change** (Weighting 20%)	
5.1	Evaluate the causes of organisational change	
	• Globalisation	13
	• Competition	13
	• Growth	13
	• Diversification	13
	• Performance	13
	• Technology	13
	• Practical analysis using political, economic, social, technological, legal and environmental (PESTLE), SWOT and Lewin's model: forces for change	13

		Chapter
5.2	Differentiate between the need for fundamental and incremental change in organisations	
	• Sector characteristics and dynamics	13
	• Takeovers, mergers and embracing cultural changes	13
	• Response to market demand	13
	• Quality and continuous improvement	13
	• Meeting customer requirements	13
5.3	Formulate plans to overcome human resistance to change and to implement change successfully within the purchasing and supply function	
	• Psychological barriers	13
	• Physical barriers	13
	• Achieving commitment from staff	13
	• Staff involvement	13
	• Devolving responsibility	13
	• Monitoring results	13
5.4	Identify and analyse the current legislation relating to employment and equality of opportunity in organisations.	
	• The Equal Pay Act 1970 (as amended)	14
	• Employment Act 2002 and Dispute Resolution Regulations (2004)	14
	• Health and Safety at Work Act 1974	14
	• EU Employment Directives, TUPE, equal treatment, working time, young people	14
	• Disability Discrimination Acts 1995 & 2005	14
	• Employment Equality (Age) Regulations 2006 and Amendment Regulations 2008	14
	• Sex Discrimination Act 1975 and Amendment Regulations 2008	14
5.5	Evaluate the impact of e-commerce and technology on the management of organisations and people, and in particular the benefit to the purchasing function	
	• Intranet	15
	• Knowledge management systems	15
	• Management information systems (MIS)/marketing information systems (MkIS)	15
	• Flexible working arrangements	15
	• Telecommunications	15
	• E-sourcing	15
	• E-procurement	15

		Chapter
5.6	Identify ways to monitor and control the impact of the change process on the performance of the supply chain and assess their effectiveness.	
	• Budget	13
	• Project measurement	13
	• Benchmarking	13
	• Auditing	13
	• Employee and stakeholder reactions	13
	• Appropriate communication programmes involving third parties internal changes	13
5.7	Assess the importance of managing continuity of performance whilst implementing change and explain how to do this.	
	• The importance of maintaining a 'business as usual' approach for managing supply	13
	• The process of internal handover from one initial/team to another	13
	• How a supplier implementation programme is organised, including the potential benefits of a trial/pilot period and ramp-up/ramp-down phases	13
	• How existing suppliers can be managed and incentivised to see out the full terms of their contracts without disruption to supply or service levels	13

How to Use Your Study Pack

Familiarisation

At this point you should begin to familiarise yourself with the package of benefits you have purchased.

- Go to www.cips.org and log on. Then go to Study and Qualify/Study Resources. Browse through the free content relating to this subject.
- Download the Quick Start Guide and print it out. Open up a ring binder and make the Quick Start Guide your first item in there.
- Now glance briefly through the Course Book (the text you're reading right now!) and the Passnotes.

Organising your study

'Organising' is the key word: unless you are a very exceptional student, you will find a haphazard approach is insufficient, particularly if you are having to combine study with the demands of a full-time job.

A good starting point is to timetable your studies, in broad terms, between now and the date of the examination. How many subjects are you attempting? How many chapters are there in the Course Book for each subject? Now do the sums: how many days/weeks do you have for each chapter to be studied?

Remember:

- Not every week can be regarded as a study week – you may be going on holiday, for example, or there may be weeks when the demands of your job are particularly heavy. If these can be foreseen, you should allow for them in your timetabling.
- You also need a period leading up to the exam in which you will revise and practise what you have learned.

Once you have done the calculations, make a week-by-week timetable for yourself for each paper, allowing for study and revision of the entire unit content between now and the date of the exams.

Getting started

Aim to find a quiet and undisturbed location for your study, and plan as far as possible to use the same period each day. Getting into a routine helps avoid wasting time. Make sure you have all the materials you need before you begin – keep interruptions to a minimum.

Begin by reading through your Quick Start Guide. This should take no more than a couple of hours, even reading slowly. By the time you have finished this you will have a reasonable grounding in the subject area. You will build on this by working through the Course Book.

Using the Course Book

You should refer to the Course Book to the extent that you need it.

- If you are a newcomer to the subject, you will probably need to read through the Course Book quite thoroughly. This will be the case for most students.
- If some areas are already familiar to you – either through earlier studies or through your practical work experience – you may choose to skip sections of the Course Book.

The content of the Course Book

This Course Book has been designed to give detailed coverage of every topic in the unit content. As you will see from pages vii–xiv, each topic mentioned in the unit content is dealt with in a chapter of the Course Book. For the most part the order of the Course Book follows the order of the unit content closely, though departures from this principle have occasionally been made in the interest of a logical learning order.

Each chapter begins with a reference to the learning objectives and unit content to be covered in the chapter. Each chapter is divided into sections, listed in the introduction to the chapter, and for the most part being actual captions from the unit content.

All of this enables you to monitor your progress through the unit content very easily and provides reassurance that you are tackling every subject that is examinable.

Each chapter contains the following features.

- Introduction, setting out the main topics to be covered
- Clear coverage of each topic in a concise and approachable format
- A chapter summary
- Self-test questions

The study phase

For each chapter you should begin by glancing at the main headings (listed at the start of the chapter). Then read fairly rapidly through the body of the text to absorb the main points. If it's there in the text, you can be sure it's there for a reason, so try not to skip unless the topic is one you are familiar with already.

Then return to the beginning of the chapter to start a more careful reading. You may want to take brief notes as you go along, but bear in mind that you already have your Quick Start Guide and Passnotes – there is no point in duplicating what you can find there.

Test your recall and understanding of the material by attempting the self-test questions. These are accompanied by cross-references to paragraphs where you can check your answers and refresh your memory.

Practising what you have learned

Once you think you have learned enough about the subject, or about a particular topic within the overall subject area, it's good to practise. Access the study resources at www.cips.org, and download a practice question on the relevant area. Alternatively, download a past exam question. Attempt a solution yourself before looking at our suggested solution or the Senior Assessor's comments.

Make notes of any mistakes you made, or any areas where your answer could be improved. If there is anything you can't understand, you are welcome to email us for clarification (course.books@cips.org).

The revision phase

Your approach to revision should be methodical and you should aim to tackle each main area of the unit content in turn. Begin by re-reading your Quick Start Guide. This gives an overview that will help to focus your more detailed study. Then re-read your notes and/or the separate Passnotes accompanying this Course Book. Then return to question practice. Review your own solutions to the practice questions you have had time to attempt. If there are gaps, try to find time to attempt some more questions, or at least to review the suggested solutions.

Additional reading

Your Study Pack provides you with the key information needed for each module but CIPS strongly advocates reading as widely as possible to augment and reinforce your understanding. CIPS produces an official reading list of books, which can be downloaded from the bookshop area of the CIPS website.

To help you, we have identified one essential textbook for each subject. We recommend that you read this for additional information.

The essential textbook for this unit is *Management and Organisational Behaviour* by J L Mullins, published by Pearson (ISBN: 978–0273–728610).

CHAPTER 1

Management and Leadership

Learning objectives and indicative content

1.1 Define the term 'management' and differentiate 'management' from 'leadership'

- Definitions of management: Fayol, Mintzberg, Drucker, Brech, Cole
- Management: planning, co-ordinating, controlling and motivating staff
- Management styles
- Leadership perspectives and styles: Hersey and Blanchard, Tannenbaum and Schmidt, Kotter, Lewin

Chapter headings

1 What is management?

2 What do managers do?

3 Management styles

4 What makes an effective manager?

5 What is leadership?

6 Leadership perspectives and styles

Introduction

Management is such a universal feature of the business and employment landscape, that you may not have thought much about what 'management' means – or might mean. For hundreds of years, people have been doing management in organisations. Yet every year there is new research and new ideas about why management is necessary; what managers actually do; and how they can do it better.

In this chapter, we explore some basic ideas about management: what does 'managing' mean, what do managers manage, and is there a 'best way' to manage? We look at some classical ideas on these topics – and also at some more modern perspectives. (In Chapter 4, we give a more extensive survey of the history of organisation and management theory, as we explore the rationale behind organisation structures.)

We then go on to discuss the most recent trend in management thinking: the distinction between 'management' and 'leadership'; whether it is important; and why managers may need to develop leadership skills.

1 What is management?

1.1 There are many different definitions of management – and some of them have been adjusted in the light of the emerging focus on 'leadership'. Here are a few to be starting with.

- Management is the process of getting results by making the best use of available human, financial and material resources. 'The most important part of management will be... getting things done through people, but managers will be concerned directly or indirectly with all other resources, including their own [experience, know-how, skill, competences and time].' (*Armstrong*)
- The key purpose of management (and leadership) is to 'provide direction, facilitate change and achieve results through the efficient, creative and responsible use of resources'. (*Management Standards Centre*)
- Management is 'a social process entailing responsibility for the effective and economical planning and regulation of the operations of an enterprise, in fulfilment of given purposes or tasks, such responsibility entailing: (a) judgement and decision in determining plans and in using data to control performance and progress against plans; and (b) the guidance, integration, motivation and supervision of the personnel composing the enterprise and carrying out its operations.' (*EFL Brech*)
- Your syllabus also mentions a definition by Cole, but it is not clear what this refers to. In his authoritative text *Management Theory and Practice* GA Cole cites many definitions from other authors, but does not himself offer any definition.

Classical management

1.2 Classical management theory, formulated by early writers such as Henri Fayol and EFL Brech, suggested that management involved certain basic functions, designed to bring system, order, rationality and consistency to the organisational environment.

1.3 *Fayol* suggested the following five functions of management.

- Planning: deterring objectives or desired results, and formulating courses of action (strategies, policies, procedures and so on) to achieve them
- Organising: establishing a structure of tasks which must be performed to achieve the objective, and allocating them to appropriate individuals and units
- Commanding: instructing and influencing people towards the accomplishment of tasks and goals
- Co-ordinating: integrating the goals and activities of individuals and groups within the organisation, through communication
- Controlling: measuring and monitoring the process of work in relation to the plan, and taking corrective action where necessary.

1.4 *Brech* identifies four main functions.

- Planning: determining strategies and methods of carrying them out, and setting performance standards
- Control: checking progress and performance against standards as a basis for correction and further planning
- Co-ordination: balancing and maintaining the team by dividing work suitably [organising] and harmonising the work of different units towards shared goals
- Motivation: inspiring, supervising and fostering morale, with the aim of getting team members to work effectively and to be committed and loyal to the group and the task.

1.5 *Peter Drucker* (an American business consultant and prolific writer on management) argued that the manager of a business has one basic function: to secure economic results. Within this basic function, he categorised basic managerial operations as follows.

- Objective setting: determining objectives, goals and targets
- Organising: classifying and dividing tasks, creating organisation structure, selecting staff
- Motivating and communicating: creating effective and committed teams
- Measuring: establishing targets and standards for individuals, units and the organisation as a whole, for the purposes of control
- Developing people: directing, supporting, challenging, training and empowering team members.

1.6 You may be able to see, in the development of management theory from Fayol to Brech to Drucker, a growing focus on the people resource – including managers themselves. Drucker also argued that the role of the manager was to provide leadership.

'The manager is the dynamic, life-giving element in every business. Without his leadership, "the sources of production" remain resources and never become production. In a competitive economy, above all the quality and performance of the managers determine the success of a business, indeed they determine its survival.'

1.7 Management can thus be seen as an **integrating factor**, which draws coherence, direction and performance from all the other processes and resources of the organisation.

1.8 It is worth clearing up any possible confusion between the terms 'management' and 'organisation'.

- Management, as we suggest above, is a process by which individuals exercise the authority given to them by virtue of their position in an enterprise, to plan and regulate its operations and deploy its resources, with a view to efficient and effective achievement of its objectives.
- Organisation is a term used for one function of management: that of establishing a structure for the tasks which must be performed to achieve the objectives of the enterprise. At the wider level, the term is therefore used to describe the structure of the enterprise itself. An organisation (company, charity, government body etc) is 'a social arrangement for achieving controlled performance in pursuit of collective goals' (*Huczynski & Buchanan*).

1.9 The study of management addresses the decisions people make about the running of the enterprise, and the social process by which those decisions are put into effect through other people. The study of organisation addresses the dynamics of systems and processes, structures and cultures, and individual and group working, by which the enterprise operates.

Organisational behaviour

1.10 The term 'organisational behaviour' has been given to 'the study of the structure, functioning and performance of organisations, and the behaviour of groups and individuals within it' (*Huczynski & Buchanan*).

Organisational behaviour concepts thus include organisation-level concepts (such as systems, structure and culture); group-level concepts (such as the dynamics of team development and decision-making, leadership, conflict and co-operation); and individual-level concepts (such as motivation, learning, perception and coping with change).

1.11 It is a multi-disciplinary study, encompassing research and concepts from psychology, sociology, anthropology, economics and political science. This reflects the wide impact which organisations of different types have on societies and individual lives, and also the many levels on which individuals engage themselves in relationships with organisations.

1.12 The study of organisational behaviour faces certain difficulties of methodology and application. People can't be studied scientifically in the way that other natural phenomena can – and it is almost impossible to exclude subjectivity from research and its interpretation. Different disciplines come up with different explanations of the same behaviours. Behavioural concepts don't allow you to predict or control behaviour: there are too many variables, not all of them within managerial control.

1.13 Nevertheless, organisational behaviour concepts and models offer workable theories to explain how different variables affect each other, and how some variables can be controlled to get desired results. The importance of the human variable, in particular, is the main reason why managers need to understand the behavioural implications of their plans and decisions.

2 *What do managers do?*

2.1 The classical approach to categorising management functions is simple and useful for management education, but it has been argued that it does not do justice to the complexity of the manager's 'job' in the real world. A rather different approach to defining management was taken by *Henry Mintzberg*, who studied what managers actually 'do'.

2.2 Mintzberg's research suggested that managers are not separate from, or 'above', the demands of everyday work. Their work is sometimes routine and often disjointed and discontinuous: they are not always able to be reflective, systematic thinkers. Despite the development of formal management information systems, managers generally prefer verbal and informal information.

2.3 Mintzberg suggested that in their daily working lives, managers fulfil a range of managerial roles: Table 1.1.

Table 1.1 *Mintzberg's managerial roles*

Nature of role	Role definition
Interpersonal Arising from a manager's formal authority or position in the organisation and unit	• **Figurehead**: a ceremonial role, representing the organisation in public • **Leader**: hiring, supervising, developing, motivating, team building and so on • **Liaison**: networking and co-ordinating with peers in other units/functions
Informational Arising from a manager's access to internal and external contacts	• **Monitor**: gathering information • **Spokesperson**: giving information on behalf of the unit or organisation • **Disseminator**: sharing information with relevant stakeholders or interested parties
Decisional Arising from a manager's formal authority and access to information, which places him in the best position to solve problems relating to the unit or department as a whole	• **Entrepreneur**: initiating action to exploit opportunities • **Disturbance handler**: responding to threats and pressures, taking corrective action • **Resource allocator**: distributing limited resources where they will be most effective • **Negotiator**: resolving conflicts and securing favourable outcomes in matters involving others

3 Management styles

3.1 Not all managers operate in the same manner. It is possible to identify a wide variety of behaviours which different managers use as their 'preferred' approach or 'style'. Many attempts have been made both to classify styles and to identify which is the most effective style for a manager to adopt.

Focus on the task or on the people?

3.2 The *Ohio State University Studies* (carried out in the 1940s) asked people to analyse and comment on the behaviour of their superiors. From their results it was easy to identify two major dimensions of managerial behaviour.

- Initiating structure – concern with organising the work to be done, the definition of roles and ways of getting jobs done.
- Consideration – concern with the social organisation of the group, maintaining good relations and giving opportunities for group involvement and participation.

3.3 This distinction, more commonly referred to today as the difference between a task-centred approach and a people-centred approach, has been very influential.

3.4 For example, the **Managerial Grid** (Figure 1.1) was developed by *Blake and Mouton*. Managers are classified on the grid in terms of their concern for people and their concern for production.

Figure 1.1 *Blake and Mouton's managerial grid*

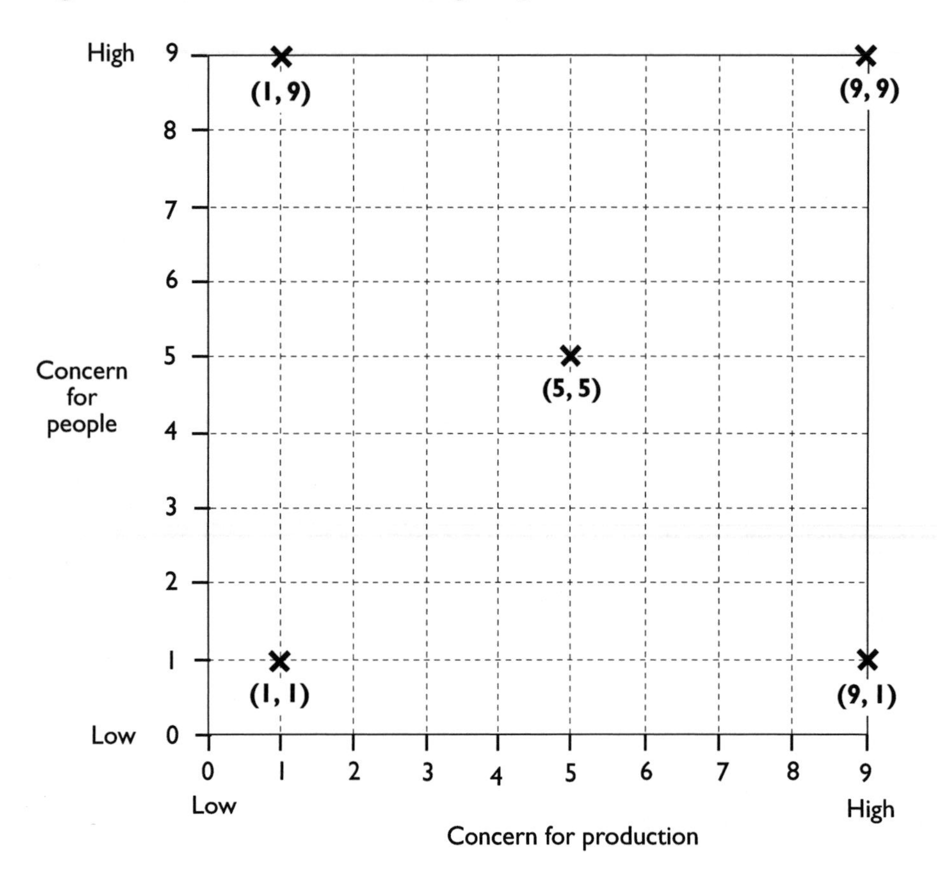

3.5 Key positions on the grid and can be explained as follows.

- 'Impoverished' (1,1): the manager exerts (and expects) minimal effort or concern for either staff satisfaction or work targets.
- 'Country club' (1,9): the manager is attentive to staff needs and has developed satisfying relationships and work culture – but with little attention to results.
- 'Task management' (9,1): the manager concentrates almost exclusively on achieving results. People's needs are virtually ignored, and work is organised so that human elements interfere to a minimal extent.
- 'Team' (9,9): the manager achieves high work performance through 'leading' committed people who identify themselves with organisational goals.
- 'Middle of the road' or 'dampened pendulum' (5,5): a manager achieves adequate performance through balancing the necessity to get work done with maintaining a satisfactory level of team morale. (Alternatively, the manager scores an *average* of 5,5 as a result of swinging from one extreme to another!)

3.6 The grid recognises that management requires a balance between concern for task and people, and that there is no necessary correlation (positive or negative) between the two. However, it assumes that high concern for both is possible at the same time – and that this is the most effective style of management. It thus offers a simple and easy-to-use diagnostic tool. It shows where the behaviour and assumptions of a manager may exhibit a lack of balance between the two dimensions and/or an unsuitably low concern in either dimension (or both).

3.7 However, critics complain that the grid oversimplifies the management role and situation: factors such as culture, technology, team members and the nature of the task are not directly considered. The model also assumes that (9,9) is the optimum style – but in some managerial contexts, this may not be so. A manager may find that a (9,1) approach is better in situations of crisis where survival is at stake, or when urgent action must be taken.

A range of management styles

3.8 The *Ashridge Management College* studies (1966) identified four management styles, which are summarised in Table 1.2 below.

Table 1.2 *Tells, sells, consults, joins*

Style	***Strengths***	***Weaknesses***
Tells (autocratic) The manager makes decisions and issues instructions which must be obeyed without question	Quick decisions can be made when required The most efficient type of leadership for highly-programmed work	Communications are one-way, neglecting feedback and potential for upward communication or team input Does not encourage initiative or commitment from subordinates: merely compliance
Sells (persuasive) The manager still makes decisions, but believes that team members must be motivated to accept them in order to carry them out properly	Team members understand the reason for decisions Team members may be more committed Team members may be able to function slightly better in the absence of instruction	Communications are still largely one-way Team members are not necessarily motivated to accept the decision Still doesn't encourage initiative or commitment
Consults (participative) The manager confers with team members and takes their views into account, although he retains the final say	Encourages motivation through greater interest and involvement Enhances the acceptability of the decision to team members Decision quality may benefit Creates upward communication	May take longer (especially if consensus is sought) Team input may not enhance the quality of the decision Consultation can be a façade for a basic 'sells' style
Joins (democratic) Manager and team members make the decision together on the basis of consensus	Fosters motivation/commitment Empowers team members to take the initiative Plus strengths of 'consults' style	May undermine manager's authority May lengthen the process May cause 'political' decisions

3.9 The Ashridge studies showed a clear preference amongst subordinates for the 'consults' style of management – although managers were most commonly perceived to be exercising a 'tells' or 'sells' style. Team members also had more positive attitudes to their work under managers who were perceived to be exercising a 'consults' style. The least favourable attitudes to work, however, were not found among team members under a 'tells' style, but among those who were unable to perceive a *consistent* style in their manager. In other words, subordinates are unsettled by a boss who chops and changes between different styles.

3.10 Other studies have identified similar styles, on a continuum between autocratic and democratic (*Tannenbaum and Schmidt*), dictatorial and *laissez-faire* (*Huneryager and Heckman*), or autocratic, democratic, *laissez-faire* (*Lippitt and White*, working under the direction of *Lewin*). Although the labels and definitions vary, style models are often talking about more or less the same things: the continuum between completely task-focused, directive behaviours on one hand, and completely people-focused, supportive behaviours on the other.

3.11 The continuum is a useful reminder that managers do not adopt extreme either/or styles, but select from a wide repertoire of behaviours, according to the demands of a particular situation. Tannenbaum and Schmidt's continuum is shown in Figure 1.2.

Figure 1.2 *Tannenbaum and Schmidt: a continuum of leadership style*

Task-oriented ←→ *Relationship-oriented*
Autocratic ←→ *Democratic*

Use of authority by the leader
Area of subordinative freedom

Manager makes decisions and enforces them
Manager makes decisions and announces them
Manager 'sells' his decisions to subordinates
Manager suggests own ideas and asks for comments
Manager suggests his own sketched ideas, asks for comments and amends his ideas as a result
Manager presents a problem, asks for ideas, makes a decision from ideas
Manager presents a problem to his group of subordinates and asks them to solve it
Manager allows his subordinates to act as they wish within specified limits

Evaluating the management style approach

3.12 The style approach provides useful insight into the nature and processes of management. It usefully stresses the value of participative leadership and, in identifying styles, it has helped in the perception of managing as a range of choices open to the manager rather than one limited and universal set of behaviours.

3.13 However, the approach is also subject to certain criticisms. Despite a level of agreement between different researchers, there are also confusions and contradictions. Perhaps the most important criticism of the style approach is that it does not consider all the variables that contribute to the operation of effective management.

- The manager's personality (or 'acting' ability) may simply not be flexible enough to utilise style theories effectively.
- The demands of the task, technology, organisation culture and other managers constrain the manager in the range of styles effectively open to him. (If the manager's own boss is authoritarian and the team are incompetent, no amount of theorising on the desirability of participative management will make it possible!)
- Consistency is important to subordinates. If a manager adopts a style suitable to the changing situation, subordinates may suffer insecurity and stress.

3.14 *Huczynski and Buchanan* note that 'There is therefore no simple recipe which the individual manager can use to decide which style to adopt to be most effective. Management style probably can be changed, but only if management values can be changed....'

3.15 It is the consideration of this wider set of variables that has led to the development of the contingency approach, which we shall now go on to examine.

4 What makes an effective manager?

Contingency theory

4.1 In essence, contingency theory sees management effectiveness as being dependent on a number of variable or contingent factors. There is no 'one right way' to lead that will fit all situations; one must lead in a manner that is appropriate to a particular situation. The management (or leadership) situation consists of factors such as the following.

- The manager's power and influence in the organisation and with the work group, affecting the extent to which a command-and-control style is possible
- The nature of the task and technology, affecting the extent to which workers require close instruction and supervision
- The skills and motivation of the work group, affecting the extent to which workers will want or expect autonomy or involvement in decision-making
- The culture of the organisation and its management, affecting the style likely to be perceived as acceptable and effective.

Situational leadership

4.2 *Hersey and Blanchard* propose a situational leadership model, in which leadership style is a combination of directive and supportive behaviours.

- Directive behaviour involves: 'clearly telling people what to do, how to do it, when to do it, and then closely monitoring their performance'.
- Supportive behaviour involves: 'listening to people, providing support and encouragement for their efforts, and then facilitating their involvement in problem-solving and decision-making'.

4.3 The most appropriate style depends on the **readiness of the team members** to perform a given task, in terms of their task ability (experience, knowledge and skills) and willingness (whether they have the confidence, commitment and motivation) to complete the task successfully.

- High-readiness teams do not need direction or support from their leader: the most appropriate leadership may be a 'delegating' style.
- High-moderate readiness teams are competent, but require supportive behaviour to build morale: the most appropriate leadership may be a 'participating' style.
- Low-moderate readiness teams require both direction and support to improve their task performance without damaging morale: the most appropriate leadership may be a 'selling' style.
- Low-readiness teams require more direction in order to secure adequate task performance: the most appropriate leadership may be a 'telling' style.

4.4 The situational model can be depicted as follows: Figure 1.3.

Figure 1.3 *Hersey and Blanchard's situational leadership model*

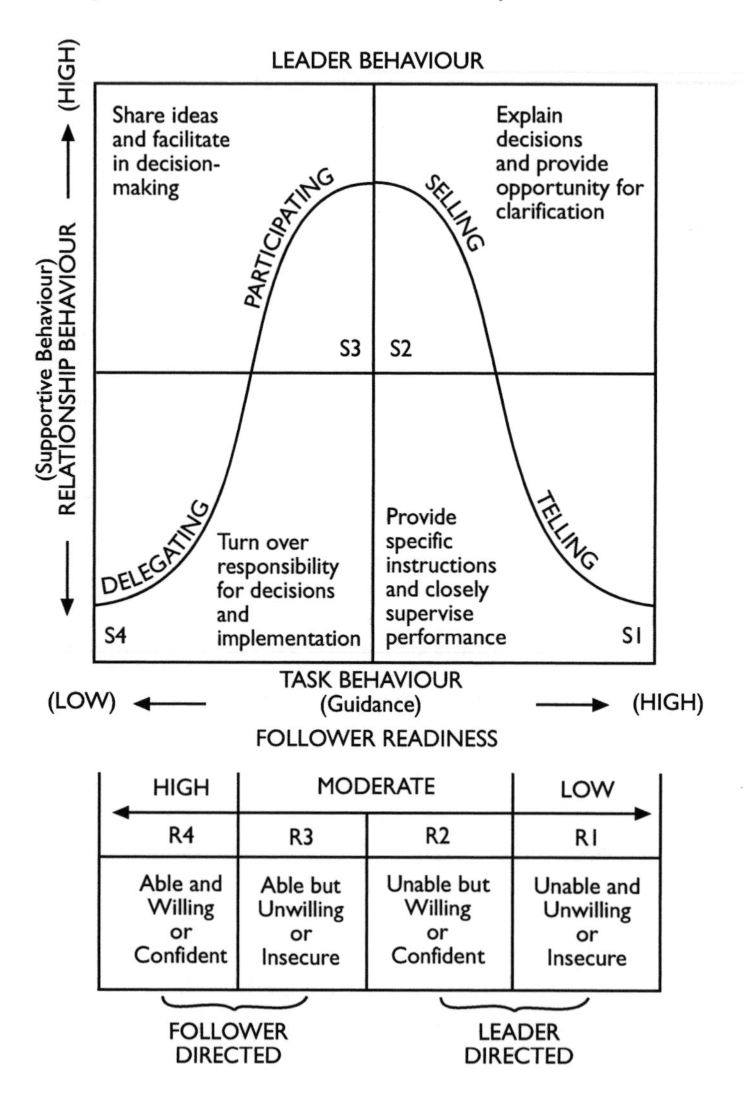

4.5 *John Adair's* **'action-centred'** (or 'functional') model is also situational. Like other contingency thinkers, Adair saw the leadership process in a context made up of three interrelated variables: task needs, the individual needs of group members and the needs of the group as a whole. These needs must be examined in the light of the whole situation, which dictates the relative priority that must be given to each of the three sets of needs. Effective leadership is identifying and acting on that priority, exercising a relevant cluster of roles to meet the needs. This is shown in Figure 1.4.

Figure 1.4 *Adair's action-centred leadership model*

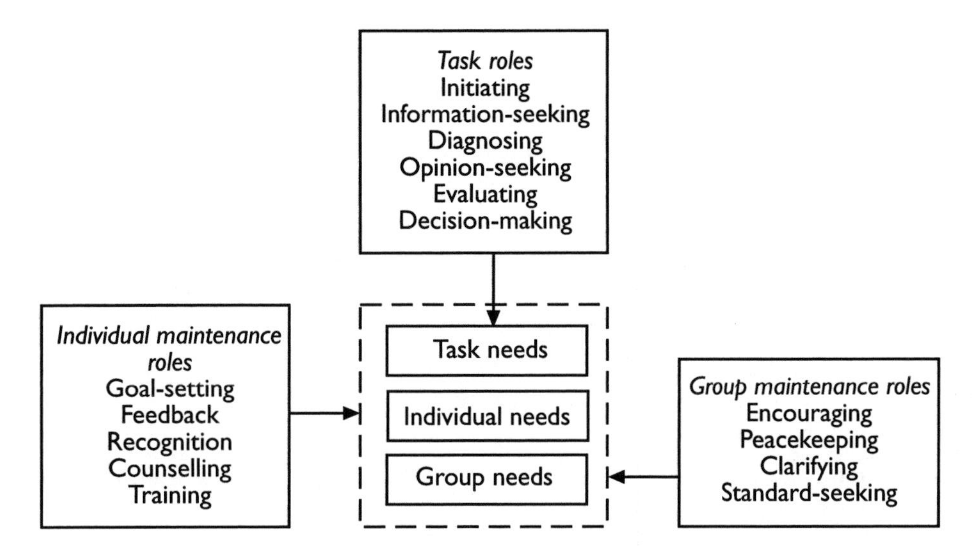

4.6 Adair argued that the common perception of leadership as 'decision-making' was inadequate to describe the range of action required by the complex situation in which the manager finds himself. He developed a scheme of leadership training based on precept and practice in each of eight leadership 'activities' (which are applied to task, team and individual): defining the task, planning, briefing, controlling, evaluating, motivating, organising and setting an example.

An appraisal of contingency theory

4.7 Contingency theory demonstrates that there is no ideal personality nor one best style for a manager. By making people aware of the factors affecting the choice of management (or leadership) style and providing a basis for increased self-awareness, the theory gives a useful starting point for development and training.

4.8 Contingency approaches have also been the object of some criticism, however.

- The key variables of task structure, power and relationships are difficult to measure in practice and may depend more on intuition than on measurement.
- The theory ignores the need for a manager to have technical competence relevant to the task – an important component in effective performance!

4.9 The major difficulty for any manager seeking to apply contingency theory is actually to modify his behaviour as the situation changes, without inconsistency which may damage team member confidence and security.

5 What is leadership?

5.1 Leadership may be defined as the process of influencing others to work willingly towards an organisation's goals and to the best of their capabilities.

Managers and leaders

5.2 The terms 'manager' and 'leader' are often used interchangeably – although 'leader' is now the more fashionable term.

5.3 *Kotter* has made a detailed and helpful distinction between leadership and management. He suggests that management is about coping with **complexity**: managerial functions are to do with logic, structure, analysis and control. Management can be exercised over processes, projects, resources, time and so on.

5.4 Leadership, on the other hand, is about coping with **change**. It can, essentially, only be exercised over people, and requires a completely different set of activities.

- Creating a sense of direction: finding a vision for something new out of the challenge of dissatisfaction with the *status quo*.
- Communicating the vision: meeting the needs of other people, giving the vision credibility.
- Energising, inspiring and motivating: stimulating others to translate the vision into achievement.

5.5 Other influential attempts to distinguish between the two concepts have been as follows.

- *Yukl* suggests that while management is defined by a formal role and position in the organisation hierarchy, leaders are given their roles by the perceptions and choice of others. Managers have subordinates: leaders have followers.
- *Zaleznik* suggests that while managers are primarily concerned with order and maintaining the *status quo*, focusing on diplomacy and decision-making processes in the organisation, leaders are more concerned with introducing new ideas and approaches, focusing on excitement, vision and empathy for people.
- *Katz and Kahn* suggest that while managers aim to secure compliance with routine organisational objectives, leaders aim to secure willingness, enthusiasm and commitment.
- *Pedler, Burgoyne & Boydell* suggest that 'leading is more concerned with finding direction and purpose in the face of critical challenges, whereas managing is about organising to achieve desired purposes – efficiently, effectively and creatively.'

Why develop managers as 'leaders'?

5.6 *Whetten and Cameron* argue that the distinction between managers and leaders is no longer very useful. 'Managers cannot be successful without being good leaders, and leaders cannot be successful without being good managers.'

5.7 Why might it be important for managers to become leaders?

- Leaders energise and support change, which is essential for survival in highly competitive and fast-changing business environments.
- Leaders secure commitment, mobilising the ideas, experience and motivation of employees – which contributes to innovation and improved quality and customer service.
- Leaders set direction, helping teams and organisations to understand their purpose and goals. This facilitates team-working and empowerment without loss of co-ordination.
- Leaders support, challenge and develop people, maximising their contribution to the organisation.
- Leaders use a facilitate-empower style (rather than a command-control style), which is better suited to the expectations of empowered teams and the need for information-sharing.

5.8 With the emphasis on empowered teamworking, the manager's role has changed. Many of the managerial functions of planning, organising and controlling work have been taken over by team decision-making processes. This has shifted the team leader's role:

- from planner to vision-creator
- from instructor to coach and facilitator
- from controller to co-ordinator
- from commander to persuader, motivator and inspirer.

6 *Leadership perspectives and styles*

Trait theories of leadership

6.1 Trait theories suggest that the best way to study leadership is to analyse the personalities of successful leaders, identify their common personality characteristics (or traits) and thus formulate a list of 'leadership traits'.

6.2 This approach has much in common with the 'great man' theory of history which states that the great events of history are set in motion by great men. Those who display leadership in one situation would probably be the leader in any other. They are leaders because of some unique and inherent set of traits that set them apart from normal people. In other words, leaders are 'born, not made': you either have the power to make others follow you, or you don't.

6.3 Various attempts have been made to determine exactly which traits are essential in a leader. A study cited by *Rosemary Stewart* contains the following 15 traits.

Judgement	Initiative	Integrity	Foresight	Energy
Drive	Human relations skill	Decisiveness	Dependability	Emotional stability
Fairness	Ambition	Dedication	Objectivity	Co-operation

6.4 There are certain problems with trait theory, which has now largely been discredited.

- It does not take account of the individuality of subordinates, or other factors in the complex leadership situation. The personal characteristics of the leader must be relevant to the characteristics, activities and goals of the followers.
- Research has produced such a varied list of traits that no set of qualities can really be said to distinguish leaders from non-leaders.
- The trait approach does not help organisations to make better team leaders: it merely allows them (in theory) to recognise a leader when they see one.

Style theories of leadership

6.5 Whether or not you find the distinction between the terms 'manager' and 'leader' useful, both sets of behaviours can be classified according to style models. (Many of the models first published using the term 'management styles' now refer to 'leadership styles': we have therefore already covered some of the main leadership models in Sections 3 and 4 above.)

6.6 *Gillen* suggests that: 'Using only one leadership style is a bit like a stopped clock: it will be right twice a day, but the rest of the time it will be inaccurate to varying degrees. Leaders need to interact with their team in different ways in different situations. This is what we mean by "leadership style".'

6.7 Some of the values used to distinguish between managers and leaders have also been identified as different styles of leadership (*Burns*).

- **Transactional leaders** see the relationship with their followers in terms of a trade: they give followers the rewards they want in exchange for service, loyalty and compliance.
- **Transformational leaders** see their role as stimulating interest, generating awareness, inspiring higher achievement and motivating others to work at levels beyond mere compliance and to think about the 'big picture'. Only transformational leadership is said to be able to change team/organisation cultures and create a new direction.

Leadership skills

6.8 Leadership theory has begun to revisit the idea of leadership traits or qualities, in a more helpful way, by examining the skills and values that contribute to effective leadership behaviours: unlike 'traits', skills and values can be learned, developed and flexibly deployed according to the needs and priorities of the leadership situation. In other words, instead of asking 'What are effective leaders like?', behavioural models ask: 'What do effective leaders do?' How do they act and speak and think?

6.9 Some of the key skills identified with leadership include:

- Interpersonal and communication skills, such as emotional intelligence (self-awareness, self-control, empathy with others and social skills), networking, influencing, negotiating, listening, counselling, coaching, giving feedback, resolving conflict and so on.

- Decision-making and problem-solving skills, including seeing the big picture and using decision-support tools
- Entrepreneurship: the ability to spot business opportunities and mobilise and deploy resources to capitalise on them
- Time-management and personal organisation, in order to maximise personal effectiveness
- Self-development: the ability to grow in self-awareness and to exploit learning opportunities (including experience) for continuous development and behavioural flexibility

6.10 A different mix of skills may be used at different levels of management. At supervisory level, for example, the emphasis may be on technical skills, while at senior management level, the emphasis will be on conceptual skills (vision creation, strategic planning and so on). Interpersonal or human skills will be equally important at all levels.

6.11 Finally, among the authorities cited by your syllabus in relation to leadership styles, there is a reference to Lewin. Like the reference to Cole under 'definitions of management' this is unclear. Kurt Lewin has made notable contributions to management research, but is not known for work in this particular area.

Chapter summary

- Organisational behaviour includes: the behaviour of individuals and groups; the structure, systems and functions of the organisation; and the dynamic effects of the environment on all of these.
- Management can be described as the efficient and effective use of financial, material, informational and human resources in pursuit of organisational goals.
- Management functions (Fayol, Drucker, Brech) broadly include: planning, organising, co-ordinating and controlling work – and motivating and developing workers.
- Being a leader is (arguably) not the same as being a manager. Leadership involves interpersonal influence, the securing of commitment (over and above compliance), and focus on change.
- Trait theories of leadership take the view that leadership qualities are inherent, not developed. Unfortunately there is no agreement among researchers adopting this line as to which personality traits good leaders do have in common!
- An alternative way of looking at the question of leadership is to adopt a behavioural approach, which emphasises what leaders actually do and their style of leadership. For example, the Ashridge Studies identified four styles – 'tells', 'sells', 'consults' and 'joins' – while Tannenbaum and Schmidt emphasised that styles represent a continuum of different behaviours, not fixed extremes. Blake and Mouton's managerial grid measures managerial style on two axes, one denoting 'concern for production' and the other 'concern for people'.
- Contingency theory asserts that there is no one 'right way' to lead that fits all situations. Leadership style has to be adapted to suit the circumstances. For example, Hersey and Blanchard suggested that leadership style should be adapted to the team's readiness (task ability and willingness) to perform a given task. John Adair proposed an 'action-centred' approach, based on managerial activities in three key roles, which in turn are based on the meeting of three key needs: task, individual and team. The relative priority to be given to these needs is dictated by the overall situation.

Self-test questions

Numbers in brackets refer to paragraphs where you can check your answers

1. Identify five functions of management and one key management task. (1.3 – 1.5)
2. What disciplines are involved in the study of organisational behaviour? (1.11)
3. Why is the study of organisational behaviour (a) difficult and (b) useful? (1.12, 1.13)
4. List the three types of managerial role (Mintzberg). (2.3)
5. What are the key scores on the Blake and Mouton managerial grid? (Figure 1.1)
6. Describe the 'tells', 'sells', 'joins' and 'consults' styles of management. (Table 1.2)
7. What are the variables that Adair identified as being related to effective leadership? (4.5)
8. How does contingency theory support the idea of leadership training? (4.7)
9. What are the distinguishing features of leadership (as opposed to management)? (5.4 – 5.5)
10. How do (a) trait theories and (b) style theories view leadership? (6.1, 6.5)

CHAPTER 2

Purchasing Management in Context

Learning objectives and indicative content

1.2 Identify the key stakeholder groups who impact directly on the purchasing function, analyse their potential impact and explain how to manage their expectations effectively

- Stakeholders: employees, customers, shareholders, suppliers, government, lenders, trustees, elected members
- Identifying and fulfilling stakeholder/customer needs: good products and service, return on investment, quality, price and measurable outcomes
- Working within ethical codes of conduct and practice
- Expectations: on time, within budget, meeting terms and conditions

1.3 Evaluate the key roles and functions of managers in the purchasing and supply function

[For full indicative content, please see page viii]

1.4 Compare and contrast the diverse purchasing management practices of the private and public sectors

[For full indicative content, please see page viii]

1.5 Create a set of rules for ethical behaviour

- What is ethics?
- CIPS ethical codes
- Corporate social responsibility

Chapter headings

1 Organisational stakeholders
2 Identifying and fulfilling stakeholder needs
3 Business ethics and corporate responsibility
4 Ethical issues in purchasing
5 Management in the purchasing and supply function
6 Purchasing management in the public and private sectors

Introduction

Managers have the right (authority) to manage – but they cannot just make decisions and manipulate resources in any way they see fit! In this chapter, we look first at the concept of 'stakeholders'. These are the people who have a legitimate stake or interest in an organisation's activity – why and how far should managers take their needs into account?

We then go on to the concept of 'ethics': why should an organisation care about the needs and interests of other people at all? And what are the guidelines for 'right' and 'wrong' conduct in the purchasing manager's role?

Finally, we focus more directly on the role of the manager specifically in the purchasing and supply function. This is only an overview: as we will see in Chapter 5, there are many ways of designing a 'job', and the exact roles and tasks required of a purchasing manager will vary from organisation to organisation.

In particular, the roles, tasks and methods will vary according to whether the organisation operates in the public or private sector. We will explore some of the key differences between the two.

1 Organisational stakeholders

1.1 Organisations are complex social systems. Depending on their type, size, orientation and sector, they may have different groups of people who own them, manage them, staff them – and for whose benefit their activities are directed. All these individuals and groups have a legitimate interest or 'stake' in the organisation's activity and performance: hence the term 'stakeholders'.

1.2 The stakeholders of an organisation include internal, connected and external groups, whose **interest** in the organisation can be summarised as follows.

- **Internal stakeholders**. The directors, managers and employees who operate within the organisation's boundaries have a key stake in the organisation's survival and growth (for continued employment and prosperity); the fulfilment of task goals (as a measure of their competence and success); and the fulfilment of their personal goals (for income, security, career, status and so on).
- **Connected stakeholders**. These include shareholders, who have a key stake, as owners, in the financial performance of the organisation. They also include:
  - Financiers, such as banks (*interest:* security of loans, return on investment).
  - Customers/consumers (*interest:* satisfaction of complex expectations and motives for purchasing a product/service; ethical business dealings; helpful service and support; accurate information).
  - Suppliers (*interest:* efficient information flow; payment as agreed; mutually beneficial long-term relationship; feedback/support to enhance service).
  - Distributors (*interest:* reliable supply; quality/added value; marketing support; earnings through discount margins or commissions; mutually beneficial long-term relationship).
- **External stakeholders**. These include:
  - Government regulatory bodies (*interest:* economic activity; tax revenue; compliance with legislation; reports and returns; social responsibility).
  - Pressure and interest groups (*interest:* awareness of a particular cause or issue, eg environmental impacts; protection of the rights and interests of the group, eg disabled workers).

- Professional bodies, trade unions and other representative groups (*interest:* protecting the interests of members; promoting professional standards and ethics).
- The local community (*interest:* employment; provision of goods and services; social responsibility and involvement).

1.3 Stakeholder groups can apply pressure to **influence** organisations in different ways and to different degrees.

- Managers exercise direct influence (formal authority or power) over planning, organisation and control. They may also exercise informal power through leadership/charisma, influencing skills (eg in negotiation), or the exercise of discretion when implementing strategy.
- Staff members may have power through control over the labour resource or through specialist knowledge or skills (expert power) to influence human resource management policy and task performance.
- Customers are (in a 'marketing oriented' business) the focus of all organisational planning and activity.
- Supply chain partners have the ability to influence supply, quality, value addition, costs and pricing decisions, efficient flow-to-market, and therefore competitive advantage. They have power through control of strategic resources, expertise (eg subcontractors), influence on strategy implementation – and perhaps interpersonal influence with managers.
- Government has the power to constrain organisational activity by legislation and regulation – and so on.

1.4 All these influences may impact on the structure, systems, policies and values of the organisation – and individual functions such as purchasing and supply. The more influence a stakeholder has, the more likely it is that managers will have to take that stakeholder's needs and wants into account.

1.5 Note that stakeholders' influence is not *just* about power to get their needs met: stakeholders also make a **contribution** to the organisation's needs and objectives. (This is often what gives them influence: they have the power to give, or withhold, something the organisation wants.) Stakeholder management is effectively a mutual exchange of benefits: a marketing process. So for example, in an ideal situation:

- Regulators fulfil the organisation's need for reliable, cost-effective guidance – which enables the organisation to fulfil the regulator's need for safe, equitable, truthful, sustainable business.
- Suppliers fulfil the organisation's need for reliable, cost-effective goods/services – which enables the organisation to fulfil its suppliers' needs for ongoing business, profit and growth.
- Employees fulfil the organisation's need for skills, knowledge, commitment and labour hours – which enables the organisation to fulfil its employees need for job security, livelihood, development and so on.

(You should be able to match needs/wants like this for each stakeholder group.) In practice, however, stakeholder and organisational objectives do not always coincide, and potential conflict must be managed.

Stakeholders of the purchasing function

1.6 In addition to 'organisational stakeholders' in general, each function, unit and project of an organisation may be said to have stakeholders, whose needs and influence must be taken into account. You should be able to identify the key stakeholders in the purchasing function, from each of the categories listed. The most obvious ones may be purchasing managers; employees; line managers on whose behalf purchases are made or to whom purchasing advice/policy is directed; suppliers; distributors; third-party service providers (eg logistics); and regulators (eg on public sector purchasing or health and safety).

The internal customer

1.7 The internal customer concept implies that any unit of the organisation whose task contributes to the task of other units (whether as part of a process, or in a staff or service relationship) can be regarded as a supplier of goods and services like any other supplier: each link in the value chain is a customer of the one before.

1.8 The task of each unit thus becomes the efficient and effective identification and satisfaction of the needs and wants of its internal customers. This helps to integrate the objectives of units throughout the value chain – and makes each unit look at what added value it is able to offer.

1.9 The internal customers of the purchasing function include: senior management and shareholders, who expect their strategic objectives to be met through supply chain management; related functions such as finance, manufacturing, warehousing and logistics which depend on efficient co-ordination with purchasing; and line managers in other functions, who expect timely supply of the right quality and quantity of resources to meet their own objectives.

The value chain

1.10 One way of gaining a deeper insight into customer needs is through value chain analysis. The value chain breaks down the firm into its strategically important activities in order to gain fuller understanding of the value of each. **Value activities** are the technologically and physically distinct activities that an organisation performs.

1.11 The concept of value should be continually assessed from the point of view of the final consumer or user of the product or service. This may be overlooked by organisations which are distanced from their final users by intermediaries such as distributors, leaving them out of touch with the realities of their markets.

1.12 According to *Michael Porter*, the business of an organisation is best described by way of a value chain in which total revenue minus total costs of all activities undertaken to develop and market a product or service yields value.

1.13 Porter's value chain, shown in Figure 2.1, displays total value and value activities.

Figure 2.1 The value chain

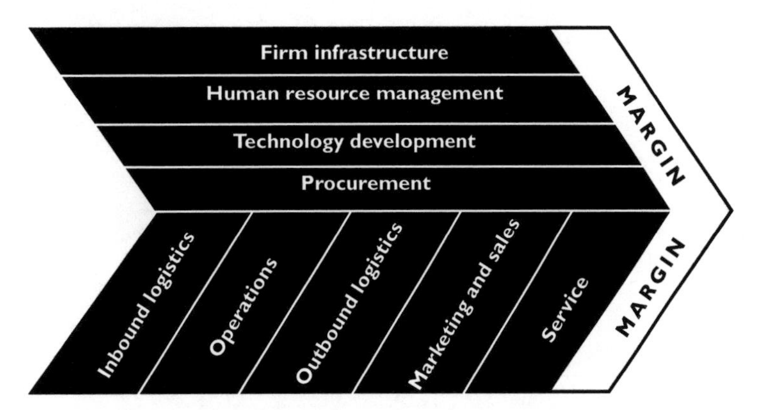

1.14 The **primary activities**, in the lower half of the value chain, show in sequence the activities performed by the organisation in converting raw material inputs to finished products and the transfer of the product/service to the buyer.

- Inbound logistics are the activities concerned with receiving, storing and handling raw material inputs.
- Operations are concerned with the transformation of the raw material inputs into finished goods or services. The activities include assembly, testing, packing and equipment maintenance.
- Outbound logistics are concerned with storing, distributing and delivering the finished goods to the customers.
- Marketing and sales are responsible for communication with the customers, eg advertising, pricing and promotion.
- Service covers all of the activities which occur after the point of sale, eg installation, repair and maintenance.

Each of these may be a source of competitive advantage.

1.15 Alongside all of these primary activities are the secondary, or support, activities of procurement, technology, human resource management and corporate infrastructure. Each of these cuts across all of the primary activities, as in the case of procurement where at each stage items are acquired to aid the primary functions. At the inbound logistics stage it may well be raw materials, but at the production stage capital equipment will be acquired, and so on.

2 *Identifying and fulfilling stakeholder needs*

2.1 Stakeholder management recognises the need to take stakeholders into account when formulating strategies and plans. For a purchasing manager, it may be helpful in several ways. It enables you to gain expert input from stakeholders at the planning stage of a project, to improve the quality of your decisions. Stakeholders are more likely to 'own' and support plans to which they have had input: this will make ongoing collaboration easier. Gaining the support of powerful stakeholders may, in turn, mobilise power and resources within the organisation in support of your plans. At the very least, sources of resistance to your plans (from stakeholders whose goals are different or incompatible with yours) can be anticipated and planned for.

2.2 A systematic approach to managing stakeholders is as follows: Figure 2.2.

Figure 2.2 *Managing stakeholders*

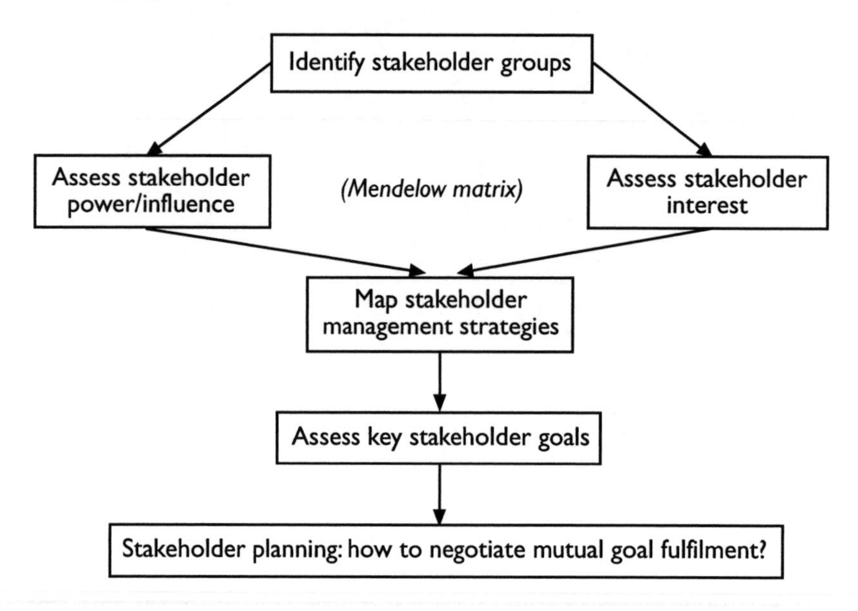

The power/interest matrix

2.3 *Mendelow's* power/interest matrix is a useful tool for mapping stakeholders according to their power to influence organisational activity and the likelihood of their showing an interest in it: Figure 2.3.

Figure 2.3: *Mendelow's power/interest matrix*

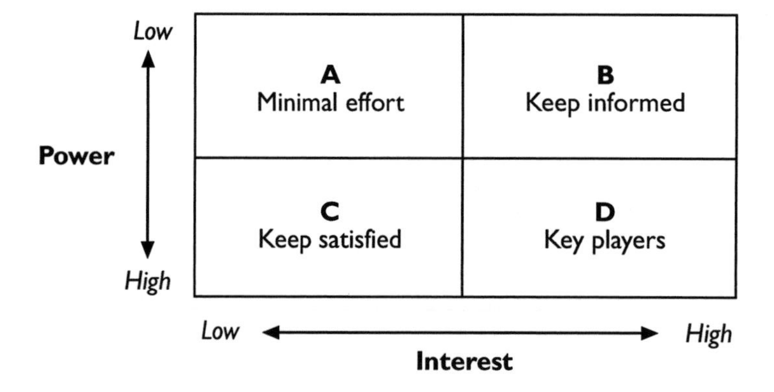

2.4 Working through each of the segments:

- Stakeholders who have neither interest nor influence in organisational activity (A) are a low-priority group: resources will not be wasted taking their goals into account, and they are likely simply to accept outcomes and directives.
- Stakeholders in segment B are important because of their high interest: they may have low direct influence, but unless they are kept 'in the loop' and understand the need for a strategy, they may seek additional power by lobbying or banding together against it. (Community and employee groups may be in this category.) The recommended strategy is to keep them informed of strategies and outcomes, through stakeholder marketing, communication and education.

- Stakeholders in segment C are important because of their high influence: they currently have low interest, but if dissatisfied or concerned, their interest may be aroused. (A large institutional shareholder may be in this category.) The recommended strategy is to keep these stakeholders satisfied.
- Stakeholders in segment D are known as 'key players': they have influence and are motivated to use it in their own interests. (Major customers and key suppliers may be in this category.) *Scholes* suggests that these stakeholders can be major drivers of change – or opponents of organisational strategy. The recommended strategy is one of early involvement and participation, so that stakeholder goals can be integrated with organisational goals as far as possible.

Stakeholder planning

2.5 Once key stakeholders have been identified, it is possible to plan a management strategy for each. You might use a standard process, such as the following.

- Goal analysis. What motivates these stakeholders? What are their goals or desired outcomes from your plans? What fears or issues might your plans raise for them? Where might they support you – and where might they oppose you?
- Desired outcomes. What do you want or need from these stakeholders? What levels of support do you want from them? What role(s) would you want them to play in your project or plans?
- Stakeholder marketing. What messages will you need to convey to these stakeholders? How can you 'sell' them the benefits of what you are proposing or doing? How can you confront and overcome any resistance?
- Relationship management. How will you manage communication to, and input from, each of these stakeholders? How will you keep your key supporters motivated? How will you win over or neutralise resistance? How will you engage the interest of potential supporters?
- Issues management. How will you raise potential issues and problems, where stakeholders' goals may differ from yours? How will you gain stakeholders' early involvement, and collaborate with them in minimising or managing the impacts?

3 *Business ethics and corporate responsibility*

Business ethics

3.1 'Ethics' are simply a set of moral principles or values about what constitutes 'right' and 'wrong' behaviour. For individuals and groups, these often reflect the assumptions and beliefs of the families, national cultures and educational environment in which their ideas developed. Ethics are also shaped more deliberately by public and professional bodies, in the form of agreed principles and guidelines which are designed to protect society's best interests.

3.2 Ethical issues may affect businesses (and public sector organisations) at three levels.

- At the **macro** level, there are the issues of the role of business and capitalism in society: the debate about globalisation, the exploitation of labour, the impacts of industrialisation on the environment and so on. This is the sphere addressed by the Ethical Trading Initiative, for example.
- At the **corporate** level, there are the issues which face an individual organisation as it formulates strategies and policies about how it interacts with its various stakeholders. Some of these matters will be covered by legislative and regulatory requirements, and an organisation may have a 'compliance based' approach to ethics which strives merely to uphold these minimal requirements. The sphere generally referred to as Corporate Social Responsibility covers policies which the organisation adopts for the good and wellbeing of stakeholders, taking a more proactive 'integrity based' approach.
- At the **individual** level, there are the issues which face individuals as they act and interact within the organisation and supply chain: whether to accept gifts or hospitality which might be perceived as an attempt to influence supplier selection, say. This is the sphere which is often covered in Codes of Ethics.

Corporate social responsibility

3.3 The term 'social responsibility' is used to describe a wide range of obligations that an organisation may feel it has towards the society in which it operates: its 'secondary' stakeholders (ie those not directly connected with the organisation, but affected by its operations). This is sometimes expressed in terms of 'externalities': the costs of business activities which are not absorbed in a product/service or paid for by consumers, but which are borne by the wider community – such as the costs of pollution, including associated costs of illness, environmental degradation and so on.

3.4 One CIPS examiner has summed up CSR as follows.

'CSR means the commitment to systematic consideration of the environmental, social and cultural aspects of an organisation's operations. This includes the key issues of sustainability, human rights, labour and community relations, and supplier and customer relations beyond legal obligations. The objective [is] to create long-term business value and contribute to improving the social conditions of the people affected by our operations.'

3.5 Any or all of the following considerations may be relevant in assessing an organisation's CSR obligations.

- **Sustainability** issues: the conservation and perpetuation of the world's limited natural resources (eg by limiting greenhouse gas emissions or logging)
- **Environmental** issues: the reduction of environment pollution, waste management, the avoidance of environmental disfigurement, land reclamation, promoting recycling, energy conservation and so on
- **Ethical trading**, business relationships and development: consumer protection; the upholding of principles of good corporate governance; improvement of working (and social) conditions for employees, suppliers and subcontractors (particularly in developing nations); avoidance of exploitation and debt minimisation; upholding ethical employment practices (such as equal opportunities and employment protection); adherence to ethical codes for fair trading and so on.

3.6 There are many ways in which a purchasing function can contribute to CSR objectives. For example, it can draw up and enforce codes of ethical practice in sourcing or adhere to the rules laid down in the CIPS ethical code and the Ethical Trading Initiative; it can encourage (or even insist on) ethical employment and/or environmental practices in its suppliers; it can adhere to health and safety, equal opportunities and other ethical practices in its own workplace and so on.

Why should an organisation set ethical standards and CSR objectives?

3.7 Various arguments have been put forward for ethical behaviour.

- It is a moral duty. (This is sometimes called a deontological position, from the Greek root word for 'obligation'.)
- It is functional or practical. (This is sometimes called a utilitarian position, from the Latin root word for 'useful'.)
- It supports organisational goals. (This is sometimes called a teleological position, from the Greek root word for 'purpose'.)

3.8 *Milton Friedman* took the view that 'the social responsibility of business is profit maximisation': to give a return on shareholders' investment. Spending funds on objectives *not* related to shareholder expectations is irresponsible: regard for shareholder wealth is a healthy discipline for management, providing accountability for decisions. The public interest is already served by profit maximisation, because the State levies taxes.

3.9 'Consequently,' argued Friedman, 'the only justification for social responsibility is **enlightened self interest**' (or ethical egoism) on the part of a business organisation. So how does CSR serve the interest of the firm?

- Law, regulation and Codes of Practice impose certain social responsibilities on organisations (eg in relation to health and safety, employment protection, consumer rights and environmental care). There are financial and operational penalties for failure to comply (eg 'polluter pays' taxes).
- Voluntary measures (which may in any case only pre-empt legal and regulatory requirements) may enhance corporate image and build a positive brand. A commonly quoted example is the environmental and sustainability strategy adopted by The Body Shop.
- Above-statutory provisions for employees and suppliers may be necessary to attract, retain and motivate them to provide quality service and commitment – particularly in competition with other employers/purchasers.
- Increasing consumer awareness of social responsibility issues create a market demand for CSR (and the threat of boycott for irresponsible firms)

3.10 However, business also needs to remember the 'enlightened' part of the equation! Profit maximisation does not, by itself, always lead to ethical behaviour – as examples of environmental and human exploitation show. (High-profile past examples include: environmental degradation caused by Shell oil refineries in Nigeria; child labour used by Nike and other Western clothing manufacturers; fraudulent reporting by Enron...)

3.11 *Mintzberg* notes that a business's relationship with society is not purely economic: a business is an open social system which makes a variety of non-economic exchanges with the society in which it operates (people, information, image), and creates a variety of non-economic impacts. Social responsibility helps to create a social climate and infrastructure in which the business can prosper in the long term.

3.12 In the same way, ethical sourcing helps to create a climate in which mutually-beneficial long-term trading relationships can be preserved. Exploitation, abuse and disappointed expectations will inevitably lead to broken relationships or reciprocal 'corner cutting' by suppliers. The modern focus on partnership in supply chains therefore puts the spotlight firmly on ethical sourcing practices.

4 Ethical issues in purchasing

Use of information

4.1 One of the key principles of business ethics is the provision of fair, truthful and accurate (not false or misleading) information. This makes unethical, for example, the practice of deliberately inflating estimates of order sizes in order to obtain a price that would not be offered if the true usage patterns were admitted.

4.2 Another key ethical principle is protecting the confidentiality of information, where appropriate. Confidential information obtained in the course of business should not be disclosed without proper and specific authority, or unless there is a legal duty to disclose it: for example, if there is suspicion of money laundering or terrorist activity.

Fair dealing

4.3 Another key principle is what might be called 'fair dealing'. A temptation may be offered, for example, where a supplier or potential supplier makes an error in a quotation or invoice; where there is potential to pay late; where quotations or tender bids are sought from suppliers where there is no intention to purchase (eg if the contract has already been awarded); or where some vendors are favoured over others in a tender situation (eg providing them with more information, or allowing post-tender negotiation). Deception or unfairness in such situations may be perceived as unethical and potentially damaging to ongoing trading relationships.

Hospitality and gifts

4.4 Another key principle of business ethics is not offering or accepting gifts or inducements which may – or may be *perceived* to – influence the recipient's decision-making. A related principle is that individuals should not make decisions (or divulge confidential information) for personal gain.

4.5 The giving of gifts and offers of hospitality are among the common courtesies of business dealings. The problem for buyers is to decide when such practices amount to an attempt to induce a favourable sourcing decision. There are obvious cases where buyer and seller collude to ensure that the seller wins a contract, the buyer in return receiving a reward: this is defined as bribery and corruption – and it is illegal in the UK (with strict legislation covering public bodies, in particular).

4.6 The more problematic cases are those where no explicit link is made between the gift and the award of business. A major difficulty may be the difference in perceptions between buyer and seller. To the seller, a gift may be merely a token of appreciation, of a kind that his organisation virtually expects him to bestow on most or all customers. To the buyer, however, the gift may become a material inducement to favour that supplier. (In international business dealings, this difference in perception may also be a cultural issue.)

Fraud prevention

4.7 Managers need to be aware of the range of activities that may be considered fraudulent – and clearly articulate organisational rules and expectations. 'Many companies have to put up with missing stationery, personal telephone calls and even the theft of mobile phones or computers. Larger scale fraud is often carried out by employees working in collusion with suppliers. Such frauds can be as simple as accepting kickbacks or they can be more complex affairs where an employee deliberately rejects goods already paid for as defective, returning them to the supplier who then resells them as new.' *(The Times,* 20/09/05)

Ethical codes and standards

4.8 As may be seen from the brief survey above, buyers are more exposed to temptation than most professionals! They control large sums of organisational funds. Their decisions typically benefit some suppliers over others – creating an incentive to try and influence those decisions. Meanwhile, it is difficult to determine wholly objective criteria for deciding between rival suppliers, allowing bias or unfairness to enter the process. Such factors place great responsibility on buyers to maintain personal ethical standards.

4.9 National and international bodies representing purchasing professionals have published ethical codes setting out (usually in fairly broad terms) what moral principles or values are used to steer conduct, and what activities are considered unethical.

CIPS ethical code

4.10 The code published by CIPS makes it clear that seeking membership of the Institute is in itself an undertaking to abide by ethical standards. Failure to do so may be dealt with according to a defined disciplinary process.

4.11 The guidance emphasises the overriding principle that members should not use a position of authority for personal gain. Equally, members have a responsibility to uphold the standing of the profession (and the Institute) by their conduct both inside and outside their employing organisations.

4.12 Specific guidance is also offered in the following areas.

- Members must disclose any personal interest which might impinge on their work activities, or which might appear to do so in the eyes of others.
- Members must respect confidentiality of information and must not use information received for personal gain. The information they provide should be true and fair.
- Members should avoid any arrangements which might prevent fair competition.

- Except for small-value items, business gifts should not be accepted.
- Only modest hospitality should be accepted. Members should not accept hospitality which might influence a business decision, or which might appear to do so.
- Any doubt on these last two points should be discussed with the individual's superior.

Management's role in promoting ethical standards

4.13 A common first step in large business organisations is to prepare written standards of conduct to which staff are expected to adhere. These will apply not just to purchasing staff, but to others in the business who may be subject to temptation or influence to behave unethically. Such written policies play an important role in raising and maintaining standards, and supporting fair disciplinary action where they are breached.

4.14 To ensure that the written policies are followed in practice, managers should ensure that they are published widely and reinforced through staff appraisal, development and training (including continuing professional development, where relevant). Performance should be monitored systematically: many buying organisations give their suppliers access to the standards, enlisting their help in identifying potential abuses. Above all, managers should foster (by example) an ethos where ethical behaviour is regarded as a positive, and key, organisational value, with zero tolerance for abuses – and open forums for discussing ethical issues of concern to staff.

The Ethical Trading Initiative

4.15 The ETI is an alliance of companies, non-governmental organisations (NGOs) and trade union organisations committed to working together to identify and promote internationally-agreed principles of ethical trade and employment, and to monitor and independently verify the observance of ethics code provisions, as standards for ethical sourcing.

4.16 The ETI publishes a code of labour practice (the 'base code') giving guidance on fundamental principles of ethical labour practices, based on international standards.

1. Employment is freely chosen.
2. Freedom of association and the right to collective bargaining are respected.
3. Working conditions are safe and hygienic.
4. Child labour shall not be used.
5. Living wages are paid.
6. Working hours are not excessive.
7. No discrimination is practised.
8. Regular employment is provided.
9. No harsh or inhumane treatment is allowed.

5 Management in the purchasing and supply function

5.1 As we noted in Chapter 1, there are several ways of looking at the purchasing manager's job.

5.2 In terms of processes (how they operate in order to ensure that tasks are performed), purchasing managers perform the functions of: planning, organising, co-ordinating, controlling and commanding.

5.3 In terms of roles (the 'hats' they wear as tasks are performed), purchasing managers may be: figureheads (at a CIPS conference, say); leaders (directing the Purchasing and Supply department); liaisons (at cross-functional management or quality meetings); information handlers; entrepreneurs (initiating new quality initiatives, perhaps); disturbance handlers (responding to unforeseen supply problems or team conflicts); resource allocators (selecting suppliers); and negotiators (not just on price, but to get purchasing policy approved by senior management, say).

The role of a purchasing and supply manager

5.4 In terms of content (what tasks are performed), the job will vary more widely according to how the purchasing/supply/logistics function is organised, and the specific job or role description developed by the organisation.

5.5 However, the broad role description of a purchasing and supply manager would typically include the following elements.

- **Purchasing**

  At an operational level, the purchasing manager may, especially in a small department, fulfil the purchaser's role. Even in a larger function, the manager may perform purchasing tasks, perhaps for large capital items, contracts over a certain value, or key suppliers. The purchaser's task can be summed up as ensuring, by ethical means, the best value/quality at the lowest price.

- **Managing resources**

  At a tactical level, managers must ensure that resources are acquired and deployed with maximum efficiency, for the effective achievement of corporate objectives. This includes planning and controlling the use of key resources such as: time (the manager's time, machine time and labour hours); finance (with attention to cost, efficiency, risk and the need for budgetary planning and control); physical resources (storage space, machinery and equipment, the transport fleet, raw materials and parts); and people (the skills, knowledge, experience and labour hours of purchasing and supply staff).

- **Advising on purchasing and supply systems**

  At a tactical level, management also involves developing systems and procedures to enable strategic objectives to be fulfilled. Purchasing and supply managers need to develop effective information, purchasing, quality, materials management, transport and other systems, in order to ensure a flow of materials and services to meet the organisation's needs.

Because these systems affect (or will be implemented and used by) other departments and links in the supply chain, managers may not have the *authority* to impose systems, procedures, standards or controls, but may have the *influence* (by virtue of their specialist expertise) to recommend them, and advise on their design and implementation.

- **Building supply chain relationships**

  This is an increasingly important role at all levels of the purchasing and supply function and management.

  At a strategic level, the building of co-operative, mutually beneficial (and therefore potentially long-lasting) relationships with the supply chain supports competitive advantage (on the basis of supply, quality or price), new product development and 'make or buy' decisions.

  At a tactical level, building effective relationships with existing sources, and developing alternative or additional sources (to meet unforeseen contingencies and planned needs) is essential to secure continuity of supply.

  Meanwhile, at an operational level, effective communication and trust supports the day-to-day planning, co-ordination and control of supply chain activity.

- **Policy development**

  'Policies' are broad statements of intent which translate strategies into guidelines for management decision-making: they allow managers to exercise their own discretion, but within clearly understood parameters. Managers in purchasing and supply will have expert input to the formulation, by the management team, of policies in regard to matters such as: environmental responsibility; ethical trading; quality management; and 'make or buy' decisions.

Multi-level management activity

5.6 Even our general survey highlights the diversity, complexity – and occasional ambiguity – of the purchasing and supply management role. For one thing, as we have noted, it may be required to operate at all levels of management: from the operational to the strategic.

5.7 This partly reflects a major shift in the role of purchasing and supply management over recent decades. For a long time, it was regarded as a secondary support or service function: an administrative handmaiden to the needs and objectives of the production function (in manufacturing contexts) or the finance function (in service/public sectors).

5.8 However, it has increasingly been recognised that, through involvement in issues such as 'make or buy' decisions, quality management, new product development and key commercial relationships, purchasing and supply have a central and strategic role in securing competitive advantage.

5.9 *Baily et al* argue that it is now possible to see purchasing (again) as a service or support activity – but in a different way and at a higher level. 'It is now widely thought, and practice reflects this thinking, that high-level purchasing expertise is best employed in determining supply strategy in line with that of the corporation, and assisting those concerned with day-to-day operations in reflecting this strategy in managing their own acquisition and use of externally sourced products and services.'

5.10 In other words, purchasing managers may now (having developed policies and systems) be able to devolve more of their day-to-day, straightforward buying activity (routine, lower-value items) to line department budget-holders – while retaining and developing their strategic roles (managing supply chains, determining overall purchasing policy, major negotiations).

'Upside-down' management?

5.11 This reflects what has been called the 'inverted pyramid'. In the traditional view, the organisation should support the objectives of management: each level of the hierarchy facilitating the activities of the one above it. Today, it is often considered that managerial activity should support the objectives of the organisation: each level of the hierarchy facilitating the activities of the one below it: Figure 2.4.

Figure 2.4 *The inverted pyramid*

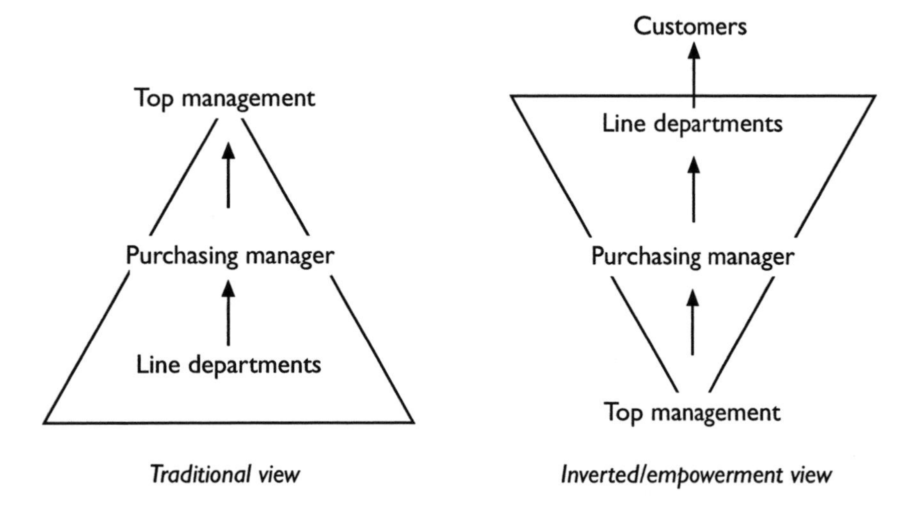

6 Purchasing management in the public and private sectors

6.1 As most readers will be aware, a private sector organisation is one that is owned by private individuals, either few in number (such as a small family business) or very numerous (as with a large company owned by millions of private shareholders). Public sector organisations on the other hand are 'owned' by the public in general: for example, the National Health Service is headed by a Government minister whose responsibility is to run the service efficiently and effectively on behalf of the general public.

6.2 A glance through standard purchasing textbooks is enough to show that private sector organisations are regarded as the main sphere of purchasing operations. Although there are some sound reasons for this (and we follow this approach in this Course Book), it would be wrong to see public sector operations as merely a trivial addition to the mainstream economic activity carried out by private sector providers. On the contrary, the spending power of public sector enterprises is enormous. Despite programmes of privatisation, the sheer range of public sector service provision is staggering: roads, law and order, education, health services, emergency services, and much more.

Private and public sector organisations

6.3 The main influence on strategic decisions in a private sector firm is the achievement of commercial objectives (generally, maximising profits), and managerial decisions are assessed on the extent to which they contribute to organisational profit or shareholder wealth. In contrast, public sector firms have a primary orientation to achieving defined service levels: providing efficient and effective services (education, transport, healthcare) and utilities (water, power) to the public, often within defined budgetary constraints and environmental/sustainability strategies.

6.4 In nearly all cases, a private sector firm will be one of several, or many, firms offering goods or services of a particular type. Consumers are free to choose between the offerings of different firms: securing competitive advantage is a large step towards realising the objective of profit maximisation. In the public sector, there has traditionally been little or no competition. (Since the 1980s, however, UK governments have sought to introduce market disciplines to the public sector eg in the form of local management of schools, customer charters and competitive tendering.)

Differences in purchasing management

6.5 The key differences are analysed by Gary J *Zenz*. His analysis forms the basis of Table 2.1 (on the following page) with our own points added.

6.6 These differences should not be overemphasised, however. An article in *Procurement Professional* recently noted that: 'key issues for the procurement profession... are as relevant for the public sector as they are for the private sector... Work is currently underway in public sectors around the world to address these issues, centred on:

- Developing standards for the assessment and ongoing development of public procurement professionals
- The greater application of strategic sourcing principles to public procurement
- The development and application of strategic procurement as a methodology that aligns strategic sourcing, supplier development and organisational strategic planning into a management mechanism and
- E-procurement systems.'

In addition, improving customer service and reducing cost inefficiencies to maximise value for money are now priorities in both sectors!

Table 2.1 *Differences between public and private sector purchasing*

Area of difference	Private sector	Public sector
Objectives	Usually, to increase profit	Usually, to achieve defined service levels
Responsibility	Buyers are responsible to directors, who in turn are responsible to shareholders	Buyers are responsible ultimately to the general public
Stakeholders	Purchasing has a defined group of stakeholders to take into account.	Purchasing has to provide value to a wider range of primary and secondary stakeholders.
Activity/process	Organisational capabilities and resources used to produce goods/services	Add value through supply of outsourced or purchased products/services. (Tend not to purchase for manufacture.)
Legal restrictions	Activities are regulated by company law, employment law, product liability law etc	Most of this applies equally to public sector, but additional regulations are present too (eg EU procurement directives)
Competition	There is usually strong competition between many different firms	There is usually no competition
Value for money	Maintain lowest cost for competitive strategy, customer value and profit maximisation.	Maintain or improve service levels within value/cost parameters.
Diversity of items	Specialised stock list for defined product/service portfolio.	Wide diversity of items/resources required to provide diverse services (eg local government authority).
Publicity	Confidentiality applies in dealings between suppliers and buyers	Confidentiality is limited because of public interest in disclosure
Budgetary limits	Investment is constrained only by availability of attractive opportunities; funding can be found if prospects are good	Investment is constrained by externally imposed spending limits
Information exchange	Private sector buyers do not exchange information with other firms, because of confidentiality and competition	Public sector buyers are willing to exchange notes and use shared e-purchasing platforms, consolidate purchases etc.
Procurement policies/procedures	Tend to be organisation-specific. Private sector buyers can cut red tape when speed of action is necessary	Tend to follow legislative directives. Public sector buyers are often constrained to follow established procedures
Supplier relationships	Emphasis on long-term partnership development where possible, to support value chain.	Compulsory competitive tendering: priority to cost minimisation and efficiency, at the expense of partnership development.

6.7 As you work through this text you will come across further references to the particular characteristics of purchasing management in the public sector.

Chapter summary

- Stakeholders are groups who have a legitimate interest or 'stake' in the activity or performance of the organisation (or specific functions or projects). Key stakeholders include: shareholders, management, employees, trade unions, investors, customers, suppliers, intermediaries, government and regulatory bodies, pressure/interest groups and the community.
- Stakeholder groups have an interest (needs, wants and concerns) and exercise power (influence and contribution). Stakeholder management involves assessing this balance (eg using Mendelow's power/interest matrix) and responding accordingly. Ideally, mutual satisfaction may be obtained – but there is often a conflict of interests.
- The internal customer concept and Porter's value chain illustrate the role of procurement in supporting other units in the organisation to produce customer value and profits.
- Business ethics are moral principles or values which steer the conduct of individuals and organisations in their internal and external dealings. Ethical codes are formulated to express these principles of conduct.
- Corporate social responsibility (CSR) describes the range of obligations that an organisation may feel it has towards secondary stakeholders in the society in which it operates, often out of a combination of ethics and self-interest.
- Managers have a key role in promoting and reinforcing ethical behaviour.
- The role of a purchasing and supply manager may include: purchasing; resource management; advising on purchasing and supply systems; building supply chain relationships and policy development. This is increasingly seen as a strategic (rather than purely operational) role.
- Purchasing management differs in the public and private sectors, in areas such as: objectives; accountabilities; the effect of competition; the number of stakeholders; the diversity of resources/services; the nature of supplier relationships; the role of legal and budgetary constraints; and the standardisation of policies and practices.

Self-test questions

Numbers in brackets refer to paragraphs where you can check your answers

1. Distinguish between internal, connected and external stakeholders. (1.2)
2. What are the primary activities in Porter's value chain? (Figure 2.1)
3. Outline a systematic approach to managing stakeholders. (Figure 2.2)
4. What strategy should be used with 'key players' in Mendelow's matrix? (2.4)
5. Give three examples of CSR issues. (3.5)
6. How does CSR serve the interests of a firm? (3.9)
7. List three principles set out in the CIPS Code of Ethics. (4.12)
8. Why is the building of supply chain relationships an important part of the purchasing manager's role? (5.5)
9. What is the 'inverted pyramid'? (5.11)
10. List six major differences between public and private sector purchasing, and one area of convergence. (Table 2.1, 6.2)

CHAPTER 3

Stakeholder Management Skills

Learning objectives and indicative content

1.6 Propose ways of reporting effectively to senior management and securing top level support and sponsorship for initiatives and implementation of plans

- Keeping your stakeholders informed
- Building a business case
- Report writing: structure, content and making it interesting
- Effective meetings
- Presenting your plans

Chapter headings

1 Communication

2 Stakeholder communication

3 Report writing

4 Effective meetings

5 Presentations

Introduction

The writer Chester Barnard described an organisation as 'a system of cooperative human activities'. *Huczynski and Buchanan* define organisations as 'social arrangements for the controlled performance of collective goals'.

Cooperative activities and social arrangements – including people management, stakeholder management and supply chain relationships – depend on communication: the transmission or exchange of information. Many of them also involve interpersonal processes, in which the dynamics of personal perceptions, influence, roles and relationships play a key part. In Chapter 1, we noted that leadership is essentially an interpersonal process.

In this chapter, we explore some of the key interpersonal and communication skills required for stakeholder management.

1 Communication

Purposes of communication

1.1 Communication is – to use the most basic definition – the transmission or exchange of information.

1.2 People communicate for a number of general reasons – any or all of which may be relevant to the task of stakeholder communication and management.

- To exchange information: giving and receiving information required in order to initiate or facilitate actions or decisions.
- To build relationships: giving information in such a way as to acknowledge and maintain the relationship between the parties – rapport, trust, respect and so on.
- To persuade: giving information in such a way as to confirm or alter the attitude of another person, securing acceptance, agreement or compliance with the communicator's views or wishes.
- To confirm: giving information that clarifies and fixes previous communication, ensuring that both parties have the same understanding and aids to recollection (including evidence, if required).

1.3 In addition, you will have a more specific purpose for communicating: an outcome that you want from the communication event or transaction. Knowing exactly what you want to achieve is an important element in successful communication.

The communication process

1.4 Effective communication is a two-way process, often shown as a 'cycle': Figure 3.1. Signals or messages are sent by the communicator and received by the other party, who sends back some form of confirmation that the message has been received and understood.

Figure 3.1 *The communication cycle*

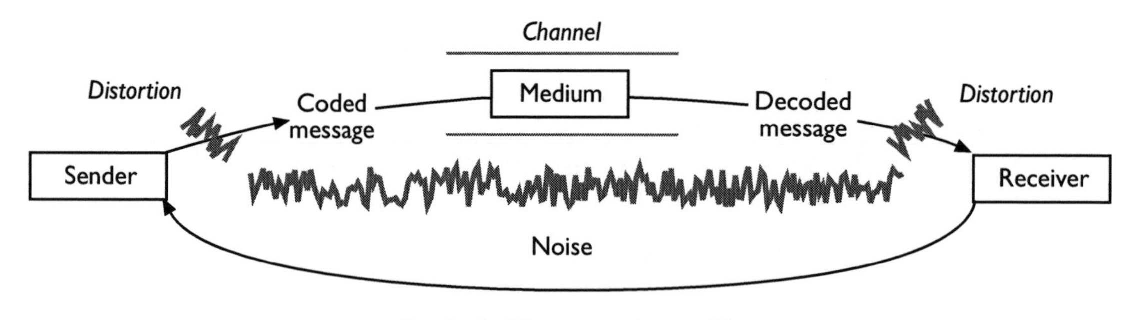

1.5 **Coding and decoding of a message**. The code or 'language' of a message may be verbal (spoken or written) or it may be non-verbal, in pictures, diagrams, numbers or body language. The needs and abilities of the target recipient should be borne in mind: not all codes (eg technical jargon, unlabelled diagrams) will be accessible to other people.

1.6 **Media and channels**. The choice of medium (letter, memo, e-mail, report, presentation, telephone call) and channel of delivery (telecom system, notice board, postal system) depends on a number of factors such as:

- Speed: a phone call, for example, is quicker than a letter
- Complexity: a written message, for example, allows the use of diagrams, figure working etc and time for the recipient to peruse it at his own pace
- Interactivity: face-to-face and phone discussion allows the flexible exchange of questions and answers, which is particularly effective in problem-solving, negotiation and conflict resolution.
- Confidentiality: private interviews or sealed letters can be limited to their intended recipients. Conversely, if swift widespread dissemination of information is required, other methods will be more appropriate: a notice board, public meeting or website, say.
- Evidence: written records are often required as confirmation of business and legal transactions
- Cost-effectiveness: for the best result at the least expense.

1.7 **Feedback** is of vital importance, making communication a two-way process. Feedback from the recipient to the sender allows both parties to check whether and to what extent the message has been received and understood. Feedback includes verbal messages ('I got your message. I'd just like to clarify...'), non-verbal cues (scratching the head in a perplexed manner, nodding, making encouraging noises – 'uh huh' – and so on), and action in response to the message. It is the communicator's responsibility to adjust the message, in response to negative or doubtful feedback, until he is satisfied that it has been correctly understood.

Written communication

1.8 Written communication is often used for formal communication in organisations, in formats such as letters, memoranda, reports, forms, briefing notes and e-mails. (We discuss report-writing, as a key technique, later in this chapter, but you should be able to use any of these formats if called on to do so.)

Oral communication

1.9 Oral communication follows the same communication cycle as written communication, with the important addition of immediate interaction: you switch between 'sending' (speaking) and 'receiving' (listening) constantly. There are also more signals to take into account, with the additional element of 'non-verbal' communication: tone of voice, and – in face-to-face discussion – body language.

1.10 Oral communication can be face-to-face (as in discussions, interviews, meetings and presentations) or audible only (as by telephone).

1.11 A particularly important area of managerial skill development is listening skills. Managers spend much of their day listening, and doing so effectively can offer important benefits: listening is a quick, direct source of information – if used accurately.

1.12 Passive listening (letting information 'wash over you') is distinguished from active listening, an approach which seeks to enter into co-operative dialogue with the speaker, in order to gain maximum understanding and empathy. Active listening involves:

- Demonstrating attention: leaning forward, maintaining eye contact
- Giving encouraging and clarifying feedback: using verbal and non-verbal encouragers (nods, uh-huhs), asking questions, summarising/paraphrasing to check your understanding
- Keeping an open mind: using your critical faculties to test the speaker's assumptions, logic and evidence – but not jumping to snap judgements
- Being patient: waiting for a suitable opening to respond, focusing on the speaker (not on planning your response)
- Paying attention to non-verbal cues and processes: listening for underlying messages and feelings (and reflecting them back – the technique of empathy – where appropriate).

Non-verbal communication

1.13 Non-verbal communication is communication without words. We convey more than half of the meaning of any given spoken message via non-verbal signals, other than the words themselves.

1.14 We can use non-verbal behaviours: instead of words (eg pointing to something to which you want to draw someone's attention); to confirm or emphasise the meaning of the words (eg nodding while saying 'yes'); to create a positive impression (eg by a firm handshake); and to seek and give appropriate feedback when communicating.

1.15 Being aware of *other* people's body language helps us to receive feedback from listeners (eg a perplexed frown); recognise another person's real or underlying feelings (eg an angry silence); and read situations so we can modify our communications accordingly.

1.16 As you can see from our examples above, there is a wide variety of non-verbal 'cues':

- Kinesic behaviour (or 'body language'): movements such as gestures, facial expressions, eye contact, body posture
- Proxemics: how near you stand or sit to others, whether you lean toward or away, what space or barriers are between you
- Paralanguage: tone of voice, speed, emphasis and other vocal qualities (*how* something is said, which may be different from the message eg in the case of sarcasm)
- Object language: personal grooming, dress, furniture, symbols

1.17 You need to be aware that no single non-verbal cue is sufficient to make an accurate diagnosis of someone's meaning or mental state. How many possible interpretations can you put on a person's frowning, for example?

Communication channels in an organisation

1.18 Formal communication channels (or flows) within an organisation may take any of the following forms.

- Downwards (in the form of instructions, team briefings, rules and policies, announcements of plans etc)
- Upwards (in the form of reporting, feedback on team briefings, suggestions etc)
- Horizontal or lateral (in the form of multidisciplinary meetings, inter-departmental information flows for coordination etc)

1.19 Any or all of these may be involved in stakeholder management. A change in policy, or the introduction of new systems, for example, will have to flow down to team members. Senior management will receive upward reports on the results of plans and negotiations (as part of a manager's general accountability), plus exception reports on unforeseen contingencies or changes (eg in supply availability or price) which may require decisions. Horizontal information flows will constantly be used to co-ordinate cross-departmental activity, from the programmed exchange of inventory usage and delivery schedule data to joint participation in quality circles.

Common communication barriers

1.20 Difficulties may occur because of general faults in the communication process. There may also be particular barriers in a work situation because of individual differences and the complexity of organisational relationships and politics. Some of the common faults and blockages in organisational communication are shown in Table 3.1.

Table 3.1 *Barriers to communication*

	Faults in the communication process
•	Distortion or omission of information by the sender
•	Misunderstanding due to lack of clarity or technical jargon
•	Noise: interference in the environment which prevents the message getting through clearly. (This may be technical eg a bad phone line or noisy office, or psychological eg emotion or prejudice.)
•	Distortion: ways in which a message is 'lost in translation' (eg use of jargon, misunderstanding).
•	Non-verbal signs (gestures, posture, facial expressions) which contradict or undermine the verbal message, so that the sender's real meaning is in doubt
•	Communication overload: the recipient is given too much information to digest in the time available
•	Differences in social, ethnic or educational background, compounded by age and personality differences, creating barriers to understanding (and/or cooperation)
•	Perceptual selectivity: people hear only what they are motivated and willing to hear
•	Perceptual bias or distortion: eg stereotyping (assessing an individual on the basis of assumptions about the group to which he belongs); halo effect (forming a general impression based on single characteristics); projection (assuming others share your thoughts and feelings); and attribution (believing yourself responsible for successes, and others as responsible for failures).
•	Lack of communication skills

Barriers in work contexts	
•	Lack of opportunity or respect for upward communication by subordinates
•	Different units/functions having different priorities/perspective, creating potential for misunderstanding
•	Different functional specialists using technical jargon
•	Organisational politics leading to competing parties withholding, distorting and mistrusting information
•	Hoarding of information, in the belief that 'knowledge is power'
•	Subordinates overloading superiors with detailed information, rather than reporting by exception or summarising
•	Subordinates avoiding being the messengers of 'bad news' (especially about their own performance)
•	Information which has no immediate use tending to be undervalued or overlooked
•	Conflict and competition, reducing the willingness to communicate effectively
•	Paranoia about confidentiality and competitive advantage, restricting openness in communication

2 Stakeholder communication

2.1 In Chapter 2, we discussed the importance of communication, education and negotiation as strategies in managing relationships with key stakeholders who have the power to support – or resist – our plans and initiatives.

2.2 In regard to supply chain relationships, *Baily et al* distinguish between transactional relationships, in which there is a simple exchange between supplier and buyer, and mutual relationships, in which 'the benefits of doing business together arise from ideas of sharing as well as exchanging'. Other areas of your CIPS studies will emphasise the process of building and maintaining supplier relations. However, you should be aware of the extent to which effective communications are crucial for managers in general, in terms of:

- Customer care and customer relations management (including internal customers)
- Teambuilding and cooperative, satisfying teamworking
- Facilitating communication, and minimising barriers caused by conflict and difference
- Motivation of team members (given people's social needs) and management of team briefings
- Managerial roles in liaison, ambassadorship and culture creation
- Influencing (applying power in a way that does not alienate others, but gains their willing compliance and even commitment).

Keeping stakeholders informed

2.3 In today's data-rich environment, information overload is as much of a problem as lack of communication. (Just think how many useless e-mails you get in the course of a day!) Information is not exchanged with stakeholders just for the sake of it – although some non-essential communication may be helpful in building relationships and maintaining regular (non-negotiatory) contact.

2.4 It is, however, important for managers to keep stakeholders informed in any of the following situations.

- New information, plans or decisions are likely to affect the stakeholder's plans or interests (so that they legitimately feel they have a 'right to know'). Employees should be informed as early as possible, for example, if a plan is made to outsource activities which might cause redundancies.
- There have been changes to data, plans or decisions previously relied upon, including unforeseen contingencies (so that they 'need to know' in order to adjust their own performance). Identified schedule or cost deviations, for example, must be notified as soon as possible to those who will be affected by the overrun, and (if significant) to more senior management.
- The information represents helpful feedback to the stakeholder, enabling them to identify a problem and take corrective action, or to reinforce and celebrate positive performance (so that they are 'grateful to know': this helps to support a partnership-style relationship).

2.5 In some cases, the right or need to know is enshrined in law. Changes cannot be made to contract terms without due notice, for example. Employee representatives must be consulted on issues which affect their interests, under EU employee involvement provisions. In other cases, exchange of information is in both parties' best interests: suppliers will need to be informed of a proposed change to e-purchasing or EDI systems, for example, in order to support collaborative development and smooth changeover.

Reporting to senior management

2.6 Reporting to senior management is an important part of the upward flow of information in an organisation. It is a key element in the control system of the organisation, providing feedback information on progress and performance in relation to objectives and plans.

2.7 However, the control information required at the senior management (strategic) level is different from the control information managers use at the operational level. Senior managers are engaged in decision-making over matters of wider scope – but less detail: responsibility for the detail is delegated to lower levels of management.

2.8 The key principles of reporting to senior management may therefore be summarised as follows.

- **Reporting by exception**, or **variance reporting**: senior managers need only be informed if progress or performance deviates from the plan, or if unforeseen issues arise for which contingency plans are not in place. (Senior managers do not expect, or want, to be 'copied' on routine inter-departmental emails!)

- **Filtered information**: routine control reports should be concise and relevant to managers' information needs and time constraints. They should be targeted and formatted to allow swift grasp of key points (eg by the use of executive summaries) and to support decision making (eg by including clear recommendations).
- **Strategic relevance**: reports and recommendations should link operational plans and activities to the strategic aims and objectives of the organisation (which are the key responsibility of senior management): profitability, competitive advantage, innovation and flexibility, social responsibility and so on.

Securing support and sponsorship

2.9 In addition to reporting as part of the control/feedback system of the organisation, upward communication is used in the 'political' process of gaining support and sponsorship for ideas, initiatives and plans. (In organisational behaviour, 'politics' refers to how power is obtained and used in organisations.)

2.10 At lower levels of the organisation, upward communication may be used simply to obtain permission or authorisation to undertake a task or make a decision that is not within the individual's delegated authority. At the higher level, this is a more complex process requiring both information and influence. It involves 'selling' your ideas; gathering support from people involved in the decision-making process; and/or getting key influencers to become sponsors or champions of your ideas, who can get them on the agenda and 'push' for them within the decision-making group. This is a form of stakeholder marketing.

2.11 The first key skill in this form of communication is therefore to select the right information gatekeepers or influencers. These may simply be senior people who have the authority to make decisions and allocate resources. They may also be individuals or groups who are recognised and respected in a given area of expertise: the people decision-makers go to for information, and listen to, when a decision on that area has to be made. (*French & Raven* called this 'expert power'.)

2.12 The second key skill is persuasion: motivating decision-makers to support or champion your plan or initiative. A persuasive report or presentation to senior management (or other key influencers) will:

- Be concise, relevant, professional and timely: not alienating recipients by wasting their time!
- Present logical, balanced, structured argument, leading to a firmly supported conclusion or recommendation. Supporting evidence need not be supplied in detail, but it should be clear that such evidence is available. (This applies in your exams, too – especially when the examiner explicitly asks you to 'justify' or 'explain the reasons for' your answer…)
- Present a business case for any proposals, plans or recommendations being put forward. This is a basic point of influencing and motivation: if you want people to do something, you have to give them a reason that makes sense to *them*, in terms of the fulfilment of *their* needs and goals. Senior managers want to know how a plan or proposal will further the strategic objectives of the business.

2.13 Formulating a business case is an important skill, because – as we saw in Chapter 1 – business performance is arguably the key responsibility of a manager. Any plan you formulate should, directly or indirectly, further the aims and objectives of the business. Can you demonstrate, or argue persuasively, that your proposal will increase revenue, or cut costs; enhance labour productivity or flexibility; offer some advantage over competitors; enhance the organisation's market share, or brand image?

3 Report writing

3.1 Reports are widely used in business, as a medium of upward communication. While they may be given verbally (eg in meetings or presentations), they are primarily a form of written communication, enabling recipients to peruse substantial, detailed and complex content at their own pace, and to refer to the material as often as required.

3.2 A business report may be informal, and presented in a variety of formats such as a discussion, a memorandum, letter or e-mail. However, there is a particular set of structural and stylistic conventions governing a formal report.

Report-writing style

3.3 Perhaps the most important feature of report-writing is the need for clarity in conveying information: business reports tend to be prepared for the use of other people. This has several consequences for report-writing style.

- **Organisation**. Material in a report is usually clearly structured, especially if it is leading up to a conclusion or recommendation. Relevant themes should be signalled by appropriate headings. The layout of the report should display data clearly and attractively. Supporting detail may be placed in separate appendices, clearly referenced in the text of the report.
- **Objectivity**. Even in a report which is designed to persuade as well as to inform, subjective value judgements and emotions should be kept out of the content and style: bias, if recognised, can undermine the credibility of the report and its recommendations. Any assumptions, evaluations and recommendations by the report writer should be clearly signalled as such, and supported with data and reasoning. Facts and findings should be balanced.
- **Impersonality**. In formal reports, impersonal constructions are often used. Instead of 'I/we found that', for example, you might write: 'It became clear that...', or '[Your Name] found that...' or 'Investigation revealed that...'.
- **User-friendliness**. The report writer needs to recognise the needs and abilities of the report user. Avoid technical 'jargon' when writing for non-specialists. Write as simply and concisely as possible. Bear in mind the type and level of detail that will interest the user and be relevant to his purpose in reading the report.

Structure and content of a short formal report

3.4 A short formal report format is often used in the context of middle management reporting to senior management, or project reports. The main feature of this format is its structure: a sequence of logical sections, each headed and referenced appropriately, for ease of navigation through the material. A typical report might include the following sections.

Heading	**Content**
Title	The title (subject) of the report, who has prepared it, for whom it is intended, the date of completion, and the status of the report (eg 'confidential' or 'urgent') where relevant
Executive summary or overview	For a longer report: the key theme, points or conclusions of the report, to enable readers to orient themselves quickly to the material.
Terms of reference (or Introduction or Background)	The scope and purpose of the report: what was to be investigated, what kind of information was required, whether recommendations were to be made and so on.
Procedure (where relevant)	The steps taken to make an investigation, collect data, set events in motion and so on.
Findings (or Analysis)	The information or proposals themselves, set out with appropriate headings and sub-headings. The content should be concise, clear and logically organised: events in chronological sequence, findings in order of importance, arguments for and against – or whatever logical relationship is appropriate.
Conclusions	Summary of the main findings or message of the report; implications for the department or business; or (if relevant) decisions or actions taken.
Recommendations (if asked for)	The suggested solution to the problem investigated, or the option chosen from discussed alternatives.
Appendices (if required)	Supporting detail, left out of the main body of the report, for clarity (clearly cross-referenced)
References	For academic reports: citing books and articles used.

3.5 It may seem superficial, but you can make your report-writing much more effective and professional simply by starting with the appropriate section headings and organising your content accordingly.

TITLE

Executive summary

I TERMS OF REFERENCE

II PROCEDURE

III FINDINGS

1. Section heading

1.1 Sub heading

Short topic paragraphs

(a) Subsidiary points
(b)

IV CONCLUSIONS

V RECOMMENDATIONS

4 *Effective meetings*

Formal meetings

4.1 Formal meetings, such as the board meeting of a company, the annual general meeting (AGM) of a society or a local council meeting, are governed by strict rules and conventions. These may establish procedure on such matters as:

- attendance rights (for members of the public or shareholders, say)
- giving notice of the meeting
- the minimum number of members required to hold the meeting (the 'quorum')
- the role of officers of the meeting (the chairperson and secretary)
- the type of business to be discussed (the 'agenda')
- procedures for discussion, adjournments, proposals, amendments, voting entitlements and methods and so on
- the binding power of decisions made upon the participants
- the form in which the proceedings and decisions should be noted and reported (the 'minutes')

4.2 We will not be discussing formal meeting requirements here: instead, we will concentrate on the leadership of meetings such as might be held for consultation, decision making or negotiation within a department or with suppliers.

The importance of effective meetings management

4.3 Managers spend a large percentage of their working week in meetings, and with flatter organisation structures and the growth of empowered teamworking, this is expected to increase. Meetings are thus both a major cost to organisations, and a major context for decision-making. A well-organised, well-aimed and well-led meeting can be extremely effective to support relationship building and maintenance, interactive explanation and/or persuasion and so on.

4.4 Face-to-face communication in general and group discussion (meetings) in particular offer several advantages.

- Generating new ideas, using group dynamics to 'bounce' ideas off one another.
- Interactive 'real time' feedback and exchange and adjustment of views, for explanation, persuasion, problem-solving and decision-making.
- Decision-making that reflects the knowledge and interests of different stakeholders, for greater quality and/or acceptance of the decision.
- Spreading information quickly through a group of people.

4.5 Poorly managed meetings can, however, be non-productive or even counter-productive for the organisation. If meetings are a significant cost, they must be efficiently utilised – but poorly managed meetings are a waste of time. If meetings are where most decisions are made, they must facilitate quality decisions – but some group dynamics (discussed further in Chapter 10) result in poor or risky decision-making.

4.6 There are several key reasons why this might be so. The terms of reference (detailing the purpose and powers of the meeting) may not be clear. The people attending may be unskilled or unwilling communicators. Above all, there may be insufficient guidance or leadership, allowing the meeting to stray from its agenda or ramble on without time limits, or allowing some participants to dominate or hijack proceedings, while others are not encouraged to contribute.

The five Ps of effective meetings

4.7 *Whetton and Cameron* suggest that there are 'five Ps' in preparing for and conducting effective meetings.

- Purpose
- Participants
- Plan
- Process
- Perspective

We will look at each of these elements in turn.

4.8 **Purpose** refers to the reason for which a meeting is held. 'Making announcements' is one function of a meeting but not, by itself, sufficient justification for holding a meeting: it can be done in more cost-effective ways. A study into meetings by 3M in 1987 concluded that: 'When information can be conveyed by a memo or phone call, when people are not prepared, when key people cannot attend, when the cost of a meeting is higher than the potential payoff, and when there is no advantage to holding a meeting, no meeting should be called.'

4.9 **Participants** refer to the number, mix and balance of individuals invited to attend.

- Meetings can fail because they are too large (discussion may be superficial and few people will get to participate) or too small (insufficient viewpoints or information).
- Meetings require a balance of skills and competencies. *Cohen, March and Olsen* suggest: problem knowers (who understand the problem), solution providers (who generate ideas), resource controllers (who can put solutions into action) and decision affirmers (who have the authority to reinforce the decision).

4.10 **Planning** refers primarily to preparation of the meeting's agenda, although it will also be necessary to make arrangements for:

- meeting space of appropriate accessibility, privacy and so on
- seating layout (reflecting the formal or informal nature of the desired interpersonal dynamics)
- table space or other facilities for those who wish to take notes
- visual aids equipment (flip charts, whiteboards, data projection and so on)
- refreshments (especially if the meeting is of long duration)

4.11 The agenda for the meeting should reflect its priorities, both in the sequencing of the items of business (so that the meeting focuses its 'best' time on the most important or difficult items) and by allotting target times for the discussion of each item. A bell curve is often used to suggest the sequencing of agenda items: see Figure 3.2. It allows for the meeting to gather, settle in and build up to important and difficult items and then to 'wind down' towards closure.

Figure 3.2 *A bell curve agenda*

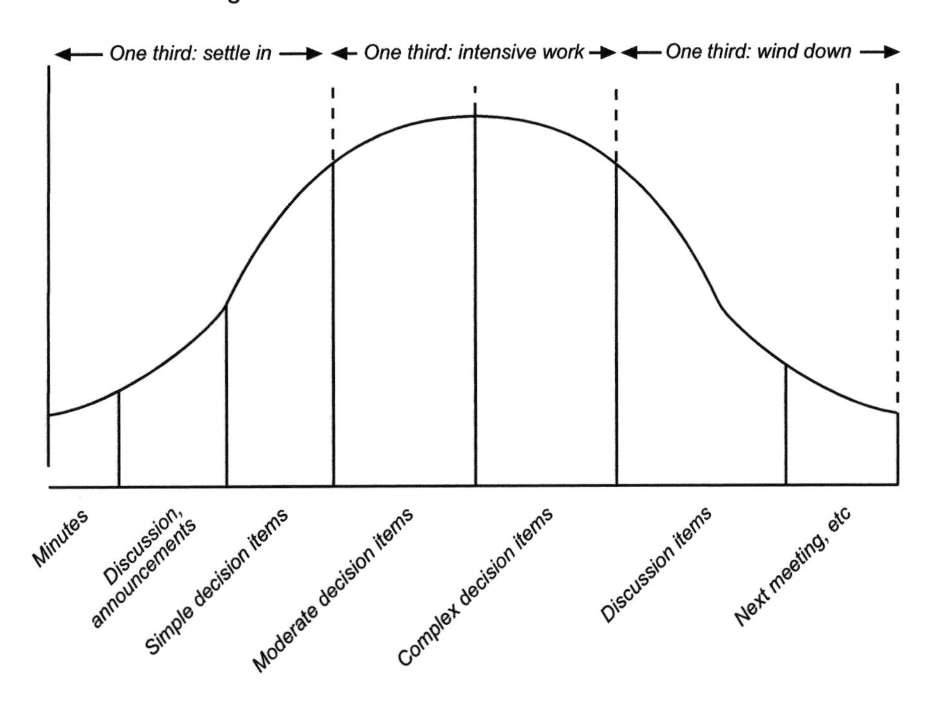

4.12 **Process** refers to the interpersonal and decision-making processes of the meeting, and the leader's efforts to ensure that all participants are allowed to contribute appropriately.

4.13 The leader should then establish a structure and ground rules for the meeting: its purpose, time frame, how closely the agenda will be followed, what kind and amount of participation is expected and so on. Different ground rules may be required for different purposes.

- The nature of brainstorming (non-evaluative, free-form ideas generation) may have to be explained, to prevent premature censorship of ideas.
- Conflict resolution meetings often apply rules of engagement whereby each party has to accurately reflect back the position just stated by the other, prior to having its own say.
- Formal meetings have detailed rules about who may contribute, when and how, including addressing all comments to the chairperson.
- Decision-making meetings often apply rules as to how decisions will be reached fairly and efficiently – by majority rule (vote), by power rule (leader decision), or by seeking consensus (general agreement).

4.14 During discussion, the role of the leader will primarily be to keep the group to its assigned tasks and time schedule, and to facilitate equitable participation among the members.

4.15 At the end of the meeting, the leader should conclude by summarising what was discussed, learned, decided or accomplished: apart from anything else, this may reinforce participants' sense that the meeting has been worthwhile. Assigned tasks and responsibilities should be reviewed to ensure that everyone knows what follow-up is required (and will be reported on at the next meeting).

4.16 **Perspective** involves looking back on meetings or series of meetings to evaluate their effectiveness. *Whetton and Cameron* suggest a KSS methodology, whereby participants are asked to assess the meeting according to:

- Keep: what went well about this meeting that we should keep or expand?
- Stop: what about this meeting was unproductive and should be abolished or phased out?
- Start: what did not happen in this meeting that should be introduced?

5 Presentations

5.1 Presentations may be used in a wide variety of purchasing contexts. As a manager, you may need to present your ideas or plans to senior management, or other stakeholders, in order to secure their agreement, support or sponsorship. As a specialist, you may need to make technical presentations to management or staff, briefing them on findings or facts relevant to their work. If you have written a report, you may be required to present it orally, to allow for interactive questions, explanations and challenges.

5.2 Presentations may therefore vary widely in the size and composition of the audience, the purpose and approach of the presentation (briefing, instruction, persuasion, entertainment and so on), the complexity and technicality of the subject matter, the length of the presentation and the formality of the occasion. All these factors will need to be taken into account.

5.3 A general approach to giving effective presentations may be described as follows.

- **F**ormulate a strategy for the specific purpose and audience
- **O**rganise the presentation content for clarity and impact
- **R**einforce oral content with appropriate visual aids
- **C**larify and emphasise the content with a confident and vivid presentation style
- **E**nd the presentation with informed responses to challenges and questions

You might use the mnemonic 'FORCE' to remember this framework.

Formulating a strategy

5.4 The **purpose** of a presentation should be expressed in specific, active terms. What do you want the audience to do/remember/believe/know/feel as a result of attending your presentation? What observable/measurable response will allow you to evaluate your success? Once you have stated your primary objective, you can work out the subsidiary objectives you need to achieve along the way.

5.5 Since your purpose is defined primarily in terms of audience response, it is important to take into account the needs, abilities and motivations of the **audience** you will be addressing. The purpose of the meeting, or topic of the conference, may indicate something of what the participants will be expecting, what they will be interested in and what they will be able to understand. In business contexts, you may know who your audience is: whether they are decision-makers, recruits/trainees, technical specialists or lay people, customers or suppliers with a particular stake in what you have to say, and so on.

The structure of the presentation

5.6 An effective introduction is vital to the presentation. It establishes credibility, gains the audience's interest and motivates them to keep attending, and gives the audience an overview of the shape and direction of the presentation. Introductions should:

- make an initial impact: arousing curiosity, setting up a problem to be solved or a question to be answered which relates to the audience's needs;
- establish credibility and congeniality, by demonstrating authority, clear thinking and/or rapport with the audience;
- give a statement of the subject and the style in which you intend to address it, to orient the audience and manage their expectations.

5.7 The structure of the main body of the presentation is critical because it facilitates or hinders the accessibility, credibility, comprehension and recall of the message. Various organisational patterns may be appropriate, according to purpose and content, as in Table 3.2: you might also bear them in mind when structuring written reports.

Table 3.2 *Approaches to organising presentation material*

Approach	Comment
Chronological order	Appropriate where events follow a time sequence: telling an anecdote, say, or explaining a process or procedure.
Causal order	Appropriate where one event causes or influences another: demonstrating the effects or consequences of a course of action, say, or tracing symptoms of a problem back to their causes.
Topical order	Covers different areas or aspects of the topic one by one or in related clusters.
Order of importance	May start with the most important point (to grab attention) or build up to the most important point (for a persuasive climax).
Order of specificity	May move from a general statement to specifics (illustrations, examples, explanations) or from specifics to a general statement (conclusion or summary).
Question-answer or problem-solution	Sets up a question, need or problem (creating strong audience motivation to listen) and answers them or proposes a solution.
Balanced or two-sided	May consist of an argument with two sides or viewpoints; a proposal which has advantages and disadvantages (pros and cons); two things which can be compared (as similar) or contrasted (as different) and so on.

5.8 The conclusion is another vital element, because people tend to rally their concentration towards the end of a talk and tend in any case to remember the last thing they hear (the principle of 'recency'). A conclusion should:

- clarify and draw together the points made into a final summary of the main idea;
- state, reinforce or imply the response required of the audience;
- give the audience a satisfying sense of closure or completeness.

Reinforcing the message with visual aids

5.9 The term 'visual aids' covers a wide variety of forms, including slides, film or video, drawing or writing on flipcharts or whiteboards, handouts, props and demonstrations. They can be used to add impact to the message; to clarify complex or detailed information; or to offer visual evidence of propositions – and to present an image of the presenter as a well-prepared communicator!

5.10 Visual aids can be counter-productive if they are the centre of attention (audience members reading handouts rather than listening); unprofessionally prepared or utilised; distracting to the speaker (having to find, manipulate, progressively unveil and retrieve them) and audience (observing all this logistics); not fully visible (too small, unclear, blocked from someone's line of sight); interfering with listening (projector noise) or audience participation (a darkened room for slides preventing note taking); and so on.

Chapter summary

- Communication is the transmission or exchange of information: it can best be modelled as a cycle.
- Communication media may be verbal (written or oral) or non-verbal. Active listening is a key skill for managers, involving engagement in a two-way process of communication.
- There are many potential barriers to communication, arising from individual perceptual selectivity and distortion, lack of skills, and noise and distortion factors in the communication situation.
- Stakeholder communication is an important part of purchasing management, for the purposes of: keeping key stakeholders informed; reporting to senior management (with an eye to reporting by exception, filtering and strategic relevance); and securing support and sponsorship (in which the key skill is persuasive communication).
- Formulating a business case for a proposal means demonstrating how it will further the aims and objectives of the business.
- Reports are primarily a form of written communication. A formal report should be highly organised (using systematic headings) and objective in style.
- Meetings are particularly valuable for making announcements, brainstorming and decision-making, because of the advantages of face-to-face communication for information-sharing, representation, persuasion and applying interpersonal skills. However, poorly managed meetings are widely regarded as non-productive or even counterproductive.
- Presentations are used in a wide variety of business contexts. They may be informational (eg for technical briefings), instructional (eg for training) or persuasive (eg for pitching proposals).

Self-test questions

Numbers in the brackets refer to the paragraphs where you can check your answers.

1 Draw a diagram of the communication cycle. (Figure 3.1)

2 Give brief guidelines for active listening. (1.12)

3 List the elements of non-verbal communication. (1.16)

4 Explain the different 'directions' of information flow in organisations. (1.18)

5 Explain the principles of (a) reporting by exception and (b) business case. (2.8, 2.12)

6 List the key headings of a formal report. (3.4)

7 What are the barriers to effective meetings? (4.6)

8 What is the role of (a) an agenda, (b) ground rules and (c) evaluation in effective meetings? (4.11, 4.13, 4.16)

9 Explain the 'FORCE' mnemonic for effective presentations. (5.3)

10 Give guidelines for the effective use of visual aids. (5.10)

CHAPTER 4

Organisation Structure

Learning objectives and indicative content

2.1 Evaluate the importance of organisational structure to the development and performance of organisations

- Rationale/background: industrial revolution to modern day
- Choice of different structures to aid management
- Organisational structures: conflicts between control and empowerment; autonomy and entrepreneurship
- Power

2.2 Evaluate the nature and scope of organisational structures and the implications of such structures for the purchasing function.

- Flat
- Functional
- Matrix
- Geographical
- Local
- Regional
- National
- International
- Global
- Centralised/decentralised

Chapter headings

1 An overview of organisation structures

2 What is organisation structure?

3 Elements of an organisation structure

4 Different structural forms

5 Inter-organisational and network structures

6 Organising the purchasing function

Introduction

Organisation structure is a key factor in organisational behaviour. We start this chapter by looking at how organisation theory has approached the question of structure: what is organisation structure designed to achieve, and how can structure be adapted to these aims?

We then go on to look at the elements of organisation structure, and how decisions about centralisation or decentralisation of authority, and span of control, change the 'shape' of organisations.

We look at different structural forms and the kinds of organisational strategies to which they are best suited.

Finally, we look at the organisation of the purchasing function.

1 An overview of organisation structures

1.1 In this introductory section, we will look at some of the key developments in organisational theory over time, and their influence on how organisations are configured and managed. The general flow of these developments has been via:

- A focus on universal principles to achieve the 'one best way' of organisation, primarily directed at production efficiency ('classical' organisation approaches, such as bureaucracy).
- A focus on adapting the organisation to changing environments and demands, primarily through key values of human relations and flexibility ('modern' approaches, including the human relations and contingency schools of thought).

1.2 *Huczynski and Buchanan* summarise the general development of organisation theories and forms as a reflection of the 'classical', 'modern' and 'post-modern' thinking of different eras: Table 4.1.

Table 4.1 *Classical, modern and post-modern organisational forms*

	Classical	**Modern**	**Post-modern**
Approx period	1880-1970 (the industrial age)	1970-1990 (the technological age)	1990- (the information age)
Organisation metaphor	Machine	Open system	Flexible tool
Organisation structure	Rigid, hierarchical chain of authority	Decentralised: delegated authority and local units	Not important: action, not 'design'
Focus	Internal processes	Human relations	Adaptability, innovation
Production focus	Mass production: efficiency	Customisation: meeting customer demands	Time to market: speed of response
Work organisation	Routine, repetitive work	Teamworking	Entrepreneurial units
Human resource	Full-time employees	Flexible working patterns	Networks, subcontractors
Control mechanism	Direct supervision, rules and procedures	Decentralisation: local problem-solving	Not important: results, not rules
Key values	Control and predictability	Quality, customer service	Change, flux, quick decisions
Approach	Find 'the one best way' (prescriptive approach)	Find 'best fit' (contingency approach)	Maximise responsiveness
Strategy for uncertainty	Avoid	Manage	Exploit

1.3 In practice, as Huczynski and Buchanan note, change is never this clear-cut, in terms of dates or features. It would be wrong to think of a smooth, linear progression from one position to another according to well-defined environmental demands. Elements of 'classical' organisation exist today (bureaucracies, for example, are surprisingly resilient), and the 'post-modern' idea of multi-skilled, empowered teamworking is not yet much in evidence. Nor (as we will see) would it necessarily be the most appropriate organisational form in all circumstances.

1.4 We will now look in more detail at how theories of organisation developed over time.

Scientific management

1.5 The emphasis in this period (1880–1930) was on the efficiency of physical production. Organisations were continually looking for ways to become more efficient and prevent waste. The industrial revolution resulted in standardisation of production and the introduction of the assembly line. A pioneer of this approach was *Fredrick W Taylor*, 'the father of scientific management'.

1.6 The key features of scientific management were as follows.

- Develop a science for each element of work, to replace the old rule-of-thumb method: the best way of doing a job.
- Apply work-study techniques to establish the most efficient operations, motions and processes by which a task could be accomplished.
- Redesign jobs so that each worker carried out only one job operation (rather than sequences of operations within the task) as a specialised job.
- Scientifically select and train workers to ensure all of the work being done is in accordance with the principles of scientific management.

1.7 Taylor's methods led to spectacular results in terms of efficiency and output. Modern management writers have appraised scientific management as follows.

- It has contributed a useful philosophy of worker and work. 'As long as industrial society endures, we shall never lose again the insight that human work can be studied systematically, can be analysed, can be improved by work on its elementary parts.' (*Drucker*)
- The micro-division of labour has been found to be profoundly unsatisfying to workers. 'By the end of the scientific management period, the worker has been reduced to the role of an impersonal cog in the machine of production. His work became more and more narrowly specialised until he had little appreciation for his contribution to the total product.... (*Hicks*)
- The rigidity and depersonalisation of the approach precludes concepts such as leadership, empowerment, flexibility and commitment, which are now considered essential in the successful management of change.

1.8 Nevertheless, elements of scientific management practice can still be seen in the use of efficiency studies and work-study techniques; assembly line production processes and machine tool automation; and the continuance of intrinsically unsatisfying jobs (with molecularised work design, close supervision and tightly timed work activities), eg in fast-food outlets and call centres.

The classical school

1.9 *Henri Fayol* was a French industrialist who popularised the concept of the 'universality of management principles'. His focus was the structure and processes of the formal organisation, and the rational principles by which it could be most effectively directed.

1.10 Although Fayol recognised that 'seldom do we have to apply the same principle twice in identical conditions' and that 'allowance must be made for different changing circumstances', he proposed certain rational principles of organisation and management. The principles which most clearly affect the configuration of the organisation include the following.

- Division of work: specialisation, in order to produce more and better outputs.
- Authority and responsibility: authority should be commensurate with responsibility.
- Scalar chain: There is a chain of authority running from the top of the organisation to the bottom, via defined lines which are also the organisation's formal channels of communication.
- Unity of command: for any action, a subordinate should receive orders from only one boss. Dual command (whether caused by imperfect demarcation between specialised departments or by superiors ignoring the proper channels of authority) is a disease.
- Unity of direction: there should be one head and one plan for each activity, so that efforts can be coordinated towards the same objectives.

Bureaucracy

1.11 *Max Weber*, a German sociologist, is the writer most associated with the concept of bureaucracy as an organisational form. He defined it as 'a continuous organisation of official functions, bound by rules'.

1.12 Bureaucracy is a pure application of rational organisational principles and of a rational/legal understanding of authority as the function of a role and position in the organisation – not an interpersonal process. Although the word has unpleasant associations to the modern ear, Weber claimed that bureaucracy is technically the most efficient form of organisation: 'from a purely technical point of view, capable of attaining the highest degree of efficiency and ... in this sense formally the most rational means of carrying out imperative control over human beings.'

1.13 Weber specified several general characteristics of bureaucracy.

- Hierarchy: each lower office is under the direct control and supervision of a higher one.
- Specialisation: work is divided into technically specialised functions.
- Impersonality: employees work within rules and regulations, according to formal procedures. There is nothing 'personal' about the authority or control applied by management.
- Rationality: 'jurisdictional areas' (areas of authority) are determined rationally. The hierarchy of authority, duties and responsibilities and measures of performance are clearly defined (eg in job descriptions).

- Uniformity: standardised performance of tasks is expected, regardless of who carries them out.
- Stability: rules, structures and continuity (irrespective of change of membership) removes ambiguity and creates a stable environment.

1.14 The very strength of bureaucratic organisation in creating rationality and stability may be seen as a weakness in environments characterised by ambiguity and change. Common criticisms of bureaucracy include the following.

- Long channels of authority and communication (referring decisions back to the top) lengthen the decision-making process, making bureaucracies notoriously inflexible and poor at responding to customer demands.
- Conformity and uniformity create ritualism and formalism, which create further rigidity and unresponsiveness, and suppress creativity, initiative and innovation.
- The personal growth of individuals is inhibited (although bureaucracies tend to attract, select and retain people with a tolerance for such conditions).
- The rigidity of centralised decision-making makes it insensitive to feedback, unable to learn, and unable to respond to changing demands and environments. Bureaucracies adjust only when forced to do so by serious problems – by which time, change is difficult, traumatic and resisted by the culture.
- Rules originally designed for efficiency take on a life of their own: they are adhered to for their own sake, even if unhelpful.
- People tend to justify poor service by citing rules, procedures and job descriptions. They do not feel personally responsible for customer satisfaction.

Human relations approach

1.15 The human relations approach developed to a large extent as a reaction to the dehumanising aspects of the approaches previously described. In the early 1920s, managers and academics were becoming increasingly aware of signs of worker alienation in the face of depersonalisation and standardisation. *Elton Mayo's* work on the famous Hawthorne experiments gave birth to the human relations movement which dominated the field of organisational behaviour during the 1940s and 1950s.

1.16 The experiments were designed to study the effect on output and morale of various changes in working conditions. Almost without exception, output increased – regardless of the changes introduced. This appeared to be due to factors such as the fact that management was giving attention to the workers, the enhanced work satisfaction that they enjoyed and a new social atmosphere which brought a marked change in their attitude to work. Further experiments proved the importance of employees' attitudes to work, to supervision and to working in groups.

1.17 The human relations school argued that an organisation was more than a formal structure or arrangement of functions. Mayo wrote: 'An organisation is a social system, a system of cliques, grapevines, informal status systems, rituals and a mixture of logical, non-logical and illogical behaviour'.

1.18 The human relations approach highlighted the need for managers to:

- Pay more attention to the needs of the workers, not just tasks and processes
- Realise that the satisfaction that individuals gain from group membership may be equal to any rewards or incentives offered by management
- Organise and reward work around groups (or teams).

The neo-human relations approach

1.19 By the early 1960s the term 'organisational behaviour' began to emerge and a behaviouralist approach to management was pioneered by Maslow, McGregor, Argyris and Herzberg. The 'neo-human relations' school differed from human relations in two important respects.

- It was concerned both with organisations (structure, tasks, reporting relationships) and people.
- It explored a wider range of human needs and motivations than simply social belonging, turning attention to the 'higher order' needs of people to develop themselves and fulfil their potential.

1.20 Recognition of people as the key organisational resource focused attention on organisational configurations which offered greater job satisfaction and harnessed the energy, ability and commitment of employees for the benefit of organisational efficiency, flexibility and innovation.

- Flatter organisation structures, with fewer layers and authority decentralised to lower levels.
- Teamworking, to fulfil social needs and create the synergy of pooled skills and expertise.
- Cross-functional and multi-skilled working, allowing workers to perform larger and more meaningful parts of the task.

Contingency approaches

1.21 Contingency theory does not ignore the lessons learned from other schools, but suggests that the best way to manage and organise work depends on the circumstances – there is no 'one best way'. Contingency approaches basically seek to identify the variable factors that influence the effectiveness of organisation structures, cultures and leadership, and to explore how they can be adjusted for a 'best fit' with the demands of the situation. In essence, contingency theory is about organisational flexibility.

1.22 Contingency approaches to organisation assert that: organisations may be structured in a variety of ways; the most appropriate organisation structure for a given situation will depend on a number of factors (discussed in Section 2 below); and most organisations exist in a changing environment and must adapt in order to survive.

1.23 *Burns and Stalker* identified that organisation structures should differ according to how stable or dynamic the market environments were. They categorised organisations along a continuum ranging from mechanistic to organic. Neither was intrinsically functional or dysfunctional; a structure's suitability depended on the stability of the market and the speed of change in the technology of the production process.

1.24 Mechanistic ('machine-like') organisations are bureaucratic. As discussed earlier, they are highly technically competent and efficient in stable conditions – but unsuited to conditions of change, because of their rigidity.

1.25 Organic ('oganism-like') organisations can adapt more easily to changing conditions. They are typified by structural and cultural fluidity and flexibility, involving:

- A 'contributive' culture of information and skill sharing, encouraging versatility (rather than specialisation) and teamworking (rather than functional departmentation)
- A 'network' structure of authority and communication, allowing decentralisation and a range of lateral relationships (crossing functional boundaries) for coordination and self-control
- Job design that allows flexible definition of tasks according to the needs of the team and changing demands
- Focus on goals and outputs rather than processes.

1.26 We will look further at flexible structures in Section 4 of this chapter.

2 What is organisation structure?

2.1 *Mullins* defines organisation structure as 'the pattern of relationships among positions in the organisation and among members of the organisation. Structure makes possible the application of the process of management and creates a framework of order and command through which the activities of the organisation can be planned, organised, directed and controlled'. *Mintzberg* defines an organisation's structure as: 'the sum total of the ways in which it divides its labour into distinct tasks and then achieves co-ordination among them'.

2.2 Formal organisation structure or design therefore consists of a framework whose purpose is as follows.

- Define work roles and relationships, so that areas and flows of authority and responsibility are clearly established
- Define work tasks and responsibilities, grouping and allocating them to suitable individuals and groups.
- Channel information flows efficiently through the organisation
- Coordinate goals and activities of different units, so that organisational goals can be efficiently achieved (ie without duplication of effort)
- Control the flow of work, information and resources, through planning, monitoring and other systems
- Support flexible working and adaptability to changing internal and external demands
- Encourage and support the commitment, involvement and satisfaction of the people who work for the organisation, by offering opportunities for participation, challenge, interest, responsibility, teamworking and so on
- Support and improve the efficiency and effectiveness of the organisation's performance through all of the above

2.3 *Drucker* argued that: 'good organisation structure does not by itself produce good performance. But a poor organisation structure makes good performance impossible, no matter how good the individual managers may be. To improve organisation structure ... will therefore always improve performance.'

2.4 Note, however, that an effective organisation structure is one that both facilitates organisational effectiveness and efficiency in the long term (taking into account the need for change) *and* meets the needs of the people working within it.

2.5 Signs that a structure may be **ineffective** therefore include problems such as:

- Slow decision/response times, due to the need to refer decisions via overly lengthy formal communication channels
- Inter-departmental conflicts, due to ambiguities or overlaps of responsibility
- Excessive layers of management (often middle management), which slows communication, increases overheads and often requires work creation to justify the positions
- Lack of co-ordination between units, seen in customer complaints, production bottlenecks, inconsistent communications, and the creation of special co-ordinating mechanisms (liaison officers, committees etc)
- High labour turnover among skilled junior staff, suggesting lack of development opportunities
- Lack of identifiable accountabilities for key tasks.

What shapes organisation structure?

2.6 There are many influences on organisation structure. There are certain internal principles and dynamics of organisation: how far power and authority are held at the top (centralised) or given to lower levels (decentralised); the span of control (the number of subordinates that can be supervised by any one superior); the division of labour; the grouping of people into working units; the need for communication channels, and so on. These determine some elements of structure, to an extent, according to internal logic.

2.7 According to contingency theory, however, there are still managerial choices to be made in order to optimise the structure. A number of contingent variables may influence structural choices and organisational development.

- The **strategic objectives** or **mission** of the organisation, and how these are broken down to define and guide the work of sub-units. Diversified organisations, for example, may require more decentralised structures.
- The **task** or 'business' of the organisation, which will determine which line or task functions are required (development, production, marketing, finance) and which support or staff functions (HR, planning, quality control, maintenance).
- The **technology** of the task may necessitate certain forms of organisation to maximise its efficiency and the needs of people.
- The **size** of the organisation. As it gets larger, its structure will get more complex: specialisation, subdivision and formalisation are required in order to control and coordinate performance (typically leading to the bureaucratisation of large organisations).

- **Geographical dispersion** may require federalised structures to take into account relevant factors at local, regional, national, international or global levels of operation.
- The **environment** of the organisation. Factors (and especially changes) in the legal, commercial, technical and social environment represent demands and constraints on organisational activity, and opportunities and threats to which organisation structure must adapt. As one example, information and communication technology (ICT) has enabled organisations to adopt looser, more network-style units or 'virtual teams'.
- The **culture and management** style of the organisation: eg the willingness of management to delegate authority and adopt more fluid facilitate-and-empower roles; organisational values about teamworking, formality, flexibility and so on.

Span of control

2.8 Span of control is one of the main internal principles of organisation. Span of control (also called 'span of management') is the number of subordinates responsible to any one superior, and is used for all levels in a management hierarchy. If three people report directly to a manager, the span of control is three: Figure 4.1.

Figure 4.1 *Span of control (3)*

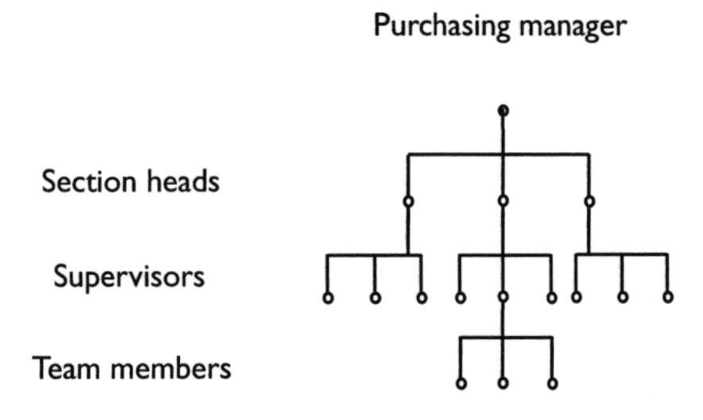

2.9 Classical theorists such as Fayol argued that the span of control should be restricted (between three and six) because while there needs to be managerial control over activities at every level of the organisation, there are also physical and mental limitations to a manager's ability to keep track of people, relationships and activities at the level of detail required.

2.10 If span of control is too wide, too much of the manager's time will be taken up with routine problems and supervision, leaving less time for higher management functions. Even so, people may not get the supervision or communication they require, because the manager is 'spread too thin'. Arguments for a **narrow** span of control include:

- Tighter control of activities
- Better communication and coordination
- More efficient use of managerial time and costs (through less supervisory activity)
- Reduced need for managers to delegate (if this is considered undesirable, eg where team members lack capability to take on responsibility)
- More efficient and satisfying teamwork, if units are organised as small groups or project teams.

2.11 If the span of control is too narrow, however, the manager may over-supervise the work of subordinates and may feel no pressure to delegate at all. The arguments for a **wide** span of control therefore include:

- More efficient use of managerial time and costs (through delegation)
- More discretion for subordinates, potentially contributing to job satisfaction, organisational flexibility and innovation.

2.12 Taking a contingency approach, the appropriate span will depend on various factors.

- The capabilities of the manager to plan, organise, coordinate and control activities, resources and people, and to manage his own time effectively
- The nature of the manager's workload, which will influence the amount of supervisory activity he will be able to handle effectively
- The capabilities of the subordinates. The more competent, trustworthy and motivated subordinates are, the easier it is to control a wider span. They may also have higher expectations in regard to delegation.
- The nature and technology of the task. A wide span is possible where the task is routine, repetitive or automated. Greater managerial input – and therefore a narrower span of control – may be required where there are more complex, interlocking tasks; where demands and technologies are constantly changing; or where there are high risks attached to errors.
- The dynamics of teamworking. If subordinates are able to communicate freely between themselves, and support each other in solving work tasks, less supervision is required and there may be a wider span of control.
- The coordinatory mechanisms of the organisation. If subordinates are geographically dispersed, or the communication systems of the organisation are inadequate, the span will need to be narrower. ICT has widened spans of control, enabling managers to coordinate data-sharing and activities more efficiently.

Control or empowerment?

2.13 The terms **centralisation** and **decentralisation** are used to refer to:

- The extent to which decision-making authority is kept close to the centre (or top) of the firm: ie the level of the hierarchy at which decisions are taken – and the extent of delegation.
- The extent to which related tasks and resources are gathered under a single functional authority or location: eg whether there is a separate purchasing function, or whether purchasing is carried out by relevant line departments.

2.14 Absolute decentralisation is not possible because any delegated authority can derive only from the top, and activities must conform to the policies decided at a higher level. But then, absolute centralisation of authority is not practical except in very small concerns, because the sheer volume of decisions would overwhelm those at the top.

2.15 The choice of organisation will depend to a certain extent on the preferences of the organisation's top management, but equally important is the size of the organisation and the scale of its activities. Thus the small business structure is likely to be centralised, and the divisional structure is likely to be decentralised.

2.16 Those who support a high degree of centralisation claim the following advantages.

- Coordinated decisions ('big picture' thinking) and closer management control, therefore less sub-optimising behaviour
- Conformity with overall objectives, rather than sub-unit goals and interests
- Standardisation of work processes and outputs, eg variety reduction and rationalisation
- Balance between the competing interests of different functions or divisions
- Increased flexibility in use of resources, given 'big picture' thinking
- Economies of scale in costs of management, finance, purchasing, production, etc
- Better decisions (in theory) arising from the proven ability and experience required to reach senior management positions
- Speedier decision-making, especially in a crisis – delegation can be time-consuming
- Effective change management where quick action and strong leadership are required

2.17 Those who advocate decentralisation suggest that centralisation has the following inherent drawbacks.

- Lower-level managers experience reduced job satisfaction, which may affect commitment and loyalty.
- Senior management may not possess detailed knowledge of all the organisation's activities, or of operational demands (especially customer demands). Higher-quality problem-solving and decision-making may be carried out by those with more technical expertise and immediate experience.
- Centralisation places stressful levels of responsibility onto senior management.
- Subordinates experience restricted opportunity for career development, which may cause difficulties in skill retention and management succession planning.
- The referral of decisions upwards to senior management takes time and restricts the responsiveness of the organisation to customer demands and environmental changes.
- Standardisation of processes and outputs may not capitalise on, or respond to, local variations in conditions or customer demands.

3 Elements of an organisation structure

3.1 *Mintzberg* provided a framework and language for discussing organisation structure, by categorising the building blocks of organisations and showing that organisations operate as a hierarchy, building from a large operating core to a small strategic apex. He suggested that there are five basic component parts in any organisation: Figure 4.2.

Figure 4.2 *Components of organisation structure*

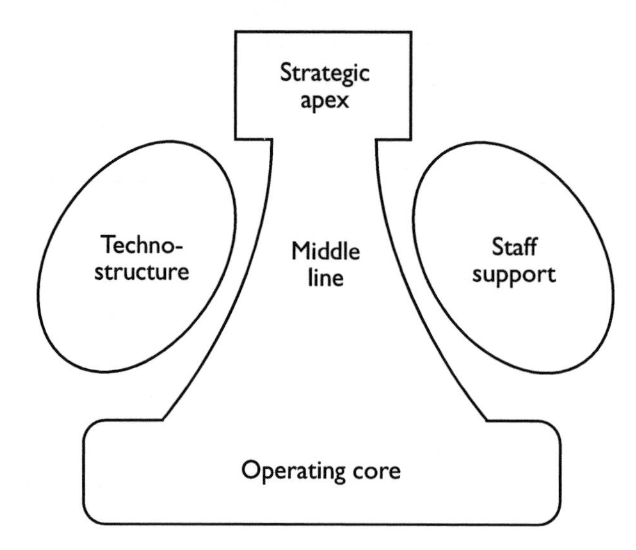

3.2 The **strategic apex** (senior management) ensures that the organisation pursues its objectives and serves the needs of its owners and stakeholders. Its tasks include strategic planning, resource allocation and boundary management (acting as ambassadors between the organisation and the outside world).

3.3 The **operating core** contains those people directly involved in production: securing inputs and processing and distributing them as outputs (goods and services).

3.4 The **middle line** (managers and supervisors) form the chain of command that runs between the strategic apex and the operating core. Its task is the organisation, planning and control of work, acting as the interface between senior management and operational employees and between the organisation and external contacts (eg the supply chain).

3.5 The **technostructure** (specialist advisers and analysts) offers technical support to the rest of the structure. Its main task is the design and maintenance of systems to standardise work throughout the organisation. Examples include strategic planning, quality control, systems analysis and design, financial control, production scheduling and HR planning.

3.6 **Staff support** offers administrative and ancillary services to the rest of the structure. Examples include personnel management, legal advice, public relations, research and development, and services such as maintenance, mail, security, reception and catering.

3.7 Mintzberg divides organisations into five broad types.

- **Simple (or entrepreneurial) structure**: a small, hierarchical organisation based on centralised control by a single leader – eg a salon owner and a team of hairdressers. Because of their small size and strong hands-on leadership, they are characterised by coherent direction, informal relationships and flexibility. Suited to small, entrepreneurial owner-managed firms. Consist mainly of the strategic apex and operating core.

- **Machine structure**: mechanistic, hierarchical, bureaucratic organisations (as already discussed). Suited to stable environments and tasks requiring strict standardisation and compliance. Tend to have many layers of middle line, and an enlarged technostructure (to standardise work procedures) and staff support.
- **Professional structure**: hierarchical, but recognising the power of professional expertise, this structure tends to be flatter and more participative than machine structures. Suited to the expectations and abilities of professional staff (doctors, lawyers, accountants). Tend to have little middle line or technostructure (since the operating core are experts), but a substantial staff support element for administrative and clerical support.
- **Divisional (independent) structure**: a number of more or less autonomous divisions, coordinated by centralised strategic and support functions. Suitable for devolved structures (such as regionally or internationally dispersed divisions) where central direction is required for brand identity, investment strategy and so on. Effectively duplicate the whole middle-line/operating-core structure within each division, reporting to the central strategic apex; the centralised technostructure and support structures appear relatively small.
- ***Ad hoc* (flexible) structure**: an organic, decentralised structure of temporary, flexible project teams and networks. Suitable for new technology (IT, R&D) businesses, consultancies, small media companies and other organisations focused on creativity and innovation. Tend to be made up of technostructure and support staff, flexibly banding together and acting as operating core where required.

3.8 We will now go on to look at a slightly different structural issue: how tasks can be grouped into departments within the middle line and operating core of the organisation. This is what is commonly referred to as types or methods of organisation.

4 Different structural forms

Departmentation

4.1 Division of labour is one of the key principles of organisation. In a very small company, people can simply share the tasks between them according to their skills. Once an organisation grows beyond a certain size, however, systematic specialisation is required. This typically involves the grouping together and allocation of specific aspects of the work to different departments. This can be done on the basis of criteria such as:

- Functional specialisation
- Geographical area or territory
- Product, brand or customer.

We will look at each of these in turn.

Functional organisation

4.2 In a functional structure, tasks are grouped together according to the common nature or focus of the task: production, sales and marketing, accounting and finance, purchasing and so on. An example of a functionally structured organisation is shown in Figure 4.3.

Figure 4.3 *Functional organisation*

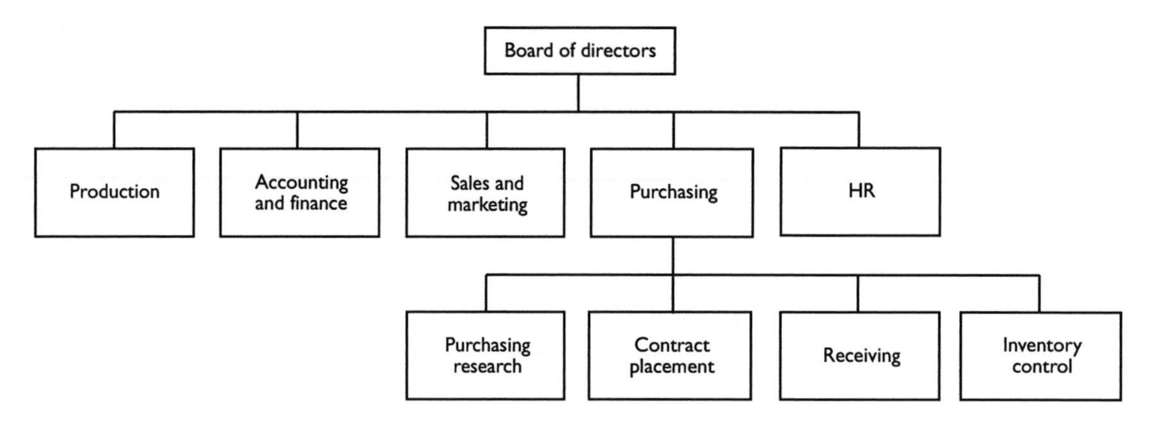

Geographical organisation

4.3 In a geographical structure, tasks are grouped together according to the region in which the activity takes place, or within which target markets or market segments are located. Multi-site organisations (eg a purchasing function organised by plant) and sales departments (with allocated 'territories') are often organised this way. An example of a geographically-structured organisation is shown in Figure 4.4.

Figure 4.4 *Geographical organisation*

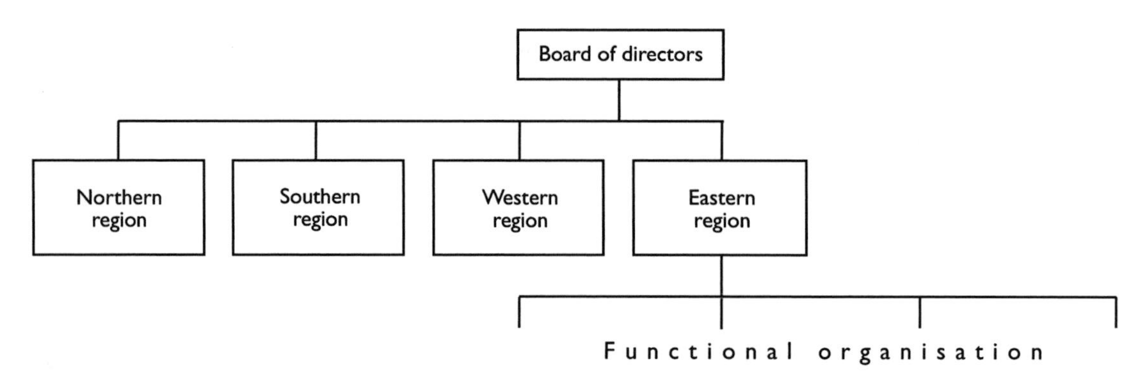

Product/brand/customer organisation

4.4 In a product structure, tasks are grouped together according to the product, product line, customer or brand they relate to. Companies with distinct brands (such as Coca Cola or Persil) often organise in this way, so that there is specialisation of brand marketing and identity – and separate brand accountabilities. Similarly, companies with key customer types, such as publishers (for example trade (bookshops), educational institutions, libraries) may group together tasks in this way. In purchasing, the equivalent may be organisation by items purchased: Figure 4.5.

Figure 4.5 *Product/brand/customer organisation*

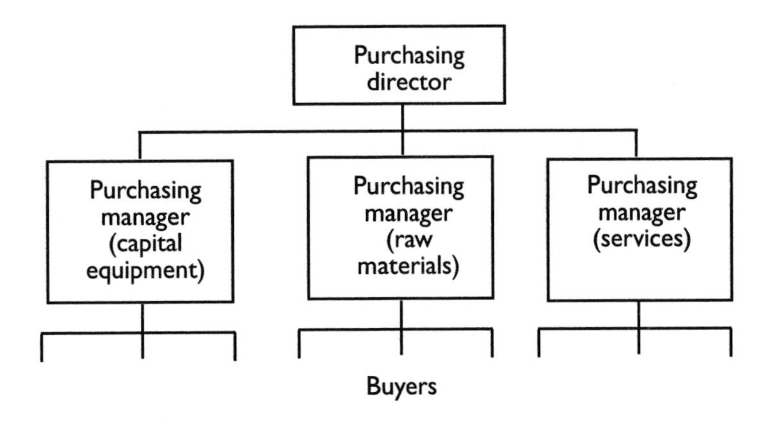

Advantages and disadvantages of different structural forms

4.5 The advantages and disadvantages of the various forms of organisation are summarised in Table 4.2.

Table 4.2 *Different structural forms*

Organisation	Advantages	Disadvantages
Functional	• Pools and focuses specialised skills and knowledge • Share specialised technology and equipment for efficiency • Facilitates the recruitment, training and management of specialist staff • Avoids duplicating functions within area/product departments: enables economies of scale	• Focuses on inputs/processes rather than outputs/customers (necessary for customer satisfaction) • Creates vertical barriers to cross-disciplinary communication (necessary to flexibility and coordination)
Geographical	• Decision-making at the interface between organisation and local stakeholders (with distinctive needs) • Cost-effective (because shorter) lines of supply and communication to local markets or plants	• Duplication of functional activities • Loss of standardisation, due to local differences
Product/brand/ customer	• Clearer accountability for the profitability of different products/brands/customer groups • Specialisation of production and marketing expertise • Coordination of different functions by product managers	• Increased managerial complexity and overhead costs • Possible fragmentation of objectives and markets

Divisionalisation

4.6 Divisionalisation is the division of the organisation into more or less autonomous strategic business units, as the business diversifies into new areas. Divisions may be:

- **Profit or investment centres within a company**. Strategic planning and other technostructure and support activities (such as finance, HR, research and development and perhaps purchasing) are undertaken at a central board or 'head office' level. Divisions may be based on function (retail division, manufacturing division), product (hardware division, software division) or region (Asian-Pacific division, European division). Each division may then be organised in an appropriate way: Figure 4.6.
- **Subsidiary companies grouped under a holding company**. When businesses grow through acquisition, or require a high degree of differentiation in product or regional divisions, they may form a group of independent public or private companies, owned or controlled by a holding company.

Figure 4.6 *Divisional structure*

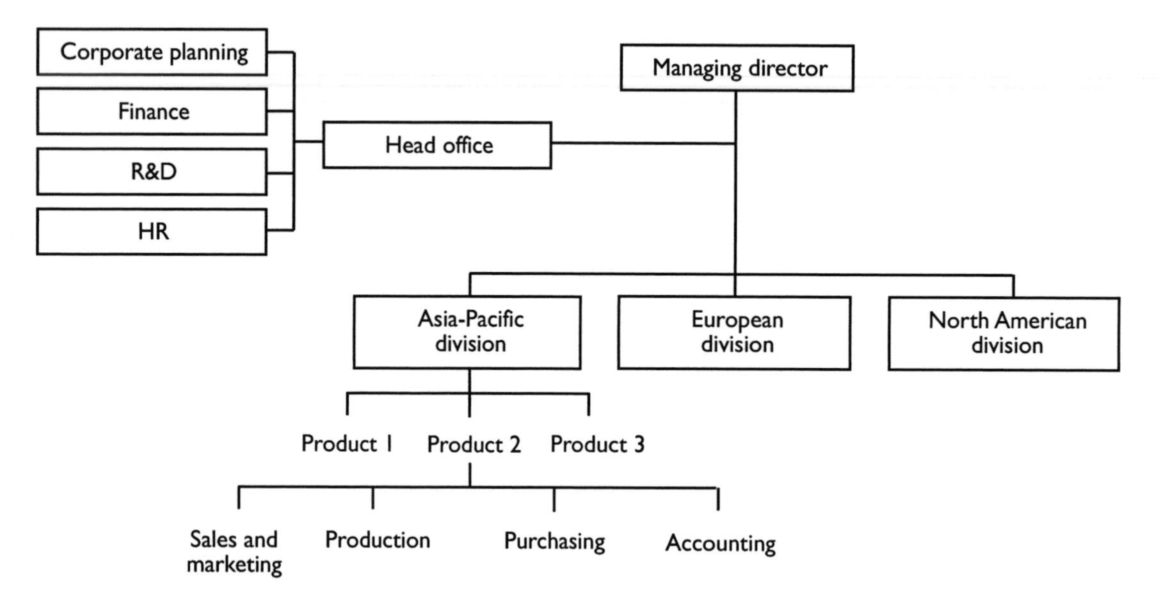

4.7 The advantages and disadvantages can be summarised as follows.

- **Advantages**
  - Clear accountability for each division as a profit/investment unit
  - Sensitivity to region/product-specific demands and opportunities
  - Efficiencies and economies of scale available from centralised functions
  - Co-ordination available from centralised strategic planning and control.
- **Disadvantages**
  - Potential fragmentation of overall objectives and markets
  - Potential conflict between central management and divisional specialists
  - Potential competition between divisions for centrally-allocated resources
  - Units may not be large enough to support managerial overheads.

Hybrid structures

4.8 'Hybrid' simply means 'crossed' or 'mixed'. As you may have noticed from the various organisation charts shown above, businesses generally combine a variety of organisational forms. For example, they may be organised by region or product at divisional level, with functional departments within each division. Hybrid structures allow the advantages of each form of organisation to be leveraged in appropriate ways: brand identity to be reinforced by a product division, for example, with regional knowledge to be capitalised on by its sales departments and economies of scale to be gained by a specialised purchasing department.

Matrix structures

4.9 The 'matrix' structure emerged at American aerospace company Lockheed in the 1950s, when its customer (the US government) became frustrated at dealing separately with a number of functional specialists when negotiating defence contracts. The concept of the 'project co-ordinator' or 'customer account manager' was born.

4.10 The essence of matrix structure is dual authority: staff in different functions or regions are responsible both to their departmental managers, in regard to the activities of the department, and to a product, project or account manager, in regard to the activities of the department related to the given product, project or account.

4.11 The matrix can be illustrated as follows, in the case of an advertising agency: Figure 4.7.

Figure 4.7 *Matrix organisation*

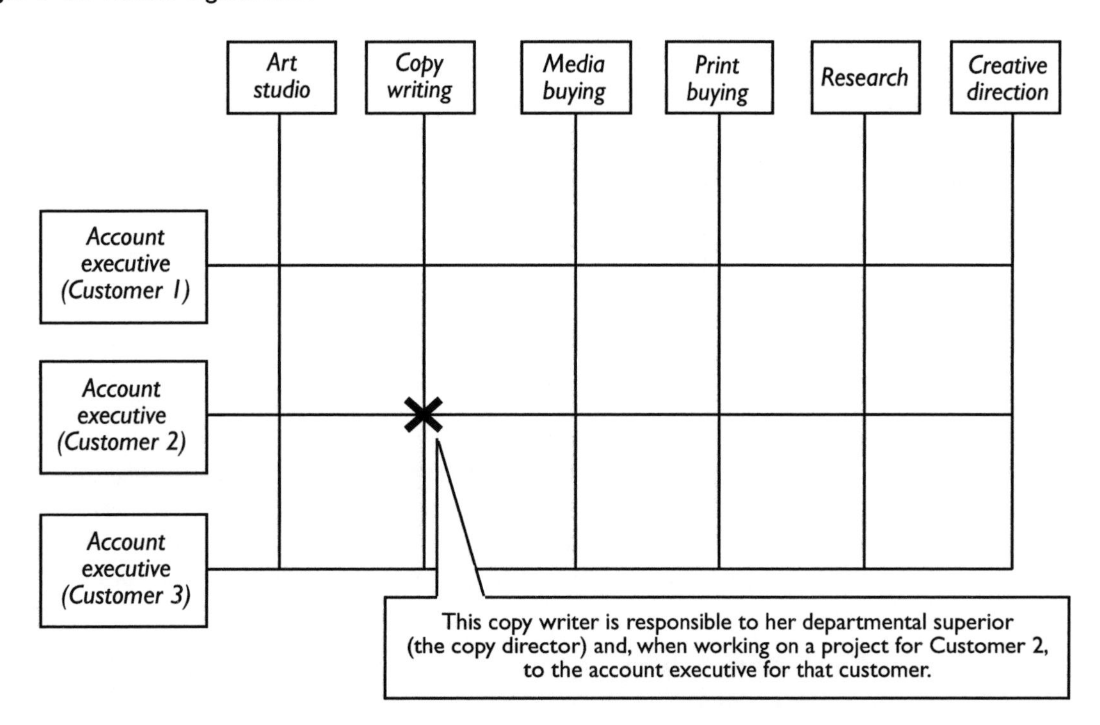

4.12 The advantages and disadvantages of matrix structure can be summarised as follows.

- **Advantages**
  - Combines functional efficiency with product/project accountability
  - Fosters interdisciplinary cooperation in pursuit of project goals
  - Develops tolerance of flexibility and ambiguity: improved change, learning
  - Focuses all functions on customer satisfaction and results: more satisfying
  - Brings conflicts of authority into the open.

- **Disadvantages**
  - Potential competition/conflict between dual managers
  - Potential stress on staff 'caught' between competing or conflicting demands
  - Potential inefficiency of ambiguous priorities and switching between tasks
  - More complex (potentially slower) decision-making processes
  - Costs of added management layer, meetings and so on.

Flexible organisational forms

4.13 We have already discussed some aspects of flexible structure (eg Burns and Stalker's 'organic' organisations, and the concept of 'adhocracy'). Modern trends in flexible organisation include the following.

- The **flattening of organisation hierarchies**. The trend is towards 'delayering', or reducing the middle line of organisations. Flatter structures are more adaptive and responsive, because there is a shorter distance between the strategic apex and the customer-facing operational core.

- **Project management structures**. Structures focus on the customer and outputs/results, rather than on internal processes and functions for their own sake. A project management orientation is being applied to the supply or services within the organisation (ie to internal customers) as well as to the external market. 'Full-service' project management can be offered by multi-functional project teams, so that the customer does not experience any vertical barriers.

- **Horizontal structures**. *Tom Peters* gives this term to structures which allow work and information to flow freely across functional boundaries, without the 'vertical barriers' created by specialisation, departmental job demarcations and formal communication channels. Peters suggests that customers' experience of the organisation is horizontal: they need to speak to different functions (sales, delivery, accounts, after-sales service) as they proceed through the purchase process. Product development and innovation, partnering, networking and learning are all horizontal activities, requiring the free exchange of information across functional boundaries.

- **Boundaryless structures** (*Milkovich and Boudreau*) are structures in which all barriers are eliminated or softened, in order to align processes for the achievement of objectives. This includes vertical/functional barriers, but also status barriers (between managers/workers), and even organisational boundaries (eg between divisions, domestic/foreign units and supply chain partners).

- **Functional flexibility** or versatility. This may be achieved by methods such as multidisciplinary teamworking (eg multifunctional project or procurement strategy teams, bringing together individuals with different skills and specialisms, across functional boundaries, so that their competencies and resources can be pooled or exchanged) and multi-skilling (where each individual within a team is functionally versatile, and able to perform a number of different tasks as required).

- **Numerical flexibility**: the ability to shrink or enlarge the labour force in response to fluctuations in demand. This may be done by: using non-standard-contract and subcontracted labour (temporary, short-contract or freelance workers); outsourcing functions to other organisations; or introducing flexible working hours schemes. In practice, an organisation may adopt a 'core-periphery' model. *Handy* proposes a 'shamrock' configuration, with various 'leaves':

  - a small, stable core of full-time permanent labour
  - a periphery of part-time and temporary labour which can be deployed flexibly according to work flow peaks and troughs
  - the option of contracting out areas of work to other service organisations
  - a possible fourth 'leaf' where work can be devolved to customers (eg through self-service, online information search and ordering, and so on).

5 Inter-organisational and network structures

5.1 Inter-organisational structures are structured relationships between two or more organisations.

5.2 *Huczynski and Buchanan* contrast the organisational relationships that exist in:

- Markets: separate firms act independently of each other, forming temporary relationships based on competition or transactions and exchanges.
- Hierarchies: an organisation forms a single, structured entity, within which all relationships are formally defined and all activities integrated, as in a bureaucracy.

5.3 In between these extremes there are inter-organisational relationships: non-market, non-bureaucratic relationships 'in which two or more organisations share resources and activities to pursue a common strategy'.

Single-hierarchy arrangements

5.4 Common approaches to extending organisational relationships, at the 'hierarchy' end of the scale, are:

- Merger, where two companies voluntarily pool the ownership interests of their respective shareholders
- Acquisition, where one firm buys the equity stake or assets of another company.

Both options result in the assets (including the human resources) of two organisations being integrated and jointly managed.

5.5 Hierarchical integration allows the firm to bring within it control over the transactions and resources that were previously conducted in the marketplace.

- Vertical integration involves increased ownership or control over the value chain. This may take the form of:
  - Backward (upstream) integration: controlling suppliers or supply chain activities (such as inbound logistics).
  - Forward (downstream) integration: controlling channels of distribution or distribution activities (such as outbound logistics).
- Lateral or horizontal integration involves increased ownership or control of competitors.

5.6 However, this lacks the flexibility of markets and contractual relationships. The alternative is non-market, non-bureaucratic relationships, based on various forms of controlled co-operation.

Structured inter-organisational relationships

5.7 Inter-organisational relationships are now significant features of the business environment because of the realisation that a single organisation's opportunities will be enhanced if alliances with other parties are entered into, in terms of:

- Access to overseas distribution channels, customers, expertise and technology, provided the other party has an established presence in the area
- Reduction in the effects of competition. As the two allies are no longer competing with each other, they can defend against existing competition better together, they can join forces against new entrants, and they can plan on the basis of known, long-term markets.
- Benefiting from economies of scale in joint production and sales
- Sharing and thereby reducing the financial and operational risk of new ventures and new products/markets
- Access to funds for expansion
- Aiding economic recovery in a region (often supported by government policy and incentives).

5.8 There are a number of popular inter-organisational forms, including: joint ventures, strategic alliances, outsourcing and franchising.

5.9 The term **joint venture** refers to a formal arrangement whereby two independent companies establish a new company which they jointly own (eg through shareholding, asset holding and profit distribution agreements) and manage. Their other businesses remain separate from this new, shared venture. Where more than two companies enter this arrangement, it is called a 'consortium'. Joint ventures have often been used to overcome barriers to entry in international markets.

5.10 The term **strategic alliance** refers to a formally structured relationship, in which two companies legally contract to cooperate in specified ways (eg purchase, supply or distribution agreements, collaborative promotions or product cross-selling) to achieve specific commercial objectives that are of benefit to both parties. Shared competitive advantage arises primarily through organisational learning: pooling competencies and resources which each firm, individually, may lack, to cope with changing technology, international markets or customer demands for integrated products/services markets. One example is the Star Alliance, in which a group of code-sharing airlines are able to cross-sell each others' connecting flight services, providing customers with 'one stop' booking and a single ticket.

5.11 **Outsourcing** involves one organisation selecting some of its tasks and delegating them, under contract, to outside companies. Many companies are currently outsourcing a range of support functions (such as cleaning and maintenance, catering, warehousing and transport, security, staff recruitment and training) and even core functions such as sales and customer service (eg in call centres). Although these are market-style contracts, they involve intimate collaboration between companies.

5.12 The benefit of outsourcing is that it allows companies to downsize and concentrate their resources on core competencies and strategic functions, becoming 'leaner' and more focused. However, recent high-profile examples (such as British Airways' problems arising from poor employee relations at Gate Gourmet, to whom it had outsourced all its catering) show that careful management is required to control the relationship, output/service quality, ethical/employment standards – and their consequences for the outsourcing organisation and its brand.

5.13 A **franchise** is a co-operative arrangement under which one party (the franchiser) sells to another party (the franchisee) the right to market its products or services, using the company's name, trademarks and technology. The contractual relationship makes the parties dependent on each other, but both parties retain their separate legal identity. Service firms are particularly appropriate franchisees: examples include fast-food businesses such as Pizza Express and KFC, office service businesses such as Kall Kwik and Mail Boxes Etc, pet grooming businesses, and so on. Franchising is a low-cost option for contractual entry into new markets, taking advantage of franchisees' local knowledge and entrepreneurial spirit.

Network organisation

5.14 The term 'network organisation' refers to a looser, dynamic, more informal affiliation of autonomous and broadly equal organisations, who exchange information and pursue ongoing (typically long-term) relationships for mutual benefit.

5.15 There are no direct contractual or financial obligations (eg investment by one company in another) shaping these relationships: they are purely based on collaboration, communication, trust and mutual advantage. *Huzcynski and Buchanan* note that: 'the formation of a network involves companies whose domains overlap in terms of products, markets, operating modes or territories, contacting one another and recognising the benefits of co-operation.' In a sense, therefore, any attempt at long-term supply chain or customer relationship management is a network.

5.16 A special form of the network concept is the **virtual organisation**, where companies (or units of a single company) collaborate, coordinate their activities and share data, using information communications technology (ICT) as their main – or only – point of contact.

5.17 Operations can be geographically dispersed, global expertise drawn on, functions outsourced and 24-hour/seven-day communication maintained – while operating (to all intents and purposes) as a single organisational entity. Tasks are typically fragmented, performed by widely dispersed individuals, but integrated by communication and data-sharing, eg via the internet – online databases, interactive websites, e-mail contact, and web-/tele-/video-conferencing. Web retailer Amazon.com is perhaps the best known virtual organisation.

5.18 The virtual organisation model is gaining popularity as an organisational structure for several reasons. Virtual organisations:

- Are supported by ongoing developments in ICT which allow data-sharing and synchronisation, interactive communication and virtual meetings (eg by webcast), across barriers of time and geographical distance
- Allow a high degree of flexibility (numerical, temporal and functional). Membership is diverse and structurally fluid enough to respond flexibly to equally diverse and changing customer/client requirements.
- Enable information and other resources to be mobilised efficiently in widely dispersed regions and specialist sectors, while allowing central control, pooled information and consistency of service and image where required
- Offer cost savings in areas such as employment (no redundancy obligations, benefits), overheads and logistics, due to the physical dispersal of (and loose contractual relationship with) members
- Exploit an increasingly knowledge-based economy, where the prime commodities are knowledge, information and expertise
- Exploit international markets, as they enable members to take advantage of local knowledge, indigenous language speakers, indigenous trading partnerships, etc.

6 Organising the purchasing function

6.1 An important organisational issue is the extent to which purchasing responsibilities should be centralised, ie placed in the hands of a single department reporting to a single executive. In service firms, in particular, it is common to find that purchasing is carried out by users or budget-holders, rather than by purchasing specialists.

6.2 Most commentators suggest that responsibilities for purchasing at a higher level (supplier selection and relationship management, contract negotiations and so on) should be centralised – ie they should lie as far as possible with purchasing specialists.

6.3 It may not always be feasible to centralise purchasing operations:

- If various divisions use and purchase entirely different materials.
- If operational sites are geographically dispersed (especially in areas where transport/communication infrastructures are less developed).

Advantages of centralised purchasing

6.4 The key advantages of centralised purchasing are as follows.

- Specialisation of purchasing staff. Each buyer can focus on a particular area (particular skills, such as contract negotiation, or particular materials and markets, such as machinery or chemicals) and develop his knowledge to greater depth, with potential to improve quality and lower costs.
- Consolidation of requirement. This reduces the frequency of small orders for a particular material; reduces transaction and transport costs; and enables buyers to obtain better prices (with economies of scale, bulk discounts, etc) and higher levels of service (as potentially significant clients). The number of suppliers is likely to be smaller, and order administration may be more streamlined.
- Greater coordination of purchasing activities. Uniform purchasing policies and procedures can be introduced, facilitating standardisation, variety reduction and (potentially) consistent quality. Staff training and development can also be undertaken more systematically.
- Avoidance of competition and conflict between purchasing divisions, due to scarcity of materials, disparities of purchasing expenditure or price anomalies.
- Skills/contacts/resources for purchasing research, which may not be available at divisional level.

6.5 If purchasing is centralised, it is usual to establish the function at head office and to appoint an overall manager or director reporting at board level. Apart from operational buying, the function will handle tasks such as planning, purchasing research, specialised buying, and negotiation of long-term contracts.

Advantages of decentralised purchasing

6.6 There are also significant advantages in devolving purchasing to local level.

- Maximised communication and coordination between purchasing and operating departments. Buyers are close to users and develop a close understanding of their needs and problems. (In centralised purchasing functions ICT should be used for regular contact and data-sharing.)
- Quicker response to operational/user needs and changes/problems by local buyers who are close to the scene of operations.
- Knowledge of, and relationships with, locally based suppliers. There are advantages – of reduced transport cost, delivery time etc – in sourcing from short distances (although these should not be overstated, given the increasing globalisation of business and the support of ICT).
- Smaller purchase quantities: sacrificing economies of scale, but reducing costs and risks of holding inventory (tied up capital, risk of deterioration/obsolescence etc).
- Accountability: divisional managers can be held accountable for performance only if they have genuine control over operations (which is not the case if procurement has been taken out of their hands.)

6.7 If purchasing is carried out at local level, it is likely that there will still be a need for a centralised purchasing function to carry out specialised activities, such as purchasing research or buying of specialised materials. Often long-term contracts may be negotiated by the central purchasing office with divisional buyers calling off requirements against the contracts.

6.8 *Lysons* suggests that a mix of centralised and decentralised purchasing is common in practice, with a division of duties somewhat as indicated by Table 4.3.

Table 4.3 *Duties of local and central purchasing functions*

Local purchasing functions	Centralised purchasing function
Small order items	Determination of major purchasing policies
Items used only by the local division	Preparation of standard specifications
Emergency purchases (to avoid disruption to production)	Negotiation of bulk contracts for a number of divisions
Items sourced from local suppliers	Stationery and office equipment
Local purchasing undertaken for social 'community' reasons	Purchasing research Staff training and development Purchase of capital assets

Chapter summary

- Theories of how organisations should be structured and managed have varied.
  - Scientific management and classical approaches emphasised efficiency and rationality (eg bureaucracy)
  - Human relations approaches switched attention from task organisation and standardisation to getting the best out of the human resource by attending to worker needs
  - Contingency theory assumes that there is no 'one best way' to organise work: the optimum depends on the organisation's environment and a best fit of internal factors (eg flexible/adoptive organisation)
- Organisation structure consists of mechanisms for division of labour and co-ordination (including formal channels of authority and communication).
- Structure is influenced by factors such as objectives, task, technology, organisation size, geography, environmental conditions and culture/management. In addition, it is shaped by internal organising principles including: centralisation/decentralisation and span of control.
- Henry Mintzberg proposed a flexible model of five components of organisational structure (strategic apex, middle line, operating core, technostructure, staff support), which are 'mixed' differently to form different types of organisational structure (simple, machine, professional, divisional, *ad hoc*).
- Organisations may be organised by function, geographical area or product/brand. Matrix organisation is a dual authority structure combining departmental management with the co-ordinating role of project/product management.
- Modern trends in organisational flexibility involve horizontal or boundaryless structures, cross-functional teamworking and functional and numerical flexibility.
- Inter-organisational forms include (in descending order of formalisation) joint ventures, strategic alliances, outsourcing and networks. Virtual organisations are elaborate networks using ICT, which allow a high degree of decentralisation.
- Purchasing may be centralised (for better control, co-ordination and economies of scale) or decentralised (for better responsiveness, specialisation and lower inventory). In practice, a mix of both will often be used.

Self-test questions

Numbers in the brackets refer to the paragraphs where you can check your answers.

1. Compare the organisation structures and metaphors of classical and modern approaches. (Table 4.1)
2. What are (a) the benefits and (b) the drawbacks of bureaucracy? (1.12, 1.13, 1.14)
3. Distinguish between organic and mechanistic organisations. (1.24, 1.25)
4. What are the purposes of formal organisation structure? (2.2)
5. What are the arguments for a narrow span of control? (2.10)
6. What are the disadvantages of centralisation? (2.17)
7. Explain Mintzberg's concept of (a) middle line, (b) technostructure and (c) professional structure. (3.4, 3.5, 3.7)
8. List the advantages and disadvantages of matrix structure. (4.12)
9. What are (a) horizontal and (b) boundaryless structures? (4.13)
10. What is vertical integration? (5.5)
11. Why is virtual organisation popular? (5.18)
12. How might responsibilities for purchasing be shared between local and centralised purchasing functions? (Table 4.3)

CHAPTER 5

Designing Purchasing Roles

Learning objectives and indicative content

2.3 Assess and evaluate methods of job design for purchasing roles

- Identifying responsibilities, associated tasks and priorities
- Updating existing roles: via job description and person specification
- Training needs analysis
- Competency frameworks
- Role mapping

Chapter headings

Introduction

A 'job' is a set of tasks or functions that are grouped together and allocated to an individual: his sphere of activity at work. For many employees, it seems as if jobs are just 'there' (or not). But the fact is that 'jobs' are the product of a great number of decisions about how the activities of the organisation can or should be divided up; what tasks naturally go together with others; how many different tasks an individual can perform effectively; whether it is more efficient or more motivating to have each individual perform a single task (repeatedly), or a variety of tasks (in sequence) – and so on.

In this chapter, we look at how the 'job' (responsibilities, tasks and priorities) of an employee in purchasing and supply can be identified, described and – where necessary – redefined or updated, in various forms.

Why is this important? So that managers know what their staff should be doing, and should be capable of doing, and are most likely to be motivated and satisfied by doing. So that they can tell staff clearly what they should be doing; select staff who are capable of doing it; train staff to do it (if necessary) and monitor staff performance to ensure that they are doing it!

1 Job design

1.1 Job design is the way in which tasks are divided or grouped to form the work responsibilities of a given job, and what decisions are made about specialisation, discretion, autonomy, variety and other job elements.

Early job design: efficient task performance

1.2 *Frederick Taylor* (discussed in Chapter 4) was an early exponent of systematic job design. His technique was to break down a complex task into the most basic component parts, which would represent the whole 'job' of a worker or group of workers. Jobs were therefore 'micro-designed': reduced to single, repetitive motions.

1.3 The micro-division of labour is based on a production line organisation of work and offers some efficiencies for this sort of work. Each task is so simple that it can be learned with little training; the effects of absenteeism and labour turnover are minimised; and tasks can be closely defined, standardised and timed, so output quantity and quality are more easily predicted and controlled. (You might recognise this form of design in packaging, quality inspection, assembly and other such jobs.)

A human relations perspective: job satisfaction

1.4 Motivation researcher *Frederick Herzberg* was among the first to suggest a systematic approach to job satisfaction and its relationship to job design. Herzberg's theory suggested that the job itself can be a source of satisfaction, offering various ways of meeting the individual's needs for personal growth.

1.5 Huczynski and Buchanan explain this by pointing out that 'the design of an individual's job determines both the kind of rewards that are available and what the individual has to do to get those rewards.'

1.6 *Hackman et al* have focused on certain core job dimensions which contribute to satisfaction.

- Skill variety: the opportunity to exercise different skills and perform different operations, as opposed to micro-specialisation and repetition
- Task identity: the integration of operations into a 'whole' task (or meaningful segment of the task), as opposed to task fragmentation
- Task significance: the task has a role, purpose, meaning and worth, according to the values of the organisation and the individual
- Autonomy: the opportunity to exercise discretion or self-management in areas such as target-setting and work methods
- Feedback: the availability of information by which the individual can assess his progress and performance in relation to expectations and targets and the opportunity to give feedback and have a voice in performance improvement.

1.7 Herzberg recommended three basic approaches to increasing worker satisfaction through job design: job rotation, job enlargement and job enrichment.

1.8 **Job rotation** is the planned transfer of staff between jobs to give greater task variety. (The documented example quotes a warehouse gang of four workers, where the worst job was seen as tying the necks of the sacks at the base of the hopper, and the best job as being the fork lift truck driver: job rotation would ensure that individuals spent equal time on all jobs.)

1.9 **Job enlargement** is an attempt to widen jobs by increasing the number of operations or tasks in which the worker is involved. This is a 'horizontal extension' of the job, which may reduce repetition and monotony. However, Herzberg noted that asking a worker to complete three separate tedious, unchallenging tasks is unlikely to motivate him more than asking him to fulfil one single tedious, unchallenging task!

1.10 **Job enrichment** is a planned, deliberate action to build greater responsibility, breadth and challenge of work into a job. This is a 'vertical extension' of the job, which is often equated with 'empowerment'. It may include removing controls over workers' actions; increasing responsibility/accountability; providing more regular feedback on performance; introducing new tasks; or allocating special assignments.

1.11 It is worth getting this in perspective. Not all workers will need or want more challenging work. And, as *Charles Handy* points out, 'Even those who want their jobs enriched will expect to be rewarded with more than job satisfaction. Job enrichment is not a cheaper way to greater productivity. Its pay-off will come in the less visible costs of morale, climate and working relationships.'

Empowerment

1.12 Empowerment involves both giving workers discretion to make decisions about how to organise their work and making workers accountable for achieving production and quality targets. (The French word for empowerment is *'responsibilisation'*.)

1.13 An interesting case study on empowerment is provided by Harvester Restaurants, where the management structure now comprises a branch manager and a 'coach' – and everyone else is a team member. All members have one or more accountabilities (recruitment, drawing up rotas, keeping track of sales targets) which are shared out by the team members at a weekly team meeting. The job of 'co-ordinator' (responsible for taking non-routine decisions) is shared by all team members on a rotating basis.

1.14 Empowerment is intended to enhance organisational effectiveness by increasing employees' job satisfaction; harnessing their creativity and 'front-line' expertise; and shortening response times at the interface with customers and suppliers.

1.15 However, there are acknowledged barriers to empowerment in practice.

- Not all employees desire more challenge or responsibility
- Not all employees are capable of exercising greater responsibility or undertaking the necessary skill development
- Managers may struggle to release control and/or to change role and style
- Empowerment is not a substitute for other rewards: it must be reinforced by recognition and/or financial rewards for exercising increased responsibility
- Empowerment may be perceived as a poor alternative to promotion or career development.

Teamworking

1.16 Teamworking is another key trend in job design. 'Team-based' job or role definitions allow individual skills to be pooled, and give workers the chance to be part of a whole meaningful task and social relationships. Teamworking is also often used in a context of shared decision-making, multi-skilling (see below), project work and empowerment – all of which offer significant job satisfactions and performance gains (as we will see in Chapter 10).

1.17 Self-managed teamworking is the most highly developed form of teamworking. They are permanent teams in which members jointly decide all the key issues of their work: processes and schedules, allocation of tasks, selection of team members, distribution of team rewards and so on. The team leader is a team member, acting in the role of facilitator: this role may be rotated as appropriate to the task.

1.18 Self-managed teams are said to offer advantages in: harnessing commitment (with gains in quality and productivity); reducing managerial costs, enhancing co-ordination and flexibility; and encouraging initiative (with gains for responsiveness and customer service). However, in a full-blown form, they are a comparatively new (and rare) phenomenon: they require skilled leadership and strong cultural support.

Multi-skilling

1.19 Multi-skilling is an alternative approach to functional flexibility. Rather than pooling different skills (eg in a multi-functional team), each individual is able to perform a number of different tasks, flexibly, as required. This involves the erosion of traditional demarcations between functional specialisms: workers are trained, organised and encouraged to operate across the boundaries of their job or craft. Instead of jobs being 'owned' by particular groups, the most appropriate individual to do a particular job should be able to do it. A well-known case study is the introduction of multi-skilling by SmithKline Beecham at its Irvine factory.

1.20 Multi-skilling offers the organisation a cost-effective, efficient way of utilising a 'leaner' workforce, particularly under the constantly changing pressures of competition, technological innovation and customer demands. If it can be achieved with the co-operation of employees and their representatives, it can end costly demarcation disputes, redundancy packages and other consequences of seemingly 'rational' job design.

1.21 All these approaches require the kind of flexible, horizontal structures we discussed in Chapter 4. In the words (quoted by Tom Peters) of a Motorola executive: 'The traditional job descriptions were barriers. We needed an organisation soft enough between the organisational disciplines so that... people would run freely across functional barriers or organisational barriers with the common goal of getting the job done, rather than just making certain that their specific part of the job was completed'.

Work-life balance

1.22 Work-life balance reflects the increasing diversity of the workforce (especially women in work) by attempting to create flexible working patterns which enable employees to balance the demands of work with the demands of home life (particularly the need to care for dependent children or elderly). It also recognises that overwork and stress are a cause of work-related ill health, and attempts to balance the desire for productivity with the need to manage work demands in a healthy and sustainable way.

1.23 Elements in work-life balance programmes (in addition to education and training in time management, delegation, stress management and so on) include:

- Flexible contracts (eg annualised hours or term-time contracts) to allow employees to plan hours around family responsibilities
- Flexi-time systems (with core periods and discretionary periods, during which hours may be debited/credited on a daily, weekly or monthly basis)
- Part-time working and job sharing.

Such measures have been supported in recent years by family-friendly and equal opportunity legislation. Under the Employment Act 2002, for example, parents of children under six years old have the right to have their requests for flexible working arrangements (changing total hours worked, when and where) seriously considered.

2 The purchasing role

2.1 It used to be a relatively simple matter to define the work performed by purchasing staff. This was because the purchasing function used to be regarded as a reactive support service, responding to the needs of other functions as they arose by performing routine clerical and administrative tasks.

2.2 This outlook has changed radically over the years. As we saw in Chapter 2, the view of the purchasing function is now typically more strategic in nature: the range of tasks to be completed is broader and the complexity of the purchasing operations is greater. However, it is still possible to distinguish a number of broad areas of responsibility.

2.3 Clerical and administrative tasks remain vital even in a more strategic environment. Record keeping, origination and processing of purchase orders and other documentation, and storage and retrieval of data are essential to the smooth running of the department. These tasks are usually to a greater or lesser degree automated and the amount of man hours expended on such activities is a declining proportion of overall purchasing effort.

2.4 Negotiating and buying are perhaps the core activities of a purchasing function. This category of work includes locating, assessing and selecting potential suppliers, as well as settling terms and conditions between buyer and seller.

2.5 Expediting, like other non-value adding activities, is increasingly tackled by automation and by approaches that seek to eliminate the need for follow-up. In an ideal world suppliers would perform exactly as required by the time required and no follow-up would be necessary. Until that happy day dawns, though, we must recognise that expediting is an essential part of purchasing work.

2.6 The importance of purchasing research has never been greater. The pace of change in the environment generally, and in supply markets in particular, make it essential to dedicate staff to monitoring activities. The objective is to improve the quality of buying by collecting, classifying and analysing relevant data to help in decision making. This area embraces economic forecasting, demand projections, analysis of prices and availability of materials, and analysis of potential suppliers.

2.7 Management of the purchasing function includes development of policies, procedures and controls; management of resources; the building of relationships within the purchasing and supply chain; and dealing with specific problems in supplier and commodity management.

3 Job analysis

3.1 The British Standards Institution describes job analysis (also known as job appraisal) as 'the determination of the essential characteristics of a job'. These essential characteristics may include the responsibilities of the job, its key tasks and priorities, the physical and social environment and conditions in which it is performed, the demands it makes on the job holder and so on.

3.2 The analysis may be carried out in different ways, depending on the nature of the job. For routine or repetitive tasks, observation of work in progress and documentary evidence of various kinds may be used to determine basic facts such as the job title, duties and tasks, reporting relationships, targets and standards applied, working conditions and so on.

3.3 For less programmed jobs, especially those which involve 'invisible' work (such as planning, people management, ideas generation, relationship-building and so on), more complex methods will be required. Interviews, questionnaires, diaries or logs may be used to gather information from job holders' managers or supervisors and/or the job holders themselves. They allow analysts to ascertain what the job entails in practice *and* how it is *perceived*, covering such qualitative issues as the difficulty of the job, discretion allowed, social skills required, the value or importance of the job and its different components and so on.

3.4 There are difficulties in carrying out job analysis. Workers may be suspicious about the purpose of the exercise, fearing that it will be used to raise standards, cut rates or rationalise staffing. There will be differences in perception between job holders and management as to the nature of the job. Many of the findings will be subjective to a greater or lesser degree, particularly in the case of unprogrammed work. In some contexts, the 'job' itself is a thing of the past, with flexible, multi-skilled staff performing whatever roles the team's goals require at a given time.

3.5 Nevertheless, job analysis is a useful exercise. When jobs fall vacant, it should be regarded as an opportunity to review and revise existing job information.

4 Job description and its variations

4.1 A job description is a broad statement of the purpose, scope, duties and responsibilities of a particular job. It is one of the products of job analysis.

Content of a job description

4.2 The precise content of a job description will vary from organisation to organisation and job to job, but might typically include the following information.

- The title of the job
- The business unit or department
- A summary of the job: its overall purpose, main functions, position in the organisation structure
- Job content: a list of the job's main tasks, including factors such as frequency, importance, difficulty, responsibility
- Key accountabilities: what the job holder is expected to achieve in key areas
- Reporting relationships: superior and subordinate positions; collaboration with other team members or departments
- Working conditions: location, special demands (health hazards, physical conditions, potential stressors, social conditions)
- Employment conditions: working hours, basis of pay and entitlements, development opportunities and so on

4.3 Figure 5.1 (on the next page) shows an example of a basic job description for a buyer in a retail environment.

The uses and limitations of job descriptions

4.4 Job descriptions provide information for:

- Recruitment and selection (indicating the requirements of the job)
- Appraisal (indicating the criteria for assessment)
- Training and development (indicating areas for improvement)
- Pay-setting (indicating job components and their value)
- Performance improvement (indicating problems in work conditions, the necessity of jobs, their relationship to each other and so on).

4.5 However, it has been argued that job descriptions are of limited usefulness and, at worst, counterproductive. They are only able to give an accurate and meaningful description of certain types of job, where the work is observable, programmed and repetitive: if a job involves variety, discretion and adaptability (as managerial jobs do), a job description will be unrealistic and constantly out of date. Job descriptions are, at best, a limited and static 'snapshot' of a job at a particular moment in time.

4.6 If job descriptions are rigidly adhered to, they can become a straitjacket: demarcation disputes may arise where people adhere strictly to the scope and territory of their job description rather than responding flexibly to customer requirements, opportunities for quality improvement or a problem which needs solving.

Figure 5.1 *Job description*

JOB DESCRIPTION

Job title	Buyer 1
Department	Books
Job summary	Operating under close supervision, (a) participates in the selection of new titles from wholesale and publisher catalogues and (b) negotiates purchase and promotion agreements with suppliers. Administers core stock replacement and purchase order processing.

Job content (general nature and level of duties performed)

1. Reviews wholesale and publisher catalogues and promotion plans, and recommends new title purchases to the bookshop manager.
2. Participates in negotiations of purchase and promotional agreements with suppliers.
3. Issues and coordinates purchase orders.
4. Processes incoming stock: coordinates release of stock and promotional materials for agreed dates; coordinates processing of discrepant supplied items; issues replacement purchase orders as required on returned items.
5. Ensures all requirements and special terms and conditions are met.
6. Approves supplier invoices for payment by the accounts department.
7. Processes returns and credits under sale-or-return agreements.
8. Actions individual customer orders, liaising with customer service staff.
9. Monitors and maintains levels of core stock titles.
10. Monitors and analyses sales of new titles to support buying and promotion decisions, and prepares report summaries for the bookshop manager.
11. Attends relevant book fairs and trade conferences.
12. Liaises with appropriate personnel in accounts, warehousing, despatch, customer services and other departments as required.

The above statements are not inteded to be an exhaustive or definitive list of the responsibilities of the job holder: flexibility in responding to marketing opportunities and customer requirements is essential.

Reports to	The bookshop manager. Close supervision is required in the areas of new title selection and negotiation of purchase/promotion agreements.
Supervises work of	N/A.
Special conditions	Some lifting may occasionally be required.
Experience/education	1-3 years retail purchasing experience (ideally in book trade). Minimum of 2 'A' levels (or equivalent).
Training provided	Initial on-the-job training offered as required. Opportunities for vocational certification after one year.
Terms and conditions	38 hours per week. Salary: see separate grading structure.
Prepared by	Personnel Dept.
Date	10 August 200X

4.7 Organisational flexibility is a hot issue in human resource management at the moment. Jobs are being redesigned to allow adaptability and responsiveness to changing task requirements, through multi-skilling, multi-disciplinary team-working, flexible working hours and so on. Indeed, commentators such as *William Bridges* and *Tom Peters* have suggested that the 'job' itself is a thing of the past: tasks and teams must be constantly redefined by customer and environmental demands.

4.8 So is there a future for job descriptions? Some organisations are working towards alternatives such as:

- Goal, competence or accountability profiles, setting out the outputs and performance levels expected of individuals and teams.
- Role definitions, setting out the part played by the job holder in meeting organisational and sub-unit objectives (stressing the purpose and contribution of competent performance in the job, rather than its task components).

Competence analysis and definition

4.9 Competence profiles, based on key success factors in a given business or sector, offer a flexible, menu-driven alternative to traditional job descriptions (and person specifications, covered below).

4.10 Competence may be defined as: 'The ability to perform activities in the jobs within an occupation to the standards expected in employment. The concept also embodies the ability to transfer skills and knowledge to new situations within the occupational area and beyond, to related occupations.' (Training, Enterprise and Education Directorate).

4.11 Competence definitions typically identify the key roles of a given occupation and break them down into areas ('units') of competence. These in turn are formulated as statements describing what a competent person should be able to do at different levels, including:

- The specific activities concerned (elements of competence)
- To what standard (performance criteria)
- In what contexts (range statement)
- With what underpinning knowledge and understanding.

4.12 Competence definitions for purchasing and supply professionals have been developed by CIPS, under the direction of the Institute of Leadership and Management, to establish what specific outcomes purchasing staff should be able to achieve.

4.13 The advantages claimed for competence-based profiles include the following.

- They can be linked directly to the strategic objectives of the organisation and to best practice in the relevant occupation or profession (such as purchasing and supply).
- They are more readily adaptable to changing circumstances and requirements, since they are non-prescriptive about job specifics.
- They can be made applicable to employees at all levels of the organisation hierarchy (although the specific behaviours expected will vary), which also helps to create consistent organisational values and practices.

Role analysis and definition

4.14 Role analysis (like job analysis) collects information relating to the work people do. But while job analysis focuses on tasks to be performed (a 'job'), role analysis focuses on the part that people play in carrying out their jobs, by working competently and flexibly. 'The concept of a role... emphasises the need for flexibility and is concerned with what people do and how they do it rather than concentrating narrowly on job content.' (Armstrong: *A Handbook of Human Resource Management Practice*).

4.15 A role profile or definition will therefore specify: the overall purpose of the role; what role holders are expected to achieve (key result areas) and what they will be held to account for (accountabilities); and the behavioural and technical competencies required to achieve acceptable levels of contribution and performance.

Learning or training specification

4.16 A learning or training specification is yet another way of defining the knowledge, skills or competences needed to achieve an acceptable level of performance – but it is used primarily as a basis for devising learning and development programmes. In other words, it focuses on defining training needs.

4.17 **Training needs analysis**, very simply, involves:

- Measuring what employees need to be *able* to do in order to perform a job competently and in line with performance standards (eg using job, role or competency analysis and descriptions);
- Measuring what employees actually *can* do (eg using self analysis, competency testing or the appraisal system of the organisation); and
- Identifying any 'gap' between the two, as a potential need for learning, training and development.

4.18 At the functional or departmental level, formal training needs analysis is most common when there is a change in the role of a department; the department is restructured; there is a change of policy (eg because of new legislation); or new systems are introduced (eg because of new technology). These scenarios present a need or opportunity to identify skill/knowledge 'gaps' (learning needs) for the whole function or department. The purchasing department takes over responsibility for transport, say, or introduces an EDI system: what does it need to be able to do now, that it did not before?

4.19 At the job level, formal training needs analysis is most common for groups of new staff, or following complaints or problems, or where new jobs have been created. What does a person in this job need to be able to do, that they may not be able to?

4.20 At the individual level, training needs analysis may be less formal, utilising self-appraisal, or ongoing feedback from a superior or mentor, say: what areas might benefit from improvement? Formal analysis may also be used: if a person is new in the job, say, or if a staff member is experiencing problems, or as part of ongoing appraisal and development planning for individuals. What does this individual need to be able to do in order to perform better, or be considered for promotion?

4.21 A typical **learning specification** would be drawn up to include the following elements.

- What the role holder(s) or individual(s) must understand (specified as learning outcomes)
- What the role holder(s) or individual(s) must be able to do (specified as learning outcomes) and
- Learning methods for each: instruction, coaching, mentoring, reading, internet research, formal training course and so on.

4.22 We cover the systematic approach to training and development in a little more detail in Chapter 12. Just be aware that the development of people is a key role of the modern manager/leader.

5 Person specification

5.1 It may sound obvious, but it is worth being clear: a 'job description' describes the job. A description of the type of person required to do the job is called a 'personnel specification' or 'person specification'.

5.2 A person specification identifies the type of person the organisation should be trying to recruit for a given job: the education, training, experience, personal attributes and competencies a job holder will need to perform the job satisfactorily.

5.3 A systematic approach was formulated by *Alec Rodger*, a pioneer of recruitment and selection systems in the UK. He suggested that 'if matching the demands of the job and the person who is to perform it is to be done satisfactorily, the requirements of an occupation (or job) must be described in the same terms as the aptitudes of the people who are being considered for it.'

Contents of a formal person specification

5.4 *Rodger's* **Seven Point Plan** draws attention to seven points about the job holder or selection candidate.

- Physical attributes (such as neat appearance or strength)
- Attainments (including educational and vocational qualifications)
- General intelligence (usually defined in terms of mental dexterity and verbal fluency)
- Special aptitudes (such as numerical proficiency or computer literacy)
- Interests (demonstrating practical abilities and social competence)
- Disposition (or manner: friendly or helpful, say)
- Background circumstances (place of residence, family situation and so on)

5.5 An alternative structure was put forward by *J Munro Fraser*, whose **Five Point Pattern of Personality** draws attention to the candidate's:

- Impact on others (including physical attributes, force of personality and interpersonal skills)
- Acquired knowledge or qualifications (including education, training and work experience)
- Innate ability (including intelligence and particular aptitudes: numerical, mechanical, artistic, linguistic and so on)
- Motivation (the ability to select and pursue appropriate behaviours to attain personal goals)
- Adjustment (emotional stability, tolerance of stress, social skills)

5.6 Whichever outline is used, the person specification should classify each feature listed as essential, desirable or contra-indicated (undesirable) for competent performance in the job. For the job of purchase expediter, for example, organisational ability might be considered essential; social skills, desirable, given the need to liaise with suppliers; and inability to work under pressure, contra-indicated.

5.7 Figure 5.2 (on the next page) shows a person specification for the book buyer's job, described in Figure 5.1, based on the Seven Point Plan.

Limitations of person specifications

5.8 A wide range of variables may be used in a person specification, including both capacities (what the job holder should be able to do) and inclinations (what the job holder should be willing to do). However, in the same way that a job description must be revised often and used flexibly, a person specification may also lose its relevance if it fails to evolve as job requirements change.

5.9 In addition, there are particular problems to avoid when developing a job description into a person specification. 'Physical attributes' and 'background circumstances', for example, may suggest criteria which may nowadays be interpreted as discriminatory: to the disabled (in the case of a speech impairment, say) or to women (for example, the contra-indication of family responsibilities or intended pregnancy) or to workers of a particular age (outlawed in the UK from 2006).

5.10 You should also be aware of the assumptions behind other criteria. (This is one of the reasons why you are required to study some of the behavioural science concepts underpinning human resource management.) The category of 'general intelligence', for example, has traditionally been measured as 'IQ' or mental dexterity, but it is now generally accepted that there are many kinds of intelligence, including emotional intelligence, practical intelligence, spatial intelligence and interpersonal intelligence – all of which might come in handy in purchasing and supply.

Figure 5.2 *Person specification*

PERSON SPECIFICATION

Job title Buyer 1

Department Books

Job description Ref (xxxx)

	Essential	*Desirable*	*Contra-indicated*
Physical attributes	Clear speech Well-groomed	Age 22-40 Strength (lifting)	Age under 22 Chronic ill-health
Attainments	2 'A' levels 1-3 years retail purchasing experience	Purchasing experience gained in book trade Vocational certificate (purchasing/book trade)	No experience of purchasing or book trade
Intelligence	Above average		Low flexibility
Aptitudes	Appreciation of market potential of new titles Organisational ability	Understanding of IT/POS systems Eye for promotional opportunities Attention to detail Negotiation skills Analysis and preparation of management information Network skills	Poor problem-solving
Interests	Reading (wide range)	Team-based or methodical activities	'Solo' interests only
Disposition	Team player Tolerant of pressure Patient/methodical	Assertive	Low tolerance of supervision Antisocial
Background circumstances	Able to work late	Within 1hr of workplace (where necessary)	

Attributes of effective purchasing staff

5.11 Purchasing staff require both general and particular attributes. Some of the most relevant general qualities are listed in Table 5.1.

Table 5.1 *General qualities required in purchasing staff*

Quality	Remarks
Honesty	Obviously – just think of the large sums of money that purchasing staff are responsible for.
Hard work	This is essential to cope with the rigours of the job at the same time as obtaining and maintaining professional expertise.
Reliability	Purchasing interfaces with many other functions. Failure in purchasing can lead to expensive disruption elsewhere.
Initiative and imagination	Purchasing tasks are rarely routine. Ability to tackle new and unexpected problems is essential.
Enthusiasm	In particular, purchasing staff require an energetic and inquiring approach to their jobs.
Interpersonal skills, including communication	Much of the effectiveness of purchasing depends on links with other functions, as well as links between purchasing personnel themselves.
Numeracy	Quantitative aspects of purchasing problems, and particularly financial aspects, cannot be overlooked.
Information gathering, processing and decision-making	A major component of purchasing effectiveness is the ability to pick out essential elements, ascertain and analyse relevant information, and arrive at logical decisions.

5.12 In addition to these general qualities, purchasing staff require particular skills, in order to perform the specialist tasks involved in the job. This is a dynamic area. Changes in the perception and activities of the purchasing function have led to a need for qualities which would have been less important at earlier stages in the development of the profession. In particular, the requirement to manage partnership relations with suppliers, and to participate in strategic planning processes, make demands on purchasing staff which were absent in an earlier era of short-term transactional relationships.

5.13 These skills can only be applied on a foundation of detailed relevant knowledge. *Saunders* suggests that relevant knowledge can be divided into three main areas.

- General knowledge of business and management, including strategic management
- Specific knowledge relating to purchasing and supply management
- Technical knowledge relating to products and processes of particular businesses

Chapter summary

- Job design is the way in which tasks are divided or grouped to form the work responsibilities of a given job.
- Core job dimensions, which can be (re)designed to enhance job satisfaction, are: skill variety, task identity, task significance, autonomy and feedback.
- Frederick Herzberg advocated three approaches to job re-design: job rotation (transfer between tasks); job enlargement (horizontal extension for more tasks); and job enrichment (vertical extension for more interest, challenge and responsibility).
- Modern trends in job design include empowerment, team working, multi-skilling and work-life balance.
- Job analysis is the process of determining the essential characteristics of a job. The output of job analysis is a job description: a statement of the purpose, scope, duties and responsibilities of a job. This may be reformulated as a person specification, describing the qualities required for competent performance of the job: ie the 'ideal' job holder.
- Job descriptions may be seen as inflexible, especially where 'jobs' themselves are becoming boundaryless. Alternatives include: goal, competence or accountability profiles and role definitions.
- Learning specifications describe the learning needs for competent performance in a job. They are developed by learning (or training) needs analysis, which identifies the gap between required and current competence (at a functional, job or individual level).

Self-test questions

Numbers in brackets refer to paragraphs where you can check your answers

1. Distinguish between (a) job design, (b) job analysis and (c) job description. (1.1, 3.1, 4.1)
2. Distinguish between (a) job description and (b) person specification. (5.1)
3. List the core job dimensions. (1.6)
4. Identify the limitation of job enlargement. (1.9)
5. List four barriers to empowerment. (1.15)
6. What is multi-skilling? (1.19)
7. List three tools of job analysis. (3.2, 3.3)
8. Identify four uses of job description. (4.4)
9. Outline the process of training needs analysis. (4.17)
10. What points are included in the 'Seven Point Plan'? (5.4)

CHAPTER 6

Organisation Culture and Cross-cultural Management

Learning objectives and indicative content

2.4 Define the term culture and assess different models of culture which may exist within organisations

- Definitions and terms associated with culture
- How organisational culture impacts on behaviour, values and assumptions
- Organisational influences of company politics, power, bureaucracy, rules and standards of behaviour
- Models of cultural strength, masculine/feminine societies, cultural values and individualism/collectivism

2.5 Evaluate methods and formulate plans for managing effectively in international or cross-cultural organisations

- Stages of planning
- Methods: managerial and leadership styles, approaches, communication and media channels
- Evaluation process of research (primary and secondary), conducting pilot schemes, gathering feedback from staff and choosing most successful option
- Considerations: cultural diversity, existing structures, codes of conduct, differing goals and expectations

Chapter headings

1 What is culture?

2 Organisation culture

3 National culture

4 International and cross-cultural management

Introduction

Organisation culture is, in simple terms, the way in which a particular organisation does things: its distinctive 'climate' and 'style'. Structure (covered in Chapter 4) and culture are often discussed together, as ways of describing an organisation and how it 'works': the formal arrangements are overlaid by a kind of collective 'personality'.

This topic underpins the practice of management – and all the material in this Course Book. A manager's approach to team leadership, motivation, decision-making, delegation, risk management and so on will depend to a large extent on the cultural values and norms of the organisation.

With the increasing internationalisation (or even globalisation) of business, there is a new emphasis on the impact of *national* cultures on organisations and management. In this chapter, therefore, we also discuss models of national culture, and how they may be useful for managing in multinational and cross-cultural contexts.

1 What is culture?

1.1 An influential writer on culture, *Geert Hofstede*, summed up culture as 'the collective programming of the mind which distinguishes the members of one category of people from another'.

1.2 In other words, culture is the shared ways of behaving and understanding that are distinctive to a particular group of people. This 'group' or category may be a nation or ethnic group, a social class, a profession or occupation, a gender, or an organisation: each may have its distinctive way of thinking and doing things. These are sometimes called 'spheres' of culture.

Elements of culture

1.3 Another influential writer on culture, *Trompenaars*, suggested that culture operates on three levels: Figure 6.1.

Figure 6.1: *Elements of culture*

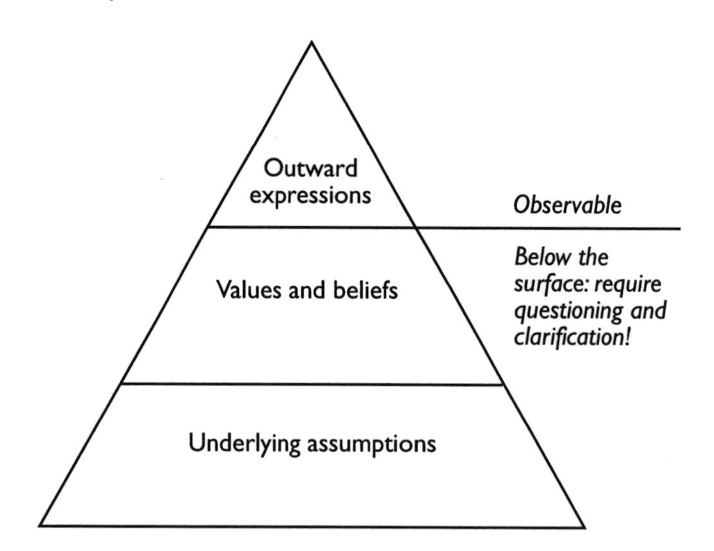

1.4 The most easily recognisable elements of culture, because they are directly observable, are its outward expressions.

- Behaviour: norms of personal and interpersonal conduct; customs and rules about the kinds of behaviour that are acceptable or unacceptable within the group
- Artefacts: products of the culture such as its music, writing and art; its myths, heroes and symbols
- Rituals: patterns of behaviour which have symbolic or traditional value, such as social formalities, ceremonies and rites of passage.

1.5 Beneath these outward expressions are the values and beliefs which give them their special meaning and significance within the culture. They may be explicit in sayings or mottos but often they are not directly expressed so much as reflected in behaviour, artefacts and rituals. So, for example, a society that believes that age deserves respect will develop behaviours honouring older people, reward seniority in organisations, create myths about wise elders and so on.

1.6 Beneath values and beliefs lie assumptions: ideas which shape the culture's ways of thinking and behaving – but which have become so ingrained that they are no longer consciously recognised or questioned. The rights of the individual, or the legitimacy of authority, may come into this category.

1.7 The 'underlying' elements of culture – like the part of the iceberg that lies under the water – are the ones that cause problems. They are difficult to manage, whether in societies or in organisations, because of the potential for misunderstanding (and, from there, conflict). An important skill of cross-cultural management, as we will see, is being aware that, when dealing with other cultures, we don't always know what it is that we don't know!

2 *Organisation culture*

2.1 Organisation culture has been defined as 'a pattern of beliefs and expectations shared by the organisation's members, and which produce norms which powerfully shape the behaviour of individuals and groups in the organisation' (*Schwartz and Davies*). It has been summed up as 'the way we do things around here'.

Manifestations of organisation culture

2.2 Organisation culture may be expressed through:

- Behaviour: informal norms (such as familiarity or formality with colleagues); rules and standards of behaviour formulated as part of the disciplinary or ethical codes of the organisation; standard procedures and channels of communication (a powerful influence in conformist bureaucratic organisations); 'short-cuts' developed in practice and so on.
- Artefacts: dress codes, office décor, symbols (eg logos), corporate marketing (mythology) and indeed all work outputs (since these reflect the organisation's values). Things such as office size, access to facilities and company cars may take on a symbolic value, reflecting status or power, say. Organisational politics (processes by which individuals and groups gain and use power in the organisation) often dictate which artefacts become valued and sought-after, and what they 'mean'.

- Rituals: business formalities, ceremonies (eg performance awards, retirement functions)
- Beliefs and values: mottos (such as 'The customer is king'; 'Get it right first time'); attitudes to matters such as quality, risk, technology, employee relations; the importance of values such as seniority, empowerment, teamworking etc.

2.3 *Johnson, Scholes and Whittington* introduce the concept of the **cultural web**, as a way of representing 'the taken-for-granted assumptions, or paradigm, of an organisation, and the behavioural manifestations of organisational culture': Figure 6.2. The elements of the web can be used as a framework to analyse organisational culture in a wide range of settings.

Figure 6.2: *The cultural web*

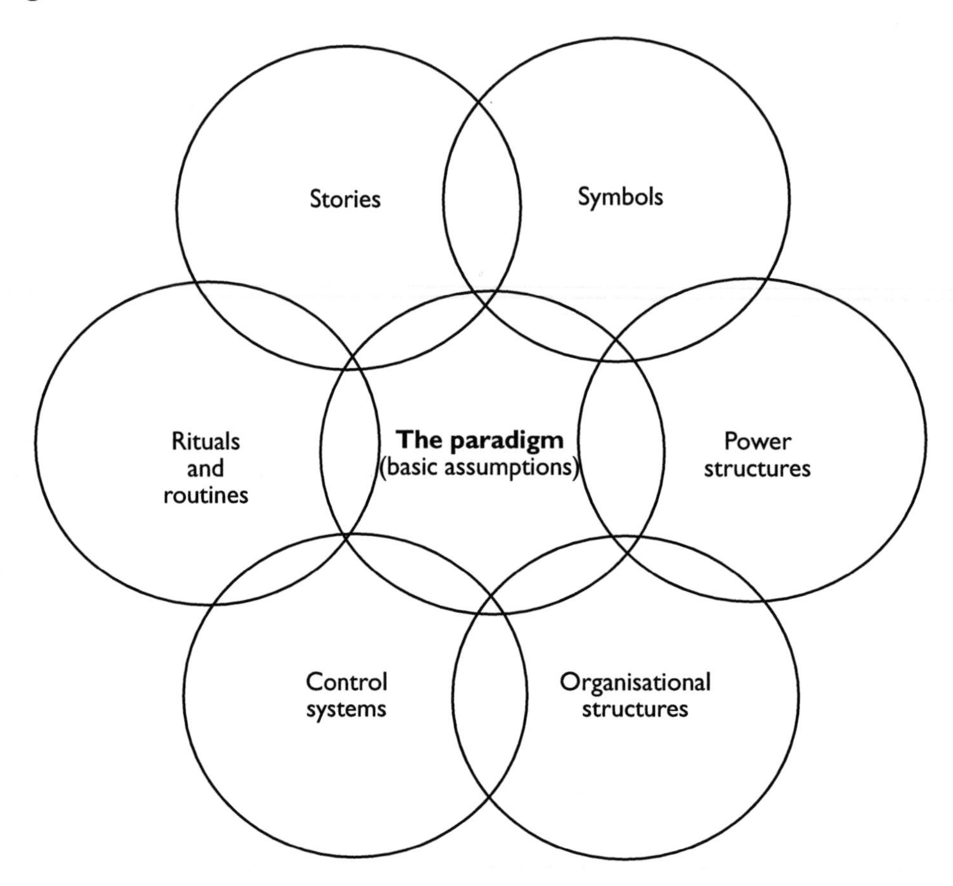

Influences on organisation culture

2.4 An organisation's culture is often shaped by its history. Since cultures develop over time and are not easy to change, they often reflect the values of the era in which the organisation was founded (hence the persistence of 'old-fashioned' bureaucratic cultures) and/or of the organisation's founder. Myths and stories about the 'heroic' early days (or 'Golden Ages') of the organisation give further power to original values.

2.5 An organisation's culture is partly shaped by its environment, as it will adopt elements of the other cultural spheres (nation, region and industry sector) in which it operates. It will also embrace some of the cultural values of influential individuals and groups within the organisation: the cultures of particular professional/occupational groups, social classes and so on. *Handy* noted that: 'Organisations are as different and varied as nations and societies of the world. They have differing cultures ... affected by events of the past and the climate of the present, by the technology of the type of work, by their aims and the type of people who work in them.'

2.6 Managers and leaders can have a strong influence on organisational culture, because they are in a position to model values and behaviours – and they have the power to influence the behaviours (and sometimes also the underlying attitudes) of subordinates. This is the basis of deliberate culture-change initiatives, as we will see later in the chapter. At the same time, organisations with a strong culture tend to recruit managers who conform to that culture, so that the 'management culture' reflects – rather than shapes – the culture of the organisation.

A model of cultural types

2.7 *Harrison* suggested that organisations could be classified into four types, differentiated by their structures, processes and management methods – and possessing, as a consequence, distinct cultural features: Table 6.1. The classification was later popularised by *Charles Handy* (using the analogy of different ancient Greek gods).

Table 6.1 *Harrison/Handy's four cultural types*

Culture	Key features	Advantages/disadvantages
Power culture (Zeus)	Power centred in a key figure, owner or founder Control through direct personal communication Little formalisation, rules or procedures	Suits small, entrepreneurial organisations of like-minded people Enables the organisation to adapt quickly in response to change
Role culture (Apollo)	Classical, rational organisation (bureaucracy) Formalised, impersonal: authority based on position, function; conformity to rules and procedures	Efficient for large organisations in stable environments Inability to change/innovate, due to rigidity
Task culture (Athena)	Management directed at outputs/results Team-based organisation: horizontally structured, flexible Valuing expertise, communication, collaboration	Fosters results/customer focus Involves/empowers staff Can be expensive (securing expertise, consensus decision-making)
Person culture (Dionysus)	Serves the interests of individuals: eg barristers working through chambers Management function administrative and supportive, rather than directive (eg bursars or registrars)	Supports individual talent and interests Rare in practice

2.8 One important point to note about this classification is the link between structure and culture. A bureaucratic structure will reflect (and be reflected by) a formalised, impersonal culture. A project structure will reflect (and be reflected by) a results-focused, collaborative culture and so on. It is not easy to change culture without addressing structural issues – and *vice versa*.

2.9 Another important point to note is that these are only classifications. Not every organisation will correspond to a particular 'type' – and different cultures may develop in different parts of the same organisation. Your purchasing department may function as a role culture – while the design or marketing department is more of a task culture.

The value of 'strong' culture

2.10 The importance of organisation culture for management was highlighted by Tom Peters and Robert Waterman, in their influential study of successful corporations: *In Search of Excellence* (1982). One of the key features of excellent companies (which consistently produce commercially viable new products and respond effectively to change) was their use of organisation culture to guide business processes and to motivate employees.

2.11 Both *Peters and Waterman* and *Deal and Kennedy* argued that cultural strength is a powerful tool for shaping the behaviour and success of an organisation. Not all organisation cultures are 'strong' – but those that *are* contribute to improved business performance.

2.12 This school of thought defined 'strong' cultures as those in which key values were widely shared and intensely held, and in which employees allowed themselves to be guided by them. In other words, as summarised by *Huczynski and Buchanan*: 'Strength refers to the degree to which employees share a commitment to a range of goals and values espoused by management, and have a high level of motivation to achieve them.'

2.13 So how does 'strong' culture improve business performance? Peters and Waterman argued as follows.

- A handful of widely shared, strongly held guiding values can replace rules, guidelines and supervision: focusing employees' attention on strategic aims such as quality, innovation and customer service, and empowering them to take initiative and responsibility in pursuit of those aims. This reduces rigidity, increases flexibility, enables change (on the basis that if values change, behaviour will follow) and develops people.
- Strong culture increases employee job satisfaction, loyalty and commitment. People need both to feel part of something meaningful and to 'shine' as stars in their own right: strong culture can satisfy both needs, by emphasising the 'family' nature of the enterprise, by building myths to reinforce the 'heroic' nature of the enterprise and by using value-laden symbols as rewards and incentives.

2.14 Strong culture is an attractive and influential idea, but empirical research has failed to show any strong correlation between strong culture and economic success. In other words, strong-culture organisations were not significantly more successful than weak-culture organisations. Nor was there any proof that culture was the determining factor in 'excellent' companies, as opposed to other organisational, market or environmental factors.

2.15 The concept of 'excellence' was in any case undermined by the subsequent failure of some of the businesses (such as IBM) on which it was based. Some commentators have argued that strong culture was not only *not* directly responsible for IBM's success (since in the same period it also enjoyed a monopoly in its market) – but may have been partly responsible for its failure. Strong culture may have created such ingrained thought and behaviour patterns that the company was unable to respond flexibly enough to the challenges of environmental change, such as the introduction of PCs.

How do you change a culture?

2.16 Cultures which are negative, unsuited to changing requirements or otherwise failing or dysfunctional can be changed! The key tools of cultural change include the following.

- Consistent expression and modelling of the new values by management (from the top down), leaders and influencers (who may need to be co-opted to the initiative by those in authority)
- Changing underlying values and beliefs, through communication, education and involvement of employees in discussing the need for new ideas and behaviours: spreading new values and beliefs and encouraging employees to 'own' them (through incentives, co-opting people to teach others and so on); and reinforcing the change (through implementation, recognition and rewards).
- Use of human resource management mechanisms to reinforce the changes: making the new values and behaviours criteria for recruitment and selection, appraisal and reward; including them in competency profiles and learning needs assessments for training and development planning; and so on. (These mechanisms are important because the organisation may need to bring in new people who will 'fit' the new culture – and squeeze out those who don't 'fit'.)

3 National culture

3.1 Different countries (or world regions) have different cultural norms, values and assumptions which influence how they do business and manage people. It is increasingly important to understand this, since managers are increasingly likely to work in organisations that have multinational or multi-ethnic elements, or in another culture.

3.2 Distinctive national features may be a source of competitive advantage in domestic and international markets (because of 'fashions' for the products or management techniques of particular cultures, and because of the synergy that may arise from diverse viewpoints and skills). However, they may also be a source of difficulties in cross-cultural business relationships and marketing (because of failure to understand underlying needs and expectations).

The Hofstede model

3.3 *Geert Hofstede* carried out major cross-cultural research at IBM in the 1980s, and formulated one of the most influential models of work-related cultural differences. The Hofstede Model describes five key dimensions of difference between national cultures, which influence all aspects of organisation and management: HR policies, communication and conflict, leadership styles, team working and so on. The five key dimensions are set out in Table 6.2.

Table 6.2 *The Hofstede model*

Dimension	Low ◄────	────► High
Power distance The extent to which unequal distribution of power is accepted.	Less centralisation, flatter organisation structures. Subordinates expect involvement and participation in decision-making. *Eg: Germanic, Anglo, Nordic*	Greater centralisation, top-down chain of command, closer supervision. Subordinates have little expectation of influencing decisions. *Eg Latin, less developed Asian*
Uncertainty avoidance The extent to which security, order and control are preferred to ambiguity, uncertainty and change	Value flexibility, creativity; generalists; variability Less task structure, written rules. Tolerance of risk, dissent, conflict, deviation from norm. *Eg Anglo, Nordic*	Value control, certainty and ritual; specialists/experts; standardisation Value task structure, rules and regulations. Need for consensus; low tolerance of deviance, dissent. *Eg Latin, Germanic, Japanese*
Individualism The extent to which people prefer to live and work in individualistic ('I') rather than collectivist ('We') ways.	Collectivist: emphasise inter-dependence, reciprocal obligation, social acceptability Organisation seen as 'family': relationship more important than task achievement Management of teams *Eg less developed Asian/ Latin*	Individualist: emphasise autonomy, individual choice and responsibility, initiative Organisation impersonal: task achievement more important than relationship Management of individuals *Eg Anglo, Nordic, more developed Latin*
Masculinity The extent to which social gender roles are distinct.	Feminine: minimise gender role differences Feminine values dominant (modesty, consensus, relationship, quality of life). *Eg Nordic*	Masculine: clearly differentiated gender roles Masculine values dominant (assertiveness, competition, decisiveness, material success). *Eg Japanese, Germanic, Anglo*
Long-term orientation The extent to which society embraces long-term devotion to traditional, forward thinking values.	Fulfilling social obligations Protecting 'face' Change can occur rapidly *Eg Anglo, Germanic*	Respect for tradition Thrift Perseverance Change may be slow *Eg Japanese*

Hall's communication model

3.4 *Edward Hall* suggested that another dimension of cultural difference is the extent to which the content and understanding of communication is influenced by its context: non-verbal aspects, underlying implications, interpersonal factors and so on.

- **Low-context** cultures (eg Germanic, Scandinavian, North American) tend to take the content of communication at face value: words say what they mean. They prefer clear, written, explicit communication. (The UK is classified as only moderately high context …)

- **High-context** cultures (eg Japanese, Asian, African, Latin American, Middle-Eastern, Southern European) interpret and exchange more complex messages. They prefer face-to-face and oral communication, and are good at developing networks and using non-verbal cues and unspoken implications. They tend to divulge less information in official/written forms

4 International and cross-cultural management

4.1 There has been increasing demand for managerial competence in working with (or within) different cultures in recent decades. Domestic skill shortages have encouraged international recruitment, supported by freedom of labour movement in blocs such as the European Economic Area. Meanwhile communications technology and e-commerce have facilitated the globalisation of markets, and there has been an increase in internal mergers, acquisitions and joint ventures as organisations have sought to operate effectively across national boundaries.

4.2 *Schneider and Barsoux* argue that 'rather than knowing what to do in Country X, or whether national or functional cultures are more important in multi-cultural teams, what is necessary is to know how to assess the potential impact of culture, national or otherwise, on performance'.

Planning cross-cultural and diversity initiatives

4.3 At the organisational level, there should be a plan to evaluate this potential impact and to implement programmes to encourage: awareness of areas of cultural difference and sensitivity; behavioural flexibility (being able to use multiple-solution models rather than 'one best way' approaches); and constructive communication, conflict resolution and problem-solving.

4.4 In particular, attention will have to be given to matters such as the following.

- **Managerial/leadership styles.** Managers' cross-cultural competence can be enhanced through: encouraging diversified work experience in international or multi-cultural settings (eg through management development); undertaking training exercises (reading, language learning, cultural briefings); networking with managers from other cultures and using them as consultants; and seeking to learn through all cross-cultural interactions.
- **Awareness training**. Relevant staff may be trained to understand the potential for problems arising from culturally-acquired assumptions: the need to recognise cultural stereotypes and move beyond them through new information and encounters with other people; the need to appreciate that 'different' does not necessarily imply 'wrong'.
- **Communication mechanisms**. Inter-cultural communication is the only way to bring cultural values and assumptions into the open, in order to limit potential misunderstanding. This cannot be done by single cultural profiles or briefings: it requires ongoing monitoring of messages, interpretations and areas of difference. Mechanisms for this kind of communication may include: cross-cultural teams; cross-cultural discussion, consultation and conflict resolution groups; cultural education and briefings; cross-cultural networking and forums (eg on the corporate intranet); and so on.

4.5 As with any major policy initiative in an organisation, this will require systematic planning and implementation.

4.6 Initial investigation may be required to identify which particular cultures are most relevant to the organisation, and areas in which cultural differences may have most impact. If an organisation is moving into a new market, forming a strategic alliance with an overseas partner, or recruiting significant numbers of staff from a particular ethnic group, for example, the need for education, awareness and communication may be clear.

4.7 Research may be carried out to explore areas of cultural difference and sensitivity which might impact on the marketing, business dealings, employment practices, managerial styles or employee relations of the organisation.

- Primary research may be carried out using interviews and surveys of individuals or representative groups, or using cross-cultural groups (to observe the impact of differences on interactions and decision-making). This research may focus on profiling another culture (its norms, beliefs and so on) or on the experience of members of that culture (areas of sensitivity, misunderstanding and so on).
- Secondary research (using published print and internet sources) may be used for similar purposes. There is a large body of published reports and briefings on cross-cultural management and business.

4.8 Once diversity or communication plans have been drawn up, the organisation may conduct pilot schemes, using single departments or small groups. This will enable them to observe the impact of initiatives, and gather feedback from staff on their experience of them, prior to rolling out the chosen option. Since cultural assumptions are so deeply embedded, the involvement of staff will be important – both in shifting values and in enhancing ownership and implementation of the programme.

4.9 It may be necessary or desirable to reinforce communication and awareness with guidelines or Codes of Conduct for cultural sensitivity and respect for diversity. Other mechanisms of organisation culture may also be used: using cross-cultural competences in recruitment, selection, appraisal and reward; planning cross-cultural learning experiences as part of training and development programmes; and so on.

Cross-cultural management issues

4.10 There is a vast range of potential differences and appropriate responses: managers will have to monitor and address them as they go. However, it is worth being aware that cultural differences may raise issues in the following areas.

- **Team-working**. 'Collective' working styles may be more congenial to some cultures than to others. Differences in social customs (gender roles, eating habits, business etiquette) may initially get in the way of co-operative working.
- **Communication**. There may be language barriers within a team or business relationship: allowances must be made for differences in fluency and understanding. There may also be different norms in regard to such matters as: the meanings attached to body language; the acceptability of displays of emotion; attitudes to conflict/consensus and so on.

- **Participation and involvement**. Some cultures prefer to raise issues or ideas one-to-one rather than in a group. Some have a problem with questioning or offering ideas to people in positions of respect/authority. In addition, there may be a need to encourage and balance diverse contributions within a cross-cultural group, to make sure that no viewpoints are excluded.
- **Conflict resolution**. Different cultures tend to have different norms and preferences in regard to the appropriateness of assertiveness, criticism or argument; the need to compromise or reach consensus; the value of competition and so on.
- **International issues**. There may be additional logistical issues in working across different time zones, developing 'virtual' teams and so on.

Managing diversity

4.11 The Western workforce is becoming increasingly diverse, not just in terms of national and ethnic backgrounds, but in terms of: the wider representation of women in the workforce; the wider variety of educational experiences and pathways leading to employment; and legislative support for the recognition of workers' rights to equality of opportunity, regardless of sexual orientation, religious affiliation, family structure, age and disability.

4.12 The concept of 'managing diversity' is based on the argument that the dimensions of individual difference on which organisations have so far focused are comparatively crude, obvious – and largely irrelevant to performance. People at work differ in all sorts of ways: personality, working style, individual needs and goals, family responsibilities and so on.

4.13 A 'managing diversity' orientation argues that an organisation should proactively seek to understand, appreciate and manage the needs of a diverse workforce. This may mean: supporting tolerance of individual differences (and outlawing discrimination and harassment); taking diversity into account when designing reward systems (eg offering 'menus' of benefits) and development programmes (taking into account potential education and qualification issues); adjusting work arrangements and environments in order to accommodate diverse family responsibilities and disabilities; and enhancing employee communications.

Chapter summary

- Culture is 'the collective programming of the mind which distinguishes members of one category of people from another' (Hofstede).
- Culture operates at three levels: outward expressions (behaviour, artefacts and rituals); values and beliefs; and underlying assumptions.
- Like other groups of people, organisations develop their own culture, style or climate: 'the way we do things around here'. Organisation culture can be analysed using the framework of the cultural web (Johnson and Scholes): underlying assumptions (or paradigm) plus behavioural manifestations (symbols, stories, rituals and routines, control systems, organisational structures and power structures).

- Harrison and Handy suggested a model of four structure/culture types: power culture (entrepreneurial); role culture (bureaucracy); task culture (project); and person culture (individuals).
- Cultural strength models argue that widely shared, intensely held values increase flexibility, quality and commitment.
- Culture can be modified by leadership vision and determination; education and communication; and supportive HR systems.
- National cultures may be classified using the Hofstede model (power distance, uncertainty avoidance, individualism, masculinity) or Hall's communication model (high context, low context).
- Cross-cultural management issues include: teamworking styles; communication differences; and international issues (time zones, virtual teams).
- Managing diversity is an approach that recognises many dimensions of difference between individuals at work.

Self-test questions

Numbers in brackets refer to paragraphs where you can check your answers

1 What are the outward expressions of culture? (1.4)

2 Draw the cultural web. (Figure 6.2)

3 What are the influences that shape organisation culture? (2.4–2.6)

4 Describe a task culture. (Table 6.1)

5 Explain the limitations of the 'cultural strength' model. (2.14, 2.15)

6 Outline an approach to culture change. (2.16)

7 What is (a) 'power distance' and (b) 'uncertainty avoidance'? (Table 6.2)

8 What is low-context communication? (3.4)

9 Outline the issues to be considered in planning a cross-cultural or diversity initiative. (4.4)

10 How might communication differences manifest themselves in cross-cultural management? (4.10)

CHAPTER 7

Decision Making Skills for Management

Learning objective and indicative content

3.1 Evaluate and apply a range of tools to make effective management choices and decisions

- Problem solving and decision making process
- Pareto analysis, Ishikawa (fishbone) diagram, strengths, weaknesses, opportunities, threats (SWOT), decision making trees, cost/benefit analysis, risk evaluation, paired comparison analysis
- Balanced scorecard (BBS)

Chapter headings

Introduction

'Decision making' is defined simply, by *Huczynski and Buchanan*, as 'the process of making choices from among several options'. In a sense, every member of an organisation makes decisions all the time: decision-making isn't the sole preserve of managers. However, the decisions taken by managers have significant impacts on the performance of the organisation – and the lives of its members. *Henry Mintzberg* suggested (as we saw in Chapter 1) that decision-making is one of the key roles of the manager.

In this chapter, we look briefly at the process of managerial problem-solving and decision-making. We then go on to describe and evaluate a number of tools and techniques which have been developed to support managers in making more effective decisions.

1 Problem solving and decision making

The rational model of decision-making

1.1 The rational model of decision-making has been central to Western thinking. It assumes that decision-making is a logical process, consisting of a sequence of steps: information is gathered, and various possible courses of action are evaluated, so the likelihood of obtaining the desired outcome (or 'best' option) is systematically increased.

1.2 This classical framework for decision-making can be illustrated as follows: Figure 7.1.

Figure 7.1: *The rational decision-making process*

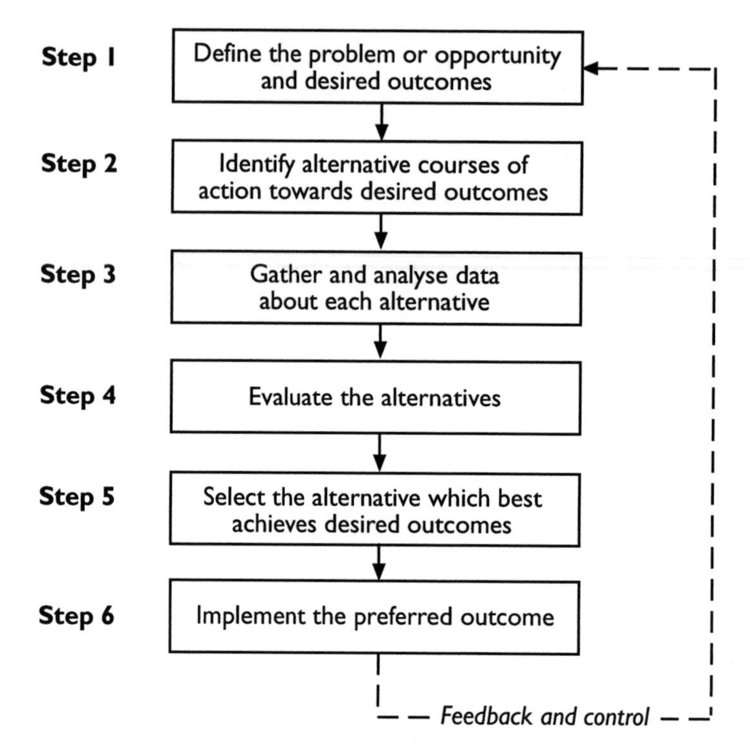

1.3 Like other classical theories of organisation, this model is founded on a belief in rationality. It assumes the ability to make decisions based on: clear and agreed goals and desired outcomes (on which consistent decision rules could be based); the availability of complete, accurate and cost-effective information; an awareness of all possible alternative courses of action – and their consequences, costs and benefits; the time and ability to take all this information into account; the ability to make logical, impersonal decisions on the basis of factual information and statistical analyses; and the ability to implement decisions based on their 'rightness' alone.

1.4 Unfortunately, reality is a bit messier than that...

Limitations of the rational approach

1.5 All decision-makers work with imperfect information. Information gathering and analysis requires time, effort, awareness and cost. In practice, it is rarely possible for a manager:

- To know exactly what goals or outcomes to pursue (given the needs of different stakeholders)
- To take into account (or even be aware of) all possible alternative courses of action
- To gather all the information (or sufficiently accurate and up-to-date information) to make a decision with any certainty
- To analyse all consequences of alternative decisions, or to predict them accurately
- To remove all subjectivity from the process, in order to process the relevant information objectively.

1.6 The attempt to gather 'all' the information required before making a decision can lead to what has been called **analysis paralysis**: a situation in which the organisation (or manager) is so concerned to gather more or better information, that no decision or action can be taken.

1.7 *March and Simon*, well-known writers on the limits to rational decision-making, point out that the process is in any case limited, or bounded, because of the nature of organisations. 'Because individuals in organisations cannot make complex decisions with complete rationality, organisations take action to limit the scope of decisions members can make... They establish rules, information channels and training programmes to narrow the range of alternatives considered in making decisions.'

1.8 Managers' decisions are therefore limited by the parameters set for them, and by the norms and values built up by the organisation's culture and systems – and, in turn, by the 'editing' of information as it passes through these systems, according to the assumptions people make about what the 'right' or 'relevant' information is. This is often called the **bounded rationality** view.

1.9 *Peters and Waterman*, from a slightly different viewpoint, add that effective decision-making is not just about rationality, but about creativity, hunches, gut reactions, politics and other unquantifiable human factors. They argue that the statistical, analytical component of the rational model has a built-in conservative bias: it stifles creativity, internal competition, innovation and flexibility – and does not take into account the importance of cultural values (including ethical values) in the 'rightness' of decisions.

1.10 *Peter Drucker* also suggests that the Western rational model focuses too exclusively on a single, objective decision-maker. He suggests that the most successful approach to decision-making is the **Japanese approach**, which:

- Does not focus on giving an answer, but on defining the question, finding out what the decision is really about – not just what the decision should be
- Focuses on alternatives, rather than on the 'right' answer
- Brings out dissenting opinions, encourages arguments and then seeks consensus.

1.11 Consensus decision-making may take longer, but decisions do not then have to be 'sold' to the people who have to implement them, and other stakeholders. Drucker argues that, contrary to the rational model, effective decisions do not flow from a 'consensus on the facts', but from 'the clash and conflict of opinions'.

Having said all that...

1.12 There are still useful analytical techniques which can be used – flexibly – to help managers in purchasing and supply to make more effective decisions.

1.13 You may already have come across some decision-making tools and techniques in your studies. There are many such techniques, depending on the nature of the decision: environmental analysis, risk analysis, supplier selection, costing and pricing, activity or project scheduling, order quantities, investment appraisal – and so on. (And remember: these are only one set of decisions, which are readily quantifiable. Human resource management decisions – what to do about an unmotivated staff member, whether to promote one individual or another – are less easily modelled using scientific methods!)

1.14 The appropriate approach depends in part on the nature of the decision in each case.

- Routine: repetitive, programmed (often low-level) decisions, involving the use of pre-established procedures or rules. One example is the re-ordering of stock items which have fallen to a certain level, at a determined order quantity.
- Adaptive: higher-level decisions which require human judgement – but can be supported or guided by relatively simple decision tools (such as SWOT analysis, decision trees or cost-benefit analysis). Examples include investment decisions, 'make or buy' or outsourcing decisions, and non-standard purchase decisions.
- Innovative: unique, first-time decisions for which there is no existing solution or model, and which require judgement and creativity. These are generally strategic decisions, such as whether to invest in new technology, or which marketing approach the firm will adopt: they are often made by professionals or top managers, on a shared/group basis.

1.15 We will now look at some of the decision-making models mentioned in the syllabus.

2 Environmental analysis

2.1 An audit of the external environment is the first step in strategic decision-making (*Johnson, Scholes and Whittington*). The total environment of an organisation can be depicted at various levels: Figure 7.2

Figure 7.2: *The organisational environment*

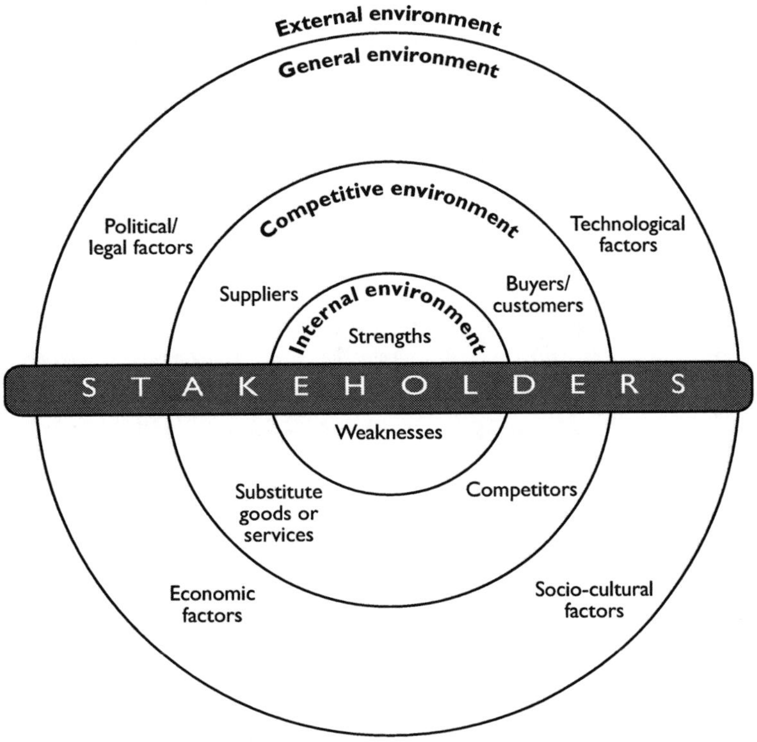

(Adapted from Dobson & Starkey (1993) and Boddy (2002))

The macro environment

2.2 Macro-environment analysis is often carried out using a PESTLE framework: Table 7.1.

Table 7.1 *The PEST/PESTLE framework*

Factors	Examples
Political	Government policy, political risk in foreign markets
Economic	Economic strength/weakness (including consumer spending); employment levels; taxation; inflation and interest rates; subsidies and grants. (On an international level: exchange rates, comparative wages/taxes, freedom of labour/capital movements, trade agreements and so on.)
Socio-cultural	Demographics (age, gender, population movements and so on); education; fashion trends; consumerism; values (eg 'green' consumers); attitudes to work.
Technological	New technology for organisational systems and processes (eg supply chain management). New technology products (eg downloaded music, plasma TV). New technology marketing (eg e-commerce).
Legal	Legislation and regulation affecting: contracts; employment; health and safety; the environment and so on.
Ecological	Consumer demand for eco-friendly products; legislation on pollution and waste management; availability of natural resources.

The micro environment

2.3 One key tool of micro-environment (industry and competitor) analysis is *Porter's* **five forces model**. Figure 7.3 displays the five forces.

Figure 7.3 *Porter's five forces model*

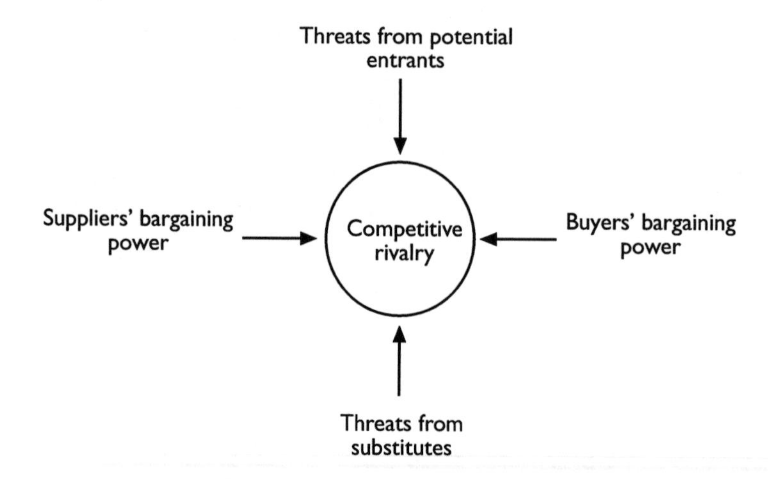

2.4 This can be used as a framework for monitoring of the competitive environment, which in turn influences the attractiveness (or profit-making potential) of the industry.

- The bargaining power of suppliers influences the cost of the materials and services the organisation needs. Suppliers are comparatively powerful within an industry when they are limited in number; when there are few substitute products/services; when when their price is a high proportion of the organisation's total product cost; or when the supplier owns the organisation (through forward integration).
- The bargaining power of buyers refers to the power of the organisation's customers. Customers are comparatively powerful within an industry when they are limited in number; when products are not highly differentiated, so that customers can switch products easily; when the customer's expenditure represents a high proportion of the organisation's revenue; or when the customer owns the supplier (through backward integration).
- The threat of new entrants to an industry influences the level of market share a business can expect to hold. A market may be protected by 'barriers to entry' which make it less attractive or viable to new entrants: for example, high capital investment requirements, low profit margins, dominant existing competitors, lack of opportunities for economies of scale for small entrants and so on.
- Substitute products influence competition by enabling customers to switch brands easily; putting pressure on the organisation to differentiate its products and ensure customer loyalty.
- The intensity of rivalry among existing firms will also influence potential profitability, because of aggressive price competition, marketing wars and so on.

SWOT analysis

2.5 Strengths, Weaknesses, Opportunities and Threats analysis is a technique of corporate appraisal, used to assess the internal resources of the organisation (or function) to cope with and/or capitalise on factors in the external environment in which it operates.

2.6 Strengths and weaknesses are internal aspects of the business that enhance or limit its ability to compete, change and thrive. Internal appraisal may cover aspects such as:

- Physical and financial resources: availability of raw materials, asset base, profitability, tax structure etc
- The effectiveness of various functions and operations: eg efficiency or quality of production, R & D expertise, purchasing integration
- The product/service portfolio, positioning and market share
- Human resources: management expertise, staff skills, flexibility etc
- The efficiency and effectiveness of systems (eg for quality control, inventory management, communication and so on)
- Structure: adaptability, efficiency, co-ordination
- Distinctive competences: things it does better than competitors

2.7 Opportunities and threats are factors in the external environment that may emerge to impact on the business. What potential do they offer to either enhance or erode competitive advantage or profitability?

2.8 The internal and external factors can be mapped in a SWOT grid as follows: Figure 7.4.

Figure 7.4: *SWOT analysis*

Internal	**Strengths** New technology Quality management systems Stable, high-quality staff Market leading brands	**Weaknesses** Low new product development Poor financial controls Non-renewable resources
External	**Opportunities** E-commerce Consumer values re quality Tax breaks for regional development	**Threats** Environmental protection law Fashion trends Aging demographic

2.9 SWOT is used to identify areas where strategic responses are required for the organisation to maintain or enhance its position in relation to the environment.

- Plan to build on strengths and/or minimise weaknesses – in order to be able to capitalise on the identified opportunities (or create new ones) and to cope better with the identified threats.
- Plan to convert threats into opportunities – by developing the strengths (and contingency plans) to counter them (more effectively than competitors), and by being prepared to learn from them.

3 Decision trees

Choosing between options by mapping their likely outcomes

3.1 A decision-tree is a type of flowchart, which can be used as a visual aid to summarise the options available for a given decision or problem, and the possible outcomes, risks and rewards of choosing each. The purpose of a decision tree is basically to help a manager to choose between particular courses of action, in order to approach decision making more systematically

3.2 *Lysons & Farrington* suggest that this tool is useful for any supply problem that can be reduced to a set of mutually exclusive decisions; with, for each decision, a set of possible outcomes; and for each outcome, an assessment of the likelihood of its occurring, and its revenues or costs.

Drawing a decision tree

3.3 A decision tree consists of the following elements.

- An initial decision point: a small square on the left hand side of the sheet of paper, which represents the decision you need to make.
- Branches: lines drawn out towards the right, representing various possible solutions or options (labelled along the line).
- The outcome of each branch/solution. If result is uncertain, draw a circle at the end of the branch. If result is another decision point, draw another square.
- Further branches from each new decision point, representing possible options.
- Further branches from each 'uncertainty' circle, representing possible outcomes.

3.4 The following example (Figure 7.5) illustrates the process.

Figure 7.5 *Decision tree: should we outsource the recruitment function?*

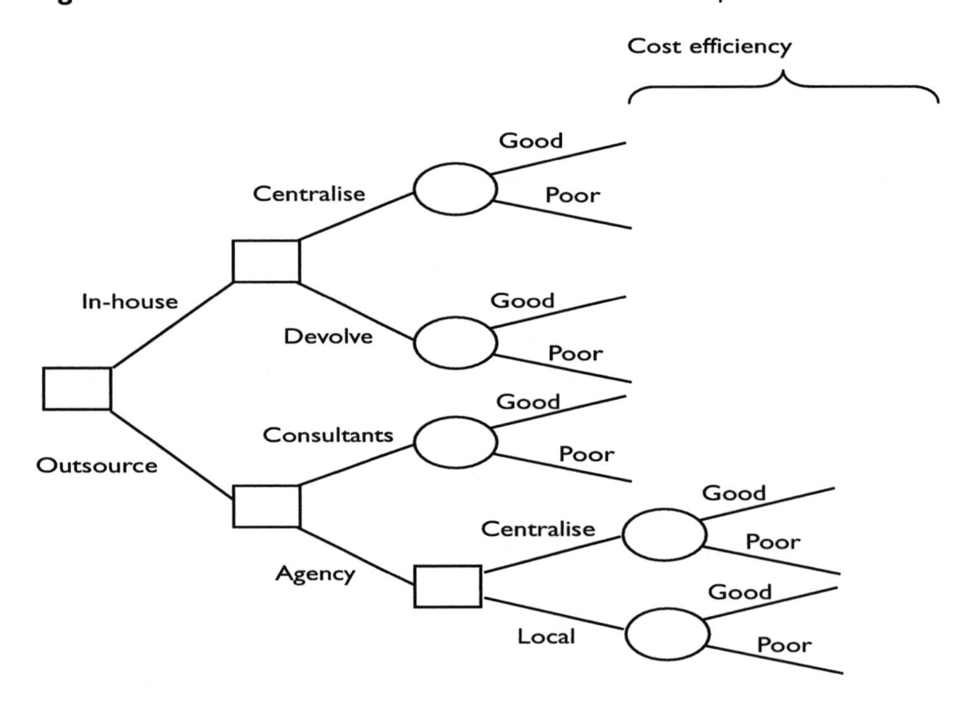

3.5 Once the decision tree has been drafted (and redrafted if necessary for clarity and completeness), you have a map of the various options and their possible outcomes. This may in itself be a useful tool for guiding group decision-making – or recording brainstorming proposals in a systematic way. There are also various ways of evaluating the options depicted on the decision tree in more detail, if you wish.

- Which is the most desirable outcome? You can assign an estimated cash value to each possible outcome.
- Which is the most likely outcome? You can assign a probability to each uncertainty point.
- Which is the 'best' decision option? You can compare the values (outcome gains *minus* costs) of each decision.

3.6 Decision trees are a useful model where the options are clearly identifiable, and where probabilities, costs and value can be assigned to them.

- They give a clear visual picture of the options and their consequences.
- They allow all options (including 'pet' ones) to be challenged.
- They allow outcomes to be quantified on the basis of value and probability, taking into account available information and best guesses.

4 Risk evaluation

4.1 Nothing is certain – however much information we gather and analyse! Every decision carries some kind of risk: the risk of making a poor investment or suffering financial loss; the risk of losing the goodwill of staff or suppliers; or the risk of environmental impacts, say. In accepting a customer's JIT sourcing policy, there is a risk that we will not be able to make the deliveries on time. In drawing up materials specifications for a product re-launch, there is a risk that the changes will not find favour with customers.

4.2 Increasingly, managers are urged not to be afraid of risk and uncertainty: they are a feature of the modern environment – and they can stimulate innovation, creativity and learning, without which the organisation may struggle to adapt and thrive. However, it is also accepted that risk must be managed, in order to reduce unacceptable impacts on the organisation and its stakeholders.

A simple risk analysis model

4.3 *Karlof & Lovingsson* suggest that risk is 'a function of the probability that an element of risk will occur and the (adverse) consequences that will result if it occurs.' This can be expressed as a simple formula.

RISK = PROBABILITY x CONSEQUENCE

Where:

- Probability is expressed as a percentage
- Consequences can be expressed as a number from 1 to 10: 1 is a small consequence, and 10 is a disastrous consequence.

4.4 So, for example, in appraising a strategy to outsource the Information Technology function, the elements of risk may be identified as follows.

Element of risk	Probability	Consequence	Risk level
Systems failure	20%	10	2
Staff strike	80%	6	4.8
Teething problems	30%	4	1.2

4.5 This analysis may be used in several ways.

- Staff strike carries the highest risk, so this may be a priority for management action.
- There may be set tolerance levels for consequence, however, so that (say) action must be taken on all risks with a potential consequence of over 7: systems failure would therefore be the priority for management action to minimise the risk.
- The various elements of risk may be mapped on a graph as follows: Figure 7.6. This enables decision guidelines to be set: no action required for 'acceptable' levels of risk; risk management required for 'moderate' risk levels; and risk avoidance or elimination for 'unacceptable' levels.

Figure 7.6 *Risk analysis*

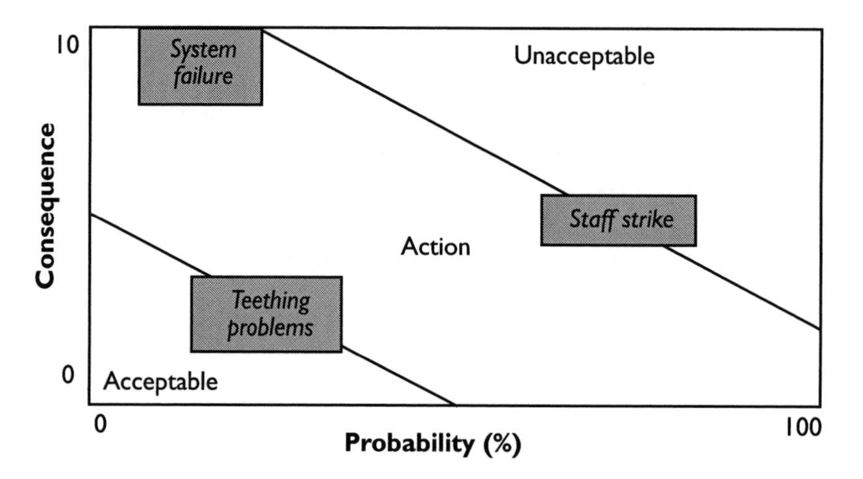

5 Cost-benefit analysis

Deciding whether to follow a course of action

5.1 Cost-benefit analysis is a fairly simple technique for deciding whether or not to pursue a particular plan or change. However creative and potentially effective your preferred solution to a problem may be, it will not be 'worth' implementing (in quantitative terms) if the costs of doing so are greater than the benefits that will accrue.

5.2 Put simply, cost-benefit analysis involves putting a monetary value to the benefits of a course of action, and deducting the costs associated with it. However, this may not be as simple as it sounds.

5.3 The benefits of a given plan may not be completely, or easily, quantifiable as a monetary value. Direct financial benefits (such as cost savings or revenue earnings) may be easy to calculate, but putting a financial value on intangible benefits may be highly subjective. (What value can be put on greater employee satisfaction or creativity, say, or the minimising of environmental impacts through better waste management?)

5.4 Similarly, costs may be difficult to analyse.

- Direct costs are those incurred directly as a result of carrying out the plan.
- Indirect costs are those which may be attributed to the plan, but would have been incurred by the organisation whether or not the plan had been carried out: management time, office space and so on.
- Opportunity costs are revenue-earning opportunities lost as a result of implementing the plan.

5.5 There are also intangible costs, which are harder to quantify: what is the cost of environmental damage, or an increase in employee stress, say? The term 'externalities' has been coined by economists to describe costs which are not absorbed in a product or service and not paid for directly by the customer, but are borne by the wider community (such as the costs of pollution control). With increasing pressure for corporate social responsibility (CSR), there is a greater interest in quantifying these kinds of costs.

5.6 As one more complicating factor, costs may be incurred, and benefits received, on an ongoing basis, over time – rather than 'up front' when a plan is implemented. Cost-benefit analysis is therefore often expressed as a payback period: the time it takes for the benefits of a change to repay its costs.

5.7 Table 7.2 shows a very simple cost benefit analysis for the introduction of a new computer-based purchasing management system. The manager making this decision believes that a computerised department will offer cost savings, enhance the efficiency of stock management and expediting, and enhance supply chain relationships – but is it *worth* doing, from a business point of view?

5.8 This manager may wish to refine his benefit estimates – perhaps using figures derived from other departments or organisations which have computerised, or from published reports on the benefits of computerised purchasing. However, it is clear from this exercise that the payback time is acceptably short: the manager is likely to go ahead with the computerisation plan.

6 Pareto analysis

Selecting the most important items to deal with or variables to alter

6.1 *Vilfredo Pareto* (1848–1923) formulated the following rule.

'In any series of elements to be controlled a selected small factor in terms of number of elements almost always accounts for a large factor in terms of effort.'

In other words, you can generate 80% of the results of a plan or job by doing just 20% of the work involved – if you can leverage your effort by picking the right 20% of items, tasks or changes to which to devote your attention!

Table 7.2 *Specimen cost benefit analysis*

Costs		£
Computer equipment:	8 PCs @ £1,000	8,000
	1 server @ £1,200	1,200
	2 printers @ £400	800
	Installation and technical support	1,800
	Purchasing management software	3,200
Staff training:	Introductory computing (6 people × £200)	1,200
	Purchasing management system (8 people × £400)	3,200
Other costs:	Lost time (20 person days @ £100 per day)	2,000
	Cost of errors/wastage through initial inefficiencies (estimate)	5,000
Total costs		**£26,400**
Benefits		
(estimate, per year)		£
Improved efficiency of ordering/expediting		20,000
Improved supplier selection and management		10,000
Improved planning/control through supply information		15,000
Total benefit (per year)		**£45,000**
Payback time: 26,400/45,000 = 0.59 year = approx. 7 months		

6.2 The Pareto principle (or '80/20 rule') is a useful technique for finding the activities or changes that will leverage your time, effort and resources to bring the biggest benefits: it is a great way of prioritising between possible courses of action.

6.3 In its simplest form, Pareto analysis involves writing out a list of the actions you could take, or the problems you are facing, in a given area – and scoring them in any way that is appropriate to your aims. If you were listing cost-reduction options, say, you could score each option on the basis of how much it would save. If you were listing sources of employee dissatisfaction, you could score them according to the number of surveyed complaints or mentions on 'exit' interviews. The items with the highest scores are those which will leverage your effort and resources for the greatest benefit.

ABC analysis

6.4 In the field of purchasing, the Pareto principle can be applied to the analysis of supply data, in the form of ABC analysis.

6.5 The Pareto principle suggests that, roughly speaking, 80% of the total value of materials will be accounted for by 20% of the items, so management effort can be leveraged by attending to that valuable 20%. ABC analysis prioritises stock into three categories:

- Category A items: the 'vital few'. Small in number but high in usage value. (Devote most managerial control effort here.)
- Category B items: 'normal' items. Medium in number, medium usage value.
- Category C items: the 'trivial many'. High in number, low usage value. (Devote least managerial control here.)

6.6 To calculate the annual usage value of each item, you simply multiply its unit value (£) by its annual usage (number of units). You can then rank all your items in descending order and identify categories.

7 Paired comparison analysis

Evaluating the relative importance of different options

7.1 Like Pareto analysis, paired comparison analysis is a tool for prioritising: weighing the relative importance of different options, so that you can choose the most important problem to solve, or select the solution that will leverage your resources most effectively to give you the greatest benefits.

7.2 The technique works as follows.

- List all the options/problems you want to compare.
- Set up a table, with your options/problems as both row and column headers.
- Block out cells on the table where you will be comparing an option with itself and where you will be duplicating a comparison.
- For each cell in the table, compare the row-headed option with the column-headed option, deciding which is more important and by how much: 0 = no difference, 3 = big difference.
- Add up the scores for each of the options.

7.3 For example, in deciding what to focus on when selecting or rating suppliers, a purchasing manager may compare the relative importance of the following factors.

	Price (A)	**Quality (B)**	**Delivery (C)**	**Environmental controls (D)**
Price (A)		A, 1	C, 1	A, 2
Quality (B)			C, 1	B, 1
Delivery (C)				C, 3
Environmental controls (D)				
	A = 3 (33.3%)	B = 1 (11.1%)	C = 5 (55.6 %)	D = 0

Suppliers should therefore be evaluated on their ability to deliver first, and then on their price. Quality and environmental controls are rather less of an issue: perhaps they are not crucial to these particular supplies, or perhaps adequate standards are in place across the board!

8 Ishikawa diagrams

Identifying and solving quality problems

8.1 Ishikawa developed a distinctively Japanese quality strategy: a broad involvement in quality involving all concerned, from top to bottom of an organisation and from start to finish of the product lifecycle.

8.2 He also developed the cause and effect analysis diagram (also known as the Ishikawa or fishbone diagram) that enables quality problems to be identified. This diagram illustrates the relationship between possible causes and effects, and helps uncover the source of the problem: Figure 7.7.

Figure 7.7 *The 5M fishbone diagram (manufacturing)*

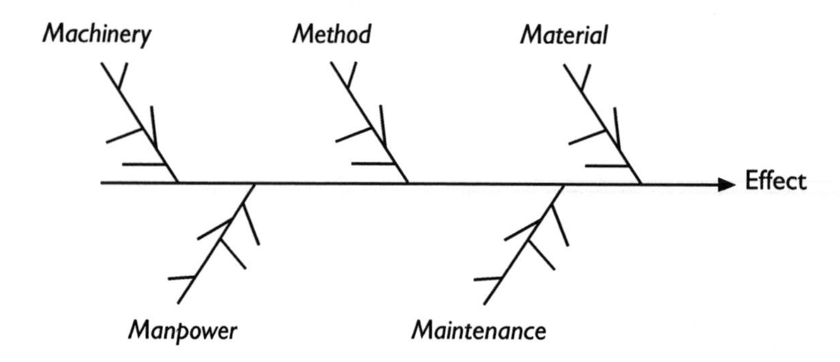

8.3 In non-manufacturing contexts, 4 Ps (policies, procedures, people and plant) is used instead.

8.4 After the basic diagram has been drawn, the main causes of problems can be expanded and treated as separate branches. These subcauses are then added to, until all possible causes have been considered.

8.5 Ishikawa developed the 'seven basic tools of quality' (7Qs) that he considered should be widely used in an organisation to analyse problems and develop improvements.

• Pareto analysis	Which are the big problems?
• Cause and effect diagrams	What causes the problems?
• Stratification	How is the data made up?
• Check sheets	How often does it occur?
• Histograms	What do the overall variations show?
• Scatter charts	What are the relationships we can deduce?
• Process control charts	Which variations to control and how?

9 The balanced scorecard

Balancing financial and non-financial values in decision-making

9.1 The balanced scorecard model was developed in 1990 by *Kaplan and Norton*. They argued that financial objectives and measures are insufficient to control organisations effectively. Organisations need other parameters and perspectives, in order to avoid the problem of 'short-termism', which arises when managers are judged by criteria which do not measure the long-term, complex effects of their decisions.

9.2 *Karlof & Lovingsson* suggest that: 'Few can withstand the simple and obvious logical underlying balanced scorecard: namely, that there are factors other than the financial which are important to control and follow up and that it can be a good idea to establish which factors these in fact are.'

9.3 Kaplan and Norton proposed four key perspectives for a balanced scorecard (sometimes called a balanced business scorecard or BBS).

- Financial – how do we create value for our shareholders?
- Customers – what do they value?
- Internal business processes – what is our internal CSF process? (CSF = critical success factors)
- Innovation and organisational learning – what new products and services do our customers need?

9.4 Other management thinkers have proposed different categories, around the same basic themes: internal perspectives (processes, efficiency, employees/co-workers, innovation/learning, organisation, products, environment/quality); external perspectives (customers, stakeholders, business environment, suppliers, community); and profit or performance perspectives (finance, economy, owners/shareholders, profit). The scorecard has been designed to balance decision-making by focusing on the interrelationship between the differing competitive pressures facing the organisation and stimulating continuous improvement.

9.5 The 'balance' of the balanced scorecard is thus between: financial and non-financial performance measures; short-term and long-term perspectives; and internal and external focus.

9.6 Working with a balanced scorecard requires describing, for each 'perspective' selected:

- The organisation's long-term goals
- The success factors established to achieve those goals
- The key activities which must be carried out to achieve those success factors
- The key performance indicators which can be used to monitor progress

9.7 According to Kaplan and Norton's model, managers' performance should be evaluated on a range of financial and non-financial key performance indicators (KPIs): Figure 7.8.

Figure 7.8 *The balanced scorecard*

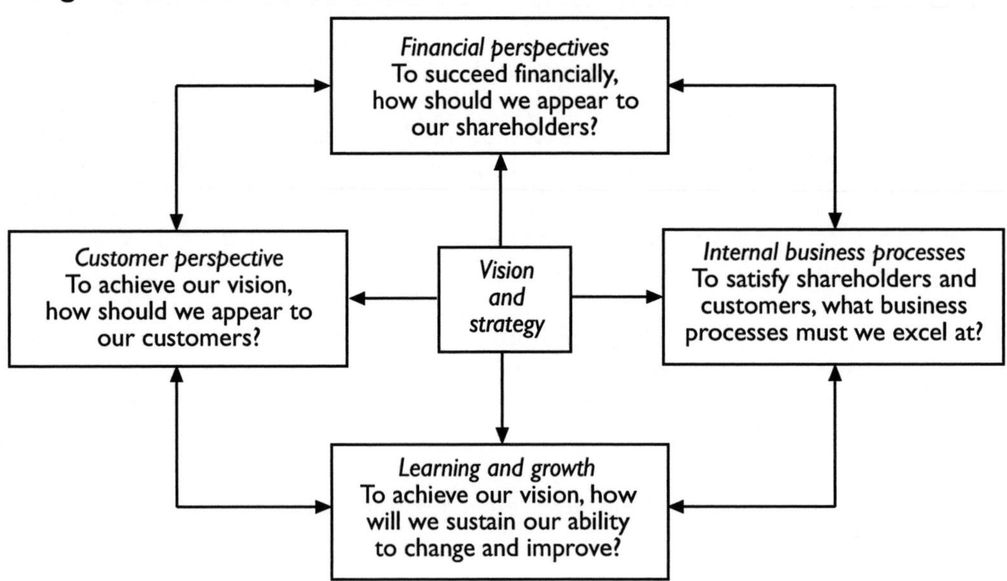

Chapter summary

- The rational model of decision making assumes that decisions can be made using a logical, sequential approach. However, all decision-makers work with incomplete and imperfect information, within limiting frameworks.
- Environmental analysis is used to audit the influence of the macro environment (eg using a PEST or PESTLE framework) and the micro or industry environment (eg using Porter's five forces model). You should be able to describe both models.
- Audits of the external and internal environment can be fed into a SWOT (strengths, weaknesses, opportunities, threats) analysis to identify strategic options.
- Other decision making tools (which you should be able to explain and apply) include:
  - Decision trees: choosing between options by mapping likely outcomes
  - Risk evaluation: eg using the equation Risk = Probability × Consequence
  - Cost-benefit analysis: a quantified comparison of 'pluses and minuses' for deciding whether to follow a course of action (often expressed as the payback period: the time it will take for benefits to repay costs)
  - Pareto analysis: prioritising the most important items to deal with or variables to alter (including ABC stock categorisation by annual usage value)
  - Paired comparison analysis: evaluating the relative importance of different options (by comparing them in all possible paired combinations)
  - Ishikawa diagrams: analysing cause and effect to identify and solve quality issues.
- The balanced scorecard is a framework of parameters and perspectives balancing financial and non-financial, short-term and long-term, and internal and external success factors. Kaplan and Norton proposed four key perspectives: finance (shareholder value), customers (customer value), internal business processes (critical success factors) and innovation and organisational learning.

Self-test questions

Numbers in brackets refer to paragraphs where you can check your answers

1. Outline the rational decision-making process. (Figure 7.1)
2. What are the features and advantages of a Japanese approach to decision-making? (1.10, 1.11)
3. What are (a) Porter's five forces and (b) PESTLE factors? (2.4, 2.2)
4. How do external/internal audit factors map to SWOT analysis? (2.8)
5. How may probability and consequence be mathematically expressed in order to derive a risk evaluation? (4.3)
6. Distinguish between direct and indirect costs. (5.4)
7. What are externalities? (5.5)
8. How would you calculate the annual usage value of items, as part of ABC analysis? (6.5)
9. What are the 5Ms and 4Ps of Ishikawa (fishbone) diagrams? (8.2, 8.3)
10. List four key perspectives of a balanced scorecard approach, and what should be described for each. (9.3, 9.6)

CHAPTER 8

Operational Planning and Control

Learning objectives and indicative content

3.2 Explain how to formulate, implement and monitor operational plans for the purchasing and supply function to achieve organisational objectives.

- Aligning plans with strategic objectives/direction of the organisation
- Agreeing objectives and targets: reducing defects, improving lead times, reducing costs
- SMART principles
- Importance of and ways to involve the team in the planning process
- Monitoring systems and processes including annual and periodic reviews
- Reporting structures

3.3 Evaluate the resource requirements for the implementation of operational plans for the purchasing function.

- People as a resource
- Financial resources
- Physical resources
- Time

Chapter headings

1 The hierarchy of planning

2 The cycle of planning and control

3 Setting objectives for purchasing

4 Monitoring and reporting

5 Managing organisational resources

Introduction

A great deal of management time is spent formulating plans. (Some managers have been known to express the opinion that 'if only they didn't have to spend so much time planning, they might have an opportunity to manage the business'.) To get value from this exercise it is important that managers have a clear view of the objectives they are seeking to achieve.

We begin this chapter by setting out the hierarchy of planning, from the 'mission statement' (which attempts to encapsulate why the organisation exists at all) right down to detailed operational plans. We then examine the processes of operational planning in the purchasing and supply function, and how various resources are assessed and allocated to implement those operational plans.

1 The hierarchy of planning

The hierarchy of objectives

1.1 Most writers agree with the idea that there is a hierarchy of objectives in organisations, just as there is a hierarchy of managers. The objectives at the top of the hierarchy are relevant to all aspects and members of the organisation, at a general level: they 'cascade down' to the more specific objectives of business units, groups and individuals. The terms commonly given to the statement of objectives at each stage of this cascade can be pictured as follows: Figure 8.1

Figure 8.1: *Hierarchy of objectives*

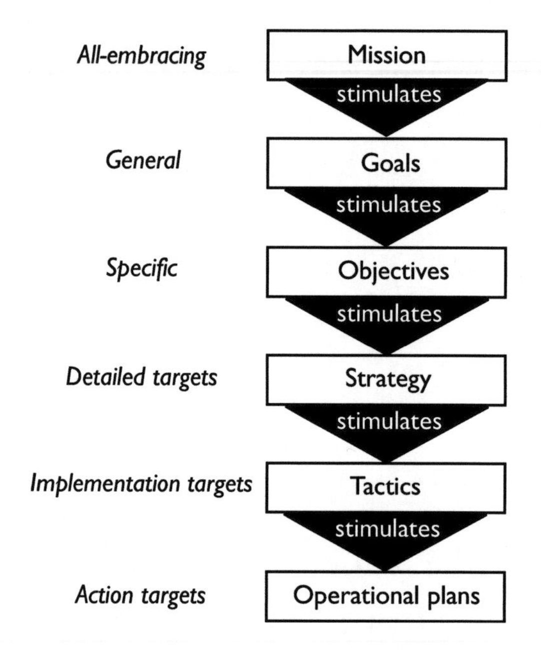

1.2 The mission of an organisation is a broad definition of the purpose of the organisation: what business are we in? what are we trying to achieve? The organisation's mission statement is usually a brief statement of the purpose, business areas and key cultural values of the organisation, stated in qualitative rather than quantitative terms. Its purpose is primarily to communicate a sense of meaning and direction to the people inside the organisation, as a guideline for activity. Most mission statements are therefore aspirational and customer-focused ('Absolutely, Positively Overnight': Fedex), although some may be competitive ('Beat Coke': Pepsi).

1.3 Goals and objectives transform the mission into targets or aims which the organisation will pursue. The terms are often used interchangeably, but it may be helpful to think of goals as statements of a desired future state ('where we want to get to'), and objectives as more specific, time-assigned, quantified targets to pursue in order to achieve each goal ('what we need to do to get there'). Objectives are quantified in order to enable you to measure progress towards meeting our goals: we will look at the characteristics of effectively-stated objectives (using the popular mnemonic SMART) later in the chapter.

Levels of planning

1.4 Plans vary in the level at which they are taken, the breadth of the business they cover, the detail they examine and the length of their horizon (or how far ahead they look).

- Strategic plans apply to the whole organisation. They focus on the broad, general direction of the organisation over the long term (say, 3–5 years. Note that 'long term' is no longer thought of in terms of 10-year plans, because of the pace of environmental change!)
- Tactical plans apply to particular divisions and functions (or strategic business units). They focus on the tasks and objectives required to pursue the chosen strategies in particular markets, over the medium term (say, 1–2 years).
- Operational plans apply to functions and departments. They focus on the specific detail of tasks, targets, resources and actions needed to implement the chosen tactics, over the short term (day to day and up to a year, say).

Integrating plans

1.5 Even from this brief description, you should appreciate the need to integrate planning activity in two directions.

- **Vertical integration** ensures that individual plans are designed to support team objectives, which are designed to support functional plans, which are designed to support organisational objectives. This is essential for purposeful activity: all efforts contribute to the goal. Purchase and supply objectives, for example, are not formulated in isolation: they further the organisation's value-adding and competitive strategies by reducing costs, improving quality and lead-times and so on.
- **Horizontal integration** ensures that the objectives of different individuals, units and functions dovetail with each other. This is essential for co-ordinated effort, reduced waste (from duplicated activity, bottlenecks or gaps) and the presentation of a coherent face to the outside world. So, for example, purchasing and supply plans must be co-ordinated with the needs of customers (defined by marketing plans), the requirements of operations (defined by operations plans) and the availability of resources (eg through HR and financial planning) and so on.

Why are goals and objectives important?

1.6 Setting effective goals is important for organisational reasons. Goals promote unity of direction, aiding co-ordination and efficient organisation: they reduce overlaps and gaps in activity. They enable limited resources to be intentionally allocated to optimise corporate performance (rather than potentially sub-optimal unit performance). They provide an objective measure against which performance can be measured and accountability maintained. They support flexibility, by focusing on end results rather than inputs (which may change).

1.7 Goal setting is also important, at an individual and team level, for behavioural reasons. Goals enable tasks to be broken down into manageable time-bounded 'chunks', while at the same time giving people a sense of their role and contribution to the whole activity of the organisation. They are important in motivation: people are motivated by the decision that it is worth expending effort to reach desired outcomes (goals), and by feedback information telling them to what extent they have achieved those goals. Goals are, for the same reason, vital in learning and change.

Why involve teams in planning?

1.8 As we will see in Chapter 10 (on teamworking and motivation), team participation in planning and decision-making is important, despite its drawbacks, for several reasons.

- People are more likely to 'own' and commit themselves to implementing plans which they have helped to formulate (both because they are more likely to understand the rationale behind the plan, and because they have made themselves jointly accountable for the success of the plan).
- Team members often have detailed experience and knowledge which can enhance the quality and practicability of the plan: knowledge of operational requirements and problems, customer needs and feedback and so on.
- Team members contribute different perspectives and ideas which may offer synergy ('no one of us is as wise as all of us') and creative/innovative solutions.
- Collaborative planning focuses the team's attention on their shared goals, which may contribute to *esprit de corps*, and minimise individual agendas and potential for conflict.
- People are likely to be more aware of their own role/responsibilities and those of others, in achieving the task – which aids co-ordination and flexibility.

1.9 Involving team members in planning can be achieved in various ways, according to the nature of the decision, the capabilities of the group, the time available, the style of the leader and so on. Weekly review and planning meetings may be held to discuss routine activity. Team members may be included in project planning discussions. Individuals may be delegated the task of preparing and updating plans, schedules and charts and presenting them to the team. The leader may propose plans for comments and suggestions by team members. And so on.

2 The cycle of planning and control

2.1 Planning is best seen as a cycle comprising a number of activities.

- Gathering information ('where are we now?')
- Developing a mission ('where do we want to get to?')
- Setting goals and objectives ('what do we need to achieve to get there?')
- Identifying actions and allocating resources ('how do we get there?')
- Implementing plans
- Monitoring and reviewing progress
- Reviewing and evaluating results (which leads us back to 'where are we now?' and starts the cycle again...)

2.2 The **control** part of this cycle is where feedback information on progress/results is gathered and compared with the plan, and corrective action taken if actual performance is deviating from the plan in a significant way. Corrective action may take the form of altering activities or resources (to bring performance back into line with the plan) or altering the plans themselves (if they were unrealistic, or if performance is exceeding planned expectations, say). We will look at this part of the cycle in Section 4.

2.3 In purchasing terms, the cycle of planning and control can be seen as follows: Figure 8.2 (adapted from van Weele's *Purchasing Management: Analysis, Planning and Practice*)

Figure 8.2 *Purchasing management as a control cycle*

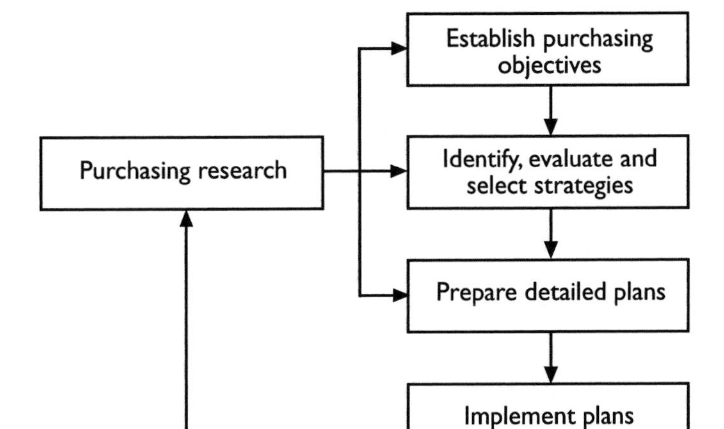

Purchasing research and strategy selection

2.4 Purchasing research plays a vital role in the process. It may be defined as 'the systematic study of all relevant factors which may affect the acquisition of goods and services, for the purpose of securing current and future requirements in such a way that the competitive position of the company is enhanced' (*van Weele*).

2.5 This research helps to identify the key objectives that purchasing must pursue, and to evaluate and select appropriate strategies. A number of information-gathering techniques may be used (some of them discussed in Chapter 7 and others which you may have come across in your studies), including:

- Environmental audit, PESTLE and SWOT analysis
- Competitive/industry analysis (eg using Porter's five forces model)
- Critical success factor analysis: what objectives must be achieved in order to secure competitive advantage
- Supply, demand and capacity forecasting: eg using statistical (trend, regression) analysis, expert opinion gathering or the Delphi technique
- Scenario planning and modelling: evaluating different futures or options, by examining the effect of changing selected variables

Purchasing objectives

2.6 The objectives of the purchasing function are varied. For example:

- To identify and select effective suppliers, and to manage relations with them in a constructive and profitable manner
- To protect the organisation's cost structure and ensure that value for money is obtained in managing the purchasing function
- To ensure availability of required materials without undue stockholding costs
- To maintain constructive relationships with other organisational functions

Purchasing plans

2.7 The selected strategies must then be converted into detailed plans capable of guiding day-to-day operational decisions. These plans should cover such issues as the following.

- Make internally or source from outside?
- Sourcing policy: single or multiple sourcing, or a combination depending on the materials concerned?
- Local or international sourcing?
- Standardisation of products or emphasis on differentiation?
- Centralise or decentralise purchasing decisions, or a combination of both depending on materials, organisation structure, available systems?
- What kind of systems to capture, analyse and share purchasing information?
- How to ensure compliance with relevant law, regulation and policy?

Monitoring and control

2.8 Once plans are in place, it is important to monitor their working in practice. To what extent are they in fact contributing to the objectives of purchasing and the organisation as a whole? What changes might be made to improve the system?

3 Setting objectives for purchasing

SMART planning principles

3.1 Planning is often considered within a 'SMART' framework. Effective objectives are:

- Specific: precise, clear and well-defined, so people know what they are committing to and accountable for.
- Measurable: related to quantified measures (reduce errors/costs by x% over x months) or qualitative measures (increase expressed customer satisfaction), so that people can assess their progress and achievement.
- Agreed: at all levels of management and between managers and teams. Objectives should emphasise teamwork as well as individual achievement.
- Realistic: achievable, given the time and resources available – even if the aim is to be 'stretching', the objective must be possible!
- Time-bounded: given a defined time-scale over which the objective will be achieved.

3.2 Some versions of the model substitute, or add:

- Stretching: objectives must be challenging enough to motivate people and bring learning, development and improvement
- Attainable: the same as 'realistic'.
- Rewarded: attainment of the objectives is linked to positive rewards of some kind
- Reviewed: plans should include a methodology and time-scales for monitoring and reviewing progress and results.

Purchasing objectives

3.3 *Baily et al* suggest the following broad statement of purchasing objectives: Table 8.1.

Table 8.1 *Objectives of purchasing and supply management*

General objectives	Specific objectives
• To supply the organisation with a flow of materials and services to meet its needs • To ensure continuity of supply by maintaining effective relationships with existing sources and by developing other sources of supply either as alternatives or to meet emerging or planned needs • To buy efficiently and wisely, obtaining by an ethical means the best value for every pound spent • To maintain sound co-operative relationships with other departments, providing information and advice as necessary to ensure the effective operation of the organisation as a whole • To develop staff, policies, procedures and organisation to ensure the achievement of these objectives	• To select the best suppliers in the market • To help generate the effective development of new products • To protect the company's cost structure • To maintain the correct quality/value balance • To monitor supply market trends • To negotiate effectively in order to work with suppliers who will seek mutual benefit through economically superior performance • To adopt environmentally responsible supply management.

Source: Baily, Farmer, Jessop & Jones (Purchasing Principles and Management)

Departmental, team and individual work objectives

3.4 As the hierarchy of planning suggests, objectives may be set at a number of levels. At the corporate level, as we have seen, they spell out the organisation's mission and strategic plans. At the departmental or functional level, they set out the specific targets or key results to be achieved by the function in order to contribute to strategic plans. At the team level, they set out the key results or contribution expected of the team, in order to achieve departmental goals. And at the individual level, they are job- or role-related: what results are individuals expected to achieve, to what standard, in what key activity areas, in order for all the higher objectives to be achieved?

3.5 As a manager, you may be required to set purchasing department objectives. More often, you will have to set and monitor individual and team objectives on a regular basis. These may take the form of:

- Quantified output or improvement targets (eg increase orders processed by 3% by 5 April; reduce wastage by 5% in the next six months; maintain inventory levels at no more than £9 million)
- Performance standards, whether quantified (eg process 90% of customer orders within 24 hours, the remaining 10% to be acknowledged same day and processed within 3 working days) or qualitative (eg performance will be up to standard if proposals for new product material specifications are fully supported by relevant data on materials and sources, justified by return-on-investment analysis, and compliant with environmental and ethical policies)
- Projects to be completed (eg report on overseas supplier ethical performance by 30 June; open distribution depot in Bristol by 15 September). *Armstrong* gives the following example of a project objective which also sets out relevant success criteria: 'Introduce a new stock control system by 30 November to provide more accurate, comprehensive and immediate information on stock and thus enable inventory targets to be achieved without prejudicing production flows or customer service levels.'
- Standing objectives: ongoing, continuous targets/standards which are a consistent part of the job (eg deliveries to be made within three days of receiving an order; ethical guidelines for purchasing are to be upheld at all times).

A range of performance measures

3.6 *Johnson* argues that a range of performance measures may be used by managers.

- External measures such as: market share, customer satisfaction and/or loyalty (eg repurchase intention, repurchase), number of new customers, number/type of customer complaints.
- Operational measures such as: on-time/in-full deliveries, number/type of errors/defects, facility/equipment utilisation, productivity, capacity (eg equipment and staff availability)
- Financial measures such as total costs and cost per customer, labour/processing/procurement/inventory costs, total revenue and revenue per customer, operating profit and profit per customer
- Development measures such as staff satisfaction, labour turnover, number of suggestions/improvements/innovations, training hours, involvement in quality teams.

3.7 In its guide *Performance Measurement of the Procurement Profession*, CIPS Australia argues that: 'Historically, procurement performance has been focused on "cost" or "savings". This narrow approach fails to address the trade-offs with quality, inventory and supplier relationships (to name a few). Due to increased focus on business results, performance measurement has been extended to broader business (risk, inventory) and operational objectives (percentage of spend)... The incentive for applying a robust performance measurement system is that both the procurement function and the broader organisation will benefit from an enhanced appreciation of procurement contributions.'

3.8 Table 8.2 shows some of the performance measurements (or metrics) recommended as part of such a 'robust' system.

Table 8.2 *Performance metrics for purchasing*

Efficiency metrics	
Cost	Procurement cost as a % of spend
Staffing	Staff per £million of spend Labour cost per employee
Productivity	Purchase orders/material receipts per employee Cost per purchase order/receipt
Technology leverage and integration	Technology cost as a % of procurement cost % of automatic (v manual) transactions % of purchase orders, RFIs/RFPs/RFQs communicated electronically to suppliers or potential suppliers
Cycle time	Hours required to complete a requisition and purchase order
Standardisation	Use of company-wide policies, commodity codes

Effectiveness metrics	
Cost savings	Annual cost savings as a % of spend
Supplier leverage	Number of suppliers per £x of spend % of suppliers providing 80% or more of the annual spend % of purchases made from preferred suppliers
Error rates	% of transactions requiring correction after process
Customer satisfaction	% of deliveries received in full and on time (IFOT)
Partnering	Procurement control over material/goods spend Use of cross-functional teams in supplier development, sourcing and negotiation Use of scoring models for suppliers
Strategic alignment	Visibility of a formal documented procurement strategy Percentage of objectives linked to business strategy % of procurement time spent on global/enterprise-wide focus

4 Monitoring and reporting

4.1 Perhaps the most neglected stage in developing a plan is to include the system and measures that will be used to monitor progress and evaluate results. *Boddy* argues that 'this happens at all levels of planning – from a project manager monitoring and controlling the detail of individual activities and tasks to a Board committee monitoring the plan for broad strategic change.'

4.2 Monitoring, ongoing progress measurement (for plan/activity adjustment) and review (looking back at performance over the planning period, in order to evaluate the process) may be carried out in various ways.

- Continuous monitoring may be possible in some systems: close supervision and/or software tools, for example, allow variance or exception reports to be produced whenever results (eg productivity, process capability, or stock levels) deviate from plan, within defined parameters or tolerances.
- Periodic reviews are often used: examining results against defined measures or targets at regular/fixed intervals. The purpose of such reviews is generally 'formative': supplying feedback information while it is still relevant for the adjustment of performance or plans.
- Annual reviews may also be used to evaluate specific plans and/or the general performance of individuals, teams and functions (eg in the case of individual performance appraisal). The purpose of such reviews is often seen as 'summative' (retrospectively evaluating performance), but this should always be regarded as feedback and identification of learning for further planning and improvement.

Project monitoring and control

4.3 Project management uses a range of control methodologies, in order to keep the complex and interrelated elements of the project 'on track'.

- End stage assessments are carried out at completion of each stage of a project, using reports from the project manager and representatives of sponsor/user groups. Plans for the following stage are reviewed and approved, and management issues (including stakeholder communication and relationships) can be raised if necessary.
- Highlight reports are submitted regularly by the project manager to the steering committee or project board. These are the principal mechanism of regular feedback control: they are often submitted monthly (or at intervals agreed at project initiation). They are basically progress reports, with brief summaries of the status of the project in regard to schedule, budget and deliverables.
- Checkpoints are used for feedback and control by the project team: they involve progress review meetings, often held weekly (more frequently than highlight reports) for continuous monitoring by team members and leaders.
- Project plans often include milestones (key stage targets) and gates (measurement points where each stage of work 'passes' or 'fails' against acceptance criteria).

4.4 Techniques such as project budgets, Gantt charts and network analysis (critical path analysis, CPA) can be used to monitor progress against specific quality, cost and schedule targets. Complex project management software (such as Microsoft Project) may be used to co-ordinate planning, progress tracking and reporting data.

4.5 There are further opportunities for feedback gathering and reporting at the end of each project. The project manager should produce a completion report, summarising the project objectives and outcomes achieved; budget and schedule variances; and any on-going issues or unfinished business (and how these will be followed up).

4.6 A post-completion audit is often used as a formal review of a programme or project, in order to assess its impact and ensure that any lessons arising from it are acknowledged and learned. Such an audit may be carried out using a survey questionnaire of all project team members and key stakeholders, or meetings to discuss what went well and what didn't.

4.7 The focus of a post-completion audit (and resulting audit report) is:

(a) Assessing whether and how far the project outcomes met the expectations of the sponsor and other stakeholders: were the deliverables up to standard, were they achieved on time and within budget and so on?

(b) Assessing the effectiveness of the management of the process: the effectiveness of the plans and structures set up for the project; the performance of individuals and teams; what problems (communication lapses, conflicts, errors, delays) might affect similar projects in future, and how they can be avoided.

5 Managing organisational resources

5.1 It should be fairly obvious from all that has been said above (and elsewhere in this Course Book) that managers are responsible for the efficient and effective deployment, utilisation and development of four key organisational resources: people, finance, physical resources, and time.

People

5.2 It is only comparatively recently that people have been seen as a resource to be developed, rather than a cost to be controlled: we will examine this development in detail in Chapter 12. Employees (their effort, time, knowledge, skills, attitudes, experience and competences) are key inputs to the transformation process (particularly in service provision).

5.3 While people can be 'managed' in some of the same ways as other assets and resources (acquired, conserved or retained, developed, deployed and utilised), there are interpersonal, behavioural and ethical issues which set 'human resource management' (and leadership) apart. People have their own interests, objectives and needs, which must be integrated with those of the organisation in order to get them to perform in the way management wants them to. People cannot be 'transformed' by operational processes in the predictable and standardised ways that materials can. They cannot (ethically) be manipulated, objectified and disposed of in the way that materials can: people have 'rights'.

5.4 Key issues in effective use of the human resource include:

- Sourcing decisions (ie recruitment and selection, outsourcing)
- Resource development (ie appraisal and learning/training/improvement planning)
- Resource utilisation (ie organising for productivity, flexible deployment, securing motivation and commitment)
- Resource disposal (ie managing employee exit, dismissals and redundancies)

5.5 At the most basic level, a manager may have to decide how many people are required for a task, and how to allocate people to tasks (or *vice versa*).

Finance

5.6 Financial resources are planned and controlled using budgets; cost estimates; cost, cost-benefit and breakeven analyses; and so on. You will cover these areas in detail, elsewhere in your CIPS studies.

5.7 Managerial performance will, at some point, be measured in financial terms, whether in cost minimisation/reduction, departmental contribution, profitability or payback period on investment. Managers are accountable for their use of financial resources, which 'belong' to other people (shareholders, investors and creditors). Expenditure budgets may be pre-determined (eg in the public sector). Cost efficiency (achieving objectives at least expense) is often a key goal.

5.8 At the most basic level, managers will need to prepare cost budgets for their activities, and implement budgetary control to monitor actual costs against estimated/budgeted expenditures.

Physical resources

5.9 Physical resources include plant and machinery; raw materials, parts and components; accessories and consumables; transport fleets; buildings and facilities and so on. Purchasing, supply and logistics managers have a key role in sourcing, developing, efficiently deploying and utilising, maintaining and replacing these items.

5.10 At the most basic level, managers will have to ensure that equipment, machinery and materials are available when required by tasks. This may, of course, include highly complex planning processes and systems, such as Materials Requirements Planning (MRP), Manufacturing Resources Planning (MRPII) and Enterprise Resource Planning (ERP).

Time

5.11 The manager's own time is a key resource (as we will see in Chapter 9). Personal time, team members' working hours and machine time are managed through scheduling or timetabling. You should be aware of a number of basic tools and techniques for doing this (checklists, diaries, personal organisers and Gantt charts).

5.12 Time management is also an element in operational effectiveness: lead times for new product development or delivery of supplies, for example; the length of the order cycle; or speed of response to customer requirements. There is often a trade-off between time, quality and cost: you can do things faster, but this may cost more – or result in quality 'short-cuts'…

Benefits of the effective management of purchasing

5.13 We hope you will realise, by now, that 'effective management of purchasing' embraces a wide range of criteria – and offers a wide range of operational, business and personal/behavioural benefits. Some of the main ones can be summarised as follows.

- Effective administration, and the efficient use of effort and resources to achieve objectives
- Reliable continuity of supply

- Improved supply chain relationships, with potential for added flexibility, value and competitive advantage
- Improved quality, through supplier selection and management, materials specification, quality control and management
- Reduced costs, through lower materials prices and purchasing costs, lower inventory holding, reduced transport/handling/storage costs, reduced materials obsolescence/deterioration and so on
- Increased flexibility and responsiveness, through reduced replenishment lead times
- Maintenance and provision of appropriate data for operations managers and other stakeholders
- Improved contribution of purchasing staff, through improved strategic awareness, commitment, productivity, flexibility, competence and knowledge

Chapter summary

- There is a hierarchy of objectives in organisations, from the mission ('what business are we in?') to goals ('where do we want to get to?') and objectives ('what do we need to achieve in order to get there?'). Planning takes place at three progressively detailed levels (strategic, tactical and operational).
- Objectives should be vertically integrated (or aligned) to ensure that individual, team and functional objectives support corporate plans; and horizontally integrated to ensure that different individual, team and functional objectives are coherent and co-ordinated.
- Goals and objectives are important for organisational direction, co-ordination and performance measurement and for individual/team motivation and learning. It is often regarded as desirable to involve team members in planning, to improve the quality and creativity of plans and to ensure commitment, coordination and flexibility in their implementation.
- Planning and control can be viewed as a cycle, from the development and implementation of plans, through the monitoring and review of results, and the adjustment of performance (or making of new plans).
- Objectives should be SMART: Specific (and/or stretching); measurable; agreed (and/or attainable); realistic (and/or rewarded and/or reviewed); and time-bounded.
- A wide range of external, operational, financial and development measures may be used by management to evaluate and control performance – including a range of specific efficiency and effectiveness metrics for procurement, eg: cost (and cost saving), staffing, productivity, technology leverage/integration, cycle time, supplier leverage, error rates and customer satisfaction.
- Monitoring and reporting may be carried out at varying intervals (continuous, periodic, annual). Project plans often have built-in progress milestones, assessments and reviews, as well as a comprehensive completion report and post-completion audit process.
- Organisational resources include people, finance, physical resources and time.

Self-test questions

Numbers in brackets refer to paragraphs where you can check your answers

1. Distinguish between goals and objectives. (1.3)
2. Describe the three levels of planning (1.4)
3. Why do purchasing plans need to be integrated with corporate plans? (1.5)
4. Outline some behaviour reasons for goal-setting. (1.7)
5. List four reasons why teams should be involved in planning. (1.8)
6. What information-gathering methods can be used to support strategy selection? (2.5)
7. Explain the acronym 'SMART' (3.1)
8. List five key objectives for a purchasing function. (Table 8.1)
9. What are (a) performance standards and (b) standing objectives? (3.5)
10. List three efficiency and three effectiveness metrics for procurement. (Table 8.2)
11. What are (a) checkpoints, (b) milestones and (c) gates in project control? (4.3)
12. Why is the human resource different from other resources? (5.3)

CHAPTER 9

Using and Delegating Authority

Learning objectives and indicative content

4.1 Evaluate the concept of authority, delegation and accountability when managing the purchasing function

- Understanding of key concepts: taking ownership, decision making, empowerment and responsibility
- Reasons: workload, prioritising, developing individuals and the team, minimising blame and achieving results
- Good time management
- The delegation process

Chapter headings

1 Power, authority and related concepts

2 Why delegate?

3 The delegation process

4 Time management

Introduction

As we saw in Chapter 1, the concepts of management and leadership are bound up with the structural – and interpersonal – issues of power and authority. What is the nature of managerial authority: what does it give a manager the 'right' to do? What (if any) is the best way to exercise power over other people: subordinates, colleagues – and perhaps even your own bosses? How do you get more power in the organisation? What's to stop people abusing their power and authority in irresponsible or unethical ways?

In the first section of this chapter, we look at the concepts of power, authority, responsibility and accountability – and why they are foundational to the way managers operate in organisations.

We then go on to look at the key concept of delegation: the process by which managers may share some of their authority with their subordinates. We saw in Chapter 4 that, from the perspective of the whole organisation, there are advantages – but also disadvantages – to 'decentralisation': letting authority flow to lower levels of the organisation hierarchy. In this chapter, we look at this from the perspective of individual managers: what tasks and decisions can or should be delegated – and how can this be done effectively?

1 Power, authority and related concepts

Power

1.1 Power may be defined as the ability to exert influence over objects, persons or situations.

1.2 *French and Raven* identify a number of different sources of power in organisations.

- Legitimate power (or 'position power'): the legal/rational, formally-conferred authority associated with a position or role in an organisation
- Expert power: the power of expertise or knowledge which is both recognised by and valued by the group, so that they are willing to be influenced by the expert
- Reward power (or 'resource power'): control over resources and rewards that are valued by the group, so that they are willing to be influenced in return for rewards
- Referent power (or 'personal power'): power emanating from the attractive and inspiring personality, image or 'charisma' of the individual
- Coercive power (or 'physical power'): the power to threaten sanctions, hand out punishments or physically intimidate others.

Definitions and distinctions

1.3 Other interrelated terms in this area may be defined as follows.

- Authority is the right to exercise power in a particular context.
- Delegation is the process by which a person or group possessing authority transfers part of that authority to another person or group.
- Responsibility is the obligation to use delegated powers appropriately. (The term is also used to mean a duty or activity assigned to a given position of authority.)
- Accountability is the liability of each person who is given authority to give an account of their use of that authority (ie their performance) to the person who delegated it to them.

1.4 'Power' is not the same as 'authority'. Authority refers to the scope and amount of discretion given to a person to make decisions by virtue of the position he holds in the organisation. It is usually conferred 'from the top down' by delegation (although it may also be conferred 'from the bottom up' – by election, for example). Power is the ability to influence – and it may not be connected to formal organisational authority. An individual may have the ability to influence others, without having positional authority to do so. Informal 'leaders' and experts are frequently in this position.

Authority and responsibility

1.5 Classical organisation theorists such as *Fayol* placed great emphasis on the need for a correspondence between authority and responsibility. *McGivering* suggests one reason why this is so. 'It is axiomatic in organisational processes that responsibility should be equal to authority, for power without corresponding responsibility is likely to lead to behaviour uncontrolled by the organisation and hence to unintended and probably undesirable consequences.' In other words, responsibility-free authority can lead to irresponsibility!

1.6 The opposite situation – responsibility without corresponding authority to carry it out – is equally dysfunctional, because of the inefficiency of struggling to obtain cooperation, and the frustration and stress it is likely to cause the individual.

Why are these concepts important for managers?

1.7 One reason why the concept of authority is important for managers is that they need to appreciate the scope and boundaries (limitations) of the authority they have been given to act and make decisions – and to influence the actions and decisions of others.

- Stepping outside the bounds of one's authority is risky: the manager is not protected by the 'legitimacy' of authority delegated by the organisation.
- Stepping outside the bounds of one's authority is a cause of poor co-ordination: the manager may be duplicating (and perhaps conflicting with) decisions and tasks which have been assigned to others.
- Stepping outside the bounds of one's authority – and into the 'territory' of others – is a major cause of conflict in organisations (as we will see in Chapter 11). It may be seen as competitive (trying to get a bigger share of limited power and resources) or deliberately undermining the authority of other managers or functions. This is part of organisational 'politics', and while it can be stimulating (where competition is in line with organisational objectives), it can also become a source of poor co-ordination and communication – and, if unchecked, a major distraction from the task.
- *Not* exercising the full extent of one's legitimate authority, however, may also be dysfunctional! This creates a 'power vacuum': if you don't exercise your authority, someone else will step in and do so – creating lack of clarity (and potential conflict) as to who the legitimate leader of the team or department is. Moreover, it is highly inefficient (and unlikely to enhance your career prospects) if you constantly refer upwards to your superior decisions which are within your own authority to make.

1.8 It is also important for managers to understand the nature of delegation. On the one hand, *McGivering* notes that: 'although it is possible to delegate both duties and the necessary authority, it is not possible to delegate responsibility. That is to say, the superior is always responsible for the actions of his subordinates and cannot escape this responsibility by delegation'. When you delegate a task to a team member, you are still responsible for the results: you don't get to 'pass the buck'! (Or as the sign on the manager's desk says: 'The buck stops here'.)

1.9 On the other hand, delegation *does* mean giving subordinates the authority required to perform tasks and make decisions. Managers should not, therefore, over-control (or micro-manage) team members, once tasks have been delegated to them. As we will see below, delegation is designed to support employees in taking initiative, where required. This is particularly important in customer- and supplier-facing roles, where decision and response times may need to be short: employees need to be empowered to take decisions themselves (within whatever parameters are set for them), rather than pass them up the chain.

1.10 Finally, it is crucial for managers to understand the concepts of responsibility and accountability. As we noted earlier, managers need to take responsibility – and recognise that they are liable to be called to account – for their plans and decisions. Otherwise, they may behave irresponsibly: carelessly, or in their own interests. At the organisational level, it is helpful to assign accountabilities for key tasks and results, so that problems can be located and dealt with in a targeted manner.

How to use authority

1.11 There still remains the question of *how* managers should use their authority. A '**command-and-control**' approach used to be the norm, and was fully validated by the nature of legitimate authority in bureaucratic organisations: people expected (and were expected) to obey instructions and to be supervised accordingly. Nowadays, with increased employee expectations, and the need for greater organisational learning and flexibility, there has been a general shift towards a '**facilitate-and-empower**' style: the manager has become a 'coach' and resource-mobiliser to support his team in fulfilling agreed objectives.

1.12 The manner in which authority or power is used is called 'management (or leadership) style'. If you need a refresher on this topic, see Chapter 1. (You might also want to look back at Chapter 4, where we surveyed the various assumptions and 'schools' of thought underpinning management styles.)

2 *Why delegate?*

Advantages of delegation

2.1 *John Adair* suggests that: 'leading managers tend to have responsibilities for more work than they can possibly execute themselves. They need to delegate some of it to others, together with some of their own positional authority.'

2.2 It is generally recognised that in any large, complex organisation, managers will have to delegate to some extent, because there are physical and mental limitations to the workload of any individual or group in authority.

2.3 The passing of routine or less important decisions down the line frees managers to prioritise, or concentrate on, the more distinctive aspects of their work (such as strategic planning, new business development, culture creation, goal articulation, staff development and so on).

2.4 Delegation may also achieve better results and enhance the quality of decisions, by involving staff who may be more qualified (by virtue of functional expertise, more detailed information or closeness to the supplier or customer) to make them.

2.5 Delegation also gives staff greater opportunities for challenge, responsibility and individual and team development. This may in turn enhance the working life and commitment/loyalty of staff, as well as helping to identify potential for promotion planning and managerial succession. (We looked at some of these broader organisational benefits of delegation in our discussion of decentralisation, in Chapter 4.)

Why don't managers delegate?

2.6 In practice, many managers are reluctant to delegate; they retain a routine workload in addition to their leading/managing functions. There are many possible reasons for this.

- The manager may have low confidence in the abilities of team members: 'If you want something done well, you do it yourself'. This may be in the manager's perception – or may be due to poor selection, training and/or motivation of staff, resulting in genuine problems of competence or attitude.
- The burden of responsibility and accountability for the mistakes of the team may put pressure on him to retain control. The organisation culture may come down hard on mistakes, rather than seeing them as 'learning opportunities'.
- He may want the familiarity of team relationships or a routine workload (particularly if he is new to, or uncomfortable in, the leadership role).
- He may feel threatened by the perception that the team could 'do the job' without his input, failing to understand the complexity of the managerial role. Empowerment implies the need for managers to change from commanders and controllers to coaches, facilitators, communication hubs and entrepreneurial resource mobilisers on behalf of the team.
- He may lack skills in time management (to appreciate the need for delegation), assertiveness (to distinguish delegation from loss of control) or delegation itself. As we will see below, skills are required for effective delegation.
- The organisational culture may be resistant to delegation, failing to promote or reward effective delegation, or regarding it as 'shirking responsibility' or 'loss of control'.

3 The delegation process

Know when to delegate

3.1 Knowing when to delegate is the first skill of effective delegation. Delegation may be possible – or positively advantageous – when trust can be placed in the competence and reliability of subordinates *and*:

- the work to be delegated is routine, repetitive or of low consequence; *or*
- the quality of the work or decision will be improved by the input of subordinates; *or*
- subordinates' involvement in, or acceptance of, a decision is important for staff morale and commitment to its implementation. (This may be the case in many decisions that will affect subordinates' work or working conditions.)

The process of effective delegation

3.2 Delegation is an interpersonal process which balances control/support (so that the superior can be confident the work will be done as required) and empowerment/challenge (so that the subordinate can exercise genuine initiative and discretion within the bounds of task requirements). This process is shown in Figure 9.1.

Figure 9.1 *The process of delegation*

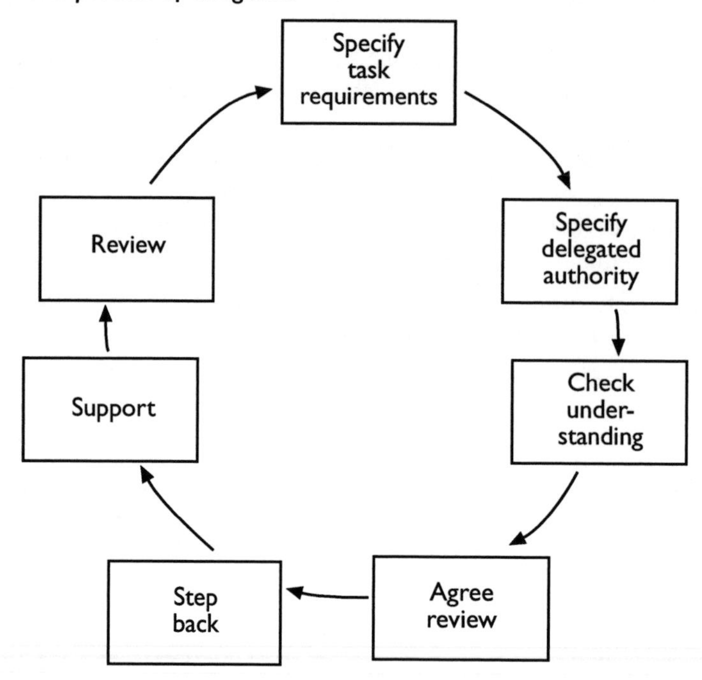

3.3 Guidelines for effective delegation would therefore be as follows.

- Clearly specify the task, and the contexts and levels of performance required: subordinates must know exactly what is expected of them.
- Clearly specify the scope and limits of the authority being delegated, setting out parameters for reporting by exception, and defining what subordinates can and cannot do without reference to the manager.
- Check subordinates' understanding. Seek feedback, give opportunities for questions and input and so on.
- Agree on methods and timescales for monitoring, reporting, progress review etc.
- Let the team member get on with the delegated task, without unnecessary interference or conspicuous monitoring (which can interfere with performance).
- Be available to support and facilitate (with additional information or instruction) where asked or required to do so, using a non-directive approach to develop the subordinate's problem-solving skills.
- Review progress at the agreed intervals. Offer constructive criticism to aid learning, and acknowledge successes and improvements.

4 Time management

What is time management?

4.1 *Adair* says that 'time is well-**managed** if: things that ought to run smoothly are doing so; and desired ends are being achieved by the economical use of time. Time is well-led [or well **spent**] if those ends are carefully thought through in terms of purpose, aims and objectives in a rapidly changing world.'

In other words, time should be used in a way that is both efficient and worthwhile.

4.2 Time management basically involves identifying objectives; prioritising tasks; time-budgeting and time-scheduling tasks; and organising and managing work to maximise the use of time and minimise disruptions. Some of the key principles of time management are set out in Table 9.1. Note principle number 8!

Table 9.1: *Adair's Ten Principles of Time Management*

1	**Develop a personal sense of time**	Learn to value your own time and other people's. Realise that time is a precious resource that should be invested, not wasted.
2	**Identify long-term goals**	Managers need to be aware of the purpose or mission of their organisation and of their job, so they know the end to which all their time and effort is to be directed. They need to define strategic aims and objectives, in order to give them long-term direction (say, over the next five years).
3	**Make medium-term plans**	Managers need to convert their aims and directions into specific plans for how to get there, with tangible goals, targets and objectives for all key areas of accountability. These tactical plans need a realistic 'time budget' and progress review at the end of the middle term (three, four, six or twelve months).
4	**Plan the day**	Objectives must be broken down into manageable steps. Compile a programme for the day, with time limits and priority ratings for all tasks: 'The daily plan is likely to take 15 minutes. In return for this investment you gain a sense of control, direction and freedom which is otherwise impossible.'
5	**Make the best use of your best time**	The quality of your concentration varies at different times. Remember the 80:20 rule: 20 per cent of your time produces 80 per cent of your high-quality output – so you need to utilise the best 20 per cent of your time to its fullest.
6	**Organise office work**	There are two key areas to efficient office work: controlling interruptions and organising paperwork. The amount of time interruptions take can be controlled through assertive time-limit setting and getting/sticking to the point. Paperwork can likewise be managed with ruthless attention to relevance and priority.
7	**Manage meetings**	As discussed in Chapter 3, attention must be paid to the relevance, value and time-management of meetings: they need to be worth the time spent in them – and, once planned, must begin and end on time.
8	**Delegate effectively**	'The benefit of effective delegation is that it gives you more time to lead and manage.'
9	**Make use of committed time**	Adair divides time into 'discretionary time' (which you can use as you see fit) and 'committed time' (which has been pre-'booked'). Committed time includes time spent travelling, eating, exercising and so on: much of this time can actually be put to better use (eg for planning or reading e-mails) with some readjustment (eg commuting by train with a laptop computer instead of by car).
10	**Manage your health**	'Time management is about the quality of your time as well as the quantity.... To give to your work and to others high quality time, you must top up your energy levels.' Adair suggests that sleep, diet, exercise, holidays and time for reflection are essential for long-term time management and the control of stress.

Chapter summary

- Power may be defined as the ability to exert influence over objects, persons or situations. It may be formally conferred by position in an organisation (positional power, or authority), or it may derive from other people's perception of the value of one's expertise, control over resources, personal charisma or coercive force.
- Authority is the right to exercise power in a given context. The scope and boundaries of authority must be observed to avoid poor co-ordination and political conflict.
- Responsibility is the obligation to use authority appropriately (and accountability is the liability to be called to account for how one has used it). Responsibility should be matched with authority to avoid irresponsible or ineffectual behaviour.
- Delegation is the process by which authority is shared with others. It is important in limiting management workload, supporting managerial priorities, enhancing decision quality and enabling individual and team development.
- As an interpersonal process, delegation balances control/support (so work is done as required) and empowerment (so subordinates can exercise genuine discretion).
- Time management is a key skill for managers, including: objective-setting; prioritising; scheduling; work organisation; and maximising time (including effective delegation).

Self-test questions

Numbers in brackets refer to paragraphs where you can check your answers

1. Explain five sources of power. (1.2)
2. Distinguish between authority, responsibility and accountability. (1.3)
3. Why should authority be matched to responsibility? (1.5, 1.6)
4. Why might exceeding the bounds of one's authority be dysfunctional? (1.7)
5. What is (and is not) transferred in the process of delegation? (1.8, 1.9)
6. List three barriers to delegation. (2.6)
7. When should a task or decision be delegated? (3.1)
8. Outline the process of effective delegation. (Figure 9.1)
9. What is the relevance of (a) planning, (b) meetings and (c) delegation to time management? (Table 9.1)
10. How can a manager control interruptions, as part of a time management strategy? (Table 9.1)

CHAPTER 10

Managing Teams

Learning objectives and indicative content

4.2 Assess techniques for building, motivating and managing successful teams within the purchasing and supply function

- What is a team/group?
- Stages of team development: Tuckman and Jensen
- Team roles: Belbin, Schutz, Holland, Cattell
- Building a balanced team
- Motivational determinants: innate drive, desire, fulfilling need
- Satisfying individual and team needs: praise, rewards, recognition, responsibility, promotion, pay
- Building relationships through leadership, with trust, fairness, equal opportunities, ethics and respect

Chapter headings

Introduction

Although human beings have been working in teams since the days of prehistoric hunting bands, the emphasis on teamworking in management theory is relatively recent. It really began 'by accident', following research at the Hawthorne plant of the General Electric Company in the 1920s. Elton Mayo's researchers found that team dynamics influenced productivity more than any changes in working conditions.

In recent decades – thanks to major issues such as labour flexibility, worker involvement and empowerment – teamworking has become a key aspect of work organisation and management.

In this chapter, we look at the ways in which groups form and operate, and how they can be 'built' and managed for effective working and member satisfaction.

We also discuss the key topic of motivation: how people can be encouraged to perform in more effective and committed ways, both individually and in teams.

1 Groups and teams

What is a group?

1.1 *Handy* defines a group as 'any collection of people who perceive themselves to be a group'. The point of this definition is the distinction it implies between a random collection of individuals and a group of individuals who share a common sense of identity and belonging.

1.2 People in organisations are drawn together into groups by a preference for smaller units where closer relationships can develop; the need to belong and to make a contribution that will be noticed and appreciated; shared space, specialism, objectives and interests; the attractiveness of a particular group activity or resources; and access to power greater than individuals could muster on their own.

Formal and informal groups

1.3 Formal groups are deliberately and rationally designed to achieve objectives assigned to them by the organisation, for which they are responsible. They are characterised by:

- membership and leadership appointed and approved by the organisation
- compliance of the members with the organisation's goals and requirements
- structured relationships of authority, responsibility, task allocation and communication.

1.4 Informal groups may spring up as a result of these formal arrangements (for example, if the members of a committee become friends), and will invariably be present in any organisation. Informal groups include workplace networks of people who regularly get together to exchange information, groups of friends who socialise outside work and so on. They have constantly fluctuating membership and structure, and leaders emerge usually through personal (rather than 'positional') power.

1.5 The purposes of informal groups are usually related to group and individual member satisfaction, rather than a particular task. However, *Stryker* claims that the informal organisation is also a 'hidden operating structure that gets the work done'. It operates via informal communication networks ('the grapevine'), 'short-cuts' and ways of doing things developed over time, and the influence of informal leaders (often by-passing communication/authority 'blockages' in the formal structure).

What is a team?

1.6 A team has been defined as 'a small group of people with complementary skills who are committed to a common purpose, performance goals and approaches for which they hold themselves basically jointly accountable.' (*Katzenbach & Smith*)

Why is teamworking so popular?

1.7 The basic work units of organisations have traditionally been specialised functional departments. In more recent times, organisations have adopted what *Peters and Waterman* called 'chunking': the breaking up of the organisation structure into small, flexible units, or teams. From the organisation's standpoint, teams have a number of advantages.

- Teams facilitate the performance of tasks which require the collective skills, experience or knowledge of more than one person or discipline. Groups have been shown to produce better evaluated (though fewer) decisions than individuals working separately.
- Teams facilitate the co-ordination of the work of different individuals or groups, because they bring them together across organisational boundaries (eg disciplines or departments) with shared goals and structured communication.
- Teams facilitate interactive communication and interpersonal relationships, and are thus particularly well-adapted for:
  - Testing and ratifying decisions, because they offer multi-source feedback and may make the decision more acceptable (by taking account of a cross-section of stakeholder views). Acceptance of the decision by a group may be important if it affects them and their work (for example, if they are responsible for carrying it out).
  - Consulting, negotiating and conflict resolution, because they allow an interactive exchange of views and influence.
  - Generating ideas, because of their potential for 'bouncing' ideas off each other and getting multiple input.
  - Collecting and disseminating information, because of the multiple networks in which the members are involved.
- Teams can motivate individuals to devote more energy and effort to achieving the organisation's goals, since:
  - They offer rewards in the form of satisfying relationships.
  - Group influences may reinforce performance, as long as the group's aims are harmonised with those of the organisation.

1.8 From the individual's standpoint, teams also perform some important functions.

- They satisfy social needs for friendship and belonging, mutual encouragement and support.
- They help individuals to develop self-image and identity (as part of something larger than themselves).
- They enable individuals to share the burdens of work responsibility and achieve more than they could do themselves.
- They enable people to make noticeable individual contributions (which bolsters their self esteem) and at the same time to share responsibility and be part of something bigger than themselves (which bolsters their sense of security). Peters and Waterman suggested that these were the key dual needs of workers.

1.9 However, there are some **problems** in using teams. Group decision-making takes longer, especially if the group seeks to reach consensus by working through disagreements (as is the preferred style in Japan). In addition, group working requires a certain amount of attention to group dynamics and group maintenance processes (as we will see a bit later): this can draw energy away from the task. Group decisions may partly be based on group norms and interests – the group's own agenda – rather than the needs of the task, or indeed of the organisation.

1.10 Team decisions have also been shown to be riskier than individual decisions. Shared responsibility blurs the individuals' sense of responsibility for the outcome of the decision. Very cohesive groups, in particular, tend to protect their consensus by ignoring 'outside' information and feedback: they become blinkered and over-confident. This effect is intensified by inter-group competition, which can result in dis-integration, lack of communication and conflict between different groups.

1.11 In addition, group norms of behaviour may restrict and inhibit individual contribution and may produce negative work results. *Elton Mayo*'s studies at the Hawthorne plant showed that groups use their power for such aims as restricting output and 'freezing out' unpopular supervisors.

1.12 You should also be aware that while 'teamworking' is regarded as a positive value in itself, there is such a thing as an ineffective team. Teamworking involves complex dynamics, roles and relationships and it is not easy to get it right. The important thing is not to have teams – but to have effective teams. (We will discuss this in more detail later in the chapter.)

2 Team formation and development

2.1 Teams are not static. They mature and develop. Four stages in this development were identified by *Tuckman* (1965).

2.2 **Forming** is the first stage, in which members try to find out about each other and about how the group is going to work: its purpose, composition, leadership and organisation are still being established. There will probably be a wariness about introducing new ideas: members will 'toe the line' in order not to make themselves unacceptable to the group. This cautious introductory period is essential, but not conducive to task effectiveness.

2.3 **Storming** is the second stage, in which members begin to assert themselves and test out roles, leadership, behavioural norms and ideas. There is more or less open conflict and competition around these areas – but this may also be a fruitful time, as more realistic targets are set, open communication develops and ideas are generated.

2.4 **Norming** is the real settling-down stage, in which agreements are reached about work, sharing, individual requirements and output expectations. Group procedures and customs will be defined and adherence secured. The enthusiasm and brain-storming of the second stage may have died down, but methodical working can be introduced and maintained.

2.5 **Performing** is the stage at which the group focuses on executing its task: the difficulties of group development no longer distract from performance.

2.6 *Tuckman and Jensen* (1977) have added further stages to the original model.

- **Dorming**: the team has been performing successfully for some time and grown complacent. It goes into a semi-automatic mode of operation, with efforts devoted primarily to the maintenance of the team itself.
- **Mourning** or **adjourning**: The team sees itself as having fulfilled its purpose, and the group disbands – either physically (eg in the case of a temporary project team) or psychologically (as the team turns to new goals, renegotiates membership roles, and returns to the forming stage for its next phase).

2.7 A group may progress through these stages quickly or slowly, may overlap stages, or may get stuck at a given stage (particularly 'storming').

Team size

2.8 The optimum size for group effectiveness has been variously estimated: some authors put the optimum primary working group at 10–12 (comparable to primitive hunting bands), while others advocate groups as small as 5–7 people. Although smaller groups limit the synergy available from pooled skills and experience, larger groups involve more complex dynamics and processes (decision-making, communication, influence and so on). Larger groups – like larger organisations – may require greater formality of rules and procedures to ensure co-ordination and control, unless group leadership and norms are very strong.

3 The dynamics of teamworking

Team member roles

3.1 Team membership may be dictated by existing arrangements, organisational appointment or election (in the case of a staff representative committee). However, where a manager is able to select team members, a mix of attributes, competencies and resources should be secured to match the needs of the task. Specialist skills and knowledge may be required (perhaps from different areas in the organisation); experience may be helpful (particularly to guide less experienced members of the team); organisational influence or access to resources (including information) may help to 'champion' the team in its competition for limited resources.

3.2 In addition to the specific requirements of its objectives, however, an effectively functioning team requires its members to adopt various task and team-maintenance roles. *R Meredith Belbin* suggests that an effective team is made up of people who, between them, fill nine roles (Table 10.1). He notes that 'strength of contribution in any one of the roles is commonly associated with particular weaknesses. These are called allowable weaknesses. Executives are seldom strong in all nine team roles.'

3.3 These team roles are not fixed within any given individual: team members can occupy more than one role, or switch roles according to need. Effective teamworking requires a mix and balance of all the roles, which between them support task functions (such as ideas generation, problem-solving, implementation and follow up) *and* team maintenance functions (support, conflict management, leadership and so on).

Table 10.1 *Belbin's team roles*

Role and description	Contribution	Allowable weaknesses
Plant		
Creative, imaginative, unorthodox	Solves difficult problems. Presents new ideas.	Ignores details. Too preoccupied to communicate effectively.
Resource investigator		
Extrovert, enthusiastic, communicative	Explores opportunities. Develops contacts.	Overoptimistic. Loses interest once initial enthusiasm has passed.
Coordinator (or Chairman)		
Mature, confident, a good chairperson	Clarifies goals, promotes decision-making, delegates well	Can be seen as manipulative. Delegates personal work.
Shaper		
Challenging, dynamic, thrives on pressure	Has the drive and courage to overcome obstacles	Can provoke others. Hurts people's feelings.
Monitor evaluator		
Sober, strategic, discerning	Sees all options. Judges accurately.	Lacks drive and ability to inspire others. Overly critical.
Teamworker		
Cooperative, mild, perceptive and diplomatic	Listens, builds, averts friction, calms the waters	Indecisive in crunch situations. Can be easily influenced.
Implementer (or Company Worker)		
Disciplined, reliable, conservative and efficient	Turns ideas into practical actions	Somewhat inflexible. Slow to respond to new possibilities.
Completer/Finisher		
Painstaking, conscientious, anxious	Searches out errors and omissions. Ensures delivery on time.	Inclined to worry unduly. Reluctant to delegate. Can be a 'nitpicker'.
Specialist		
Single-minded, self-starting, dedicated	Provides knowledge and skills in rare supply	Contributes only on a narrow front. Dwells on technicalities. Overlooks the 'big picture'.

Source: Team Roles at Work, R Meredith Belbin (Butterworth-Heinemann)

Other research into team roles

3.4 The work of Belbin is by far the best known contribution to the study of group roles. However, the revised syllabus examinable from November 2009 also mentions three other researchers: Schutz, Holland and Cattell. This is slightly unexpected, since all of these are known primarily as authorities on personality assessments rather than on group working. However, we will attempt to show how such research can be relevant to the operation of a group.

3.5 William C *Schutz* (1958) proposed a theory of interpersonal orientation based on the belief that individuals actively seek to establish compatibility with others in their social interactions, because relationships fulfil certain basic human needs: the need for inclusion (ie belonging), the need for control (ie enjoying a balance of influence in relationships) and the need for affection. He developed a concept known as FIRO: **fundamental interpersonal relations orientation.**

3.6 To assess the relative importance placed on each of these needs by different individuals Schutz developed a questionnaire, comprising 54 questions. Each question invites the respondent to consider how often he performs particular behaviours. The responses are evaluated and the individual's personality orientation is determined.

3.7 The FIRO model suggests that a compatible group (ie a group of individuals with similar needs) will work together and perform better than groups composed of people with desires that clash.

3.8 Schutz's FIRO model can also be used to identify issues that arise for the group and need to be dealt with at each stage of its development. These issues may be repeated a number of times during the life of the group, but they follow broadly in sequence as the group develops.

- **Inclusion issues**: 'in or out'. ('Can I identify with group goals and feel I have sufficient in common with others in the group to choose to stay and be involved in group activity?')
- **Control issues**: 'top or bottom'. ('Can I also be different and have some say in the running of the group?')
- **Affection issues**: 'near or far'. ('Do I trust and value the group sufficiently to lower my defences, to share and commit to group goals?')

3.9 Unlike other models of group development (eg Tuckman and Jensen), Schutz doesn't deal specifically with a termination stage. However, he talks of the above stages reversing themselves as the group ends: members disengage emotionally, become pre-occupied with control issues again, and finally resolve the inclusion issue as the group disbands.

3.10 John *Holland* (1985) devised a model of types of orientation and their relation to career choice. His orientations included: realistic, investigative, artistic, social, enterprising, conventional (sometimes referred to as Holland's hexagram). It is not at all clear how this is relevant to group roles.

3.11 Raymond B *Cattell* is a prolific author on intelligence testing and many other topics in psychology. He is best known for his '16PF' personality profiling methodology, but has also written on 'group psychodynamics'. Some of the many modelling techniques he devised might possibly be applied to group behaviour (eg his 'anxiety index': low stress groups arguably may behave differently from high stress groups).

Team cohesion

3.12 Co-operative groups have been shown to be more effective than competitive groups, where individuals focused on their own contributions rather than the group's shared performance (*Deutsch*). We will discuss some techniques of 'team building' (creating cohesive groups) below, but the basic dynamics of team cohesion are as follows.

- Team identity: the sense of being a team (sometimes called '*esprit de corps*' or 'team spirit')
- Team solidarity: loyalty to the group, so that team members put in extra effort for the group and in support of its norms and values
- Commitment to shared goals: cooperation in the interests of team objectives. These may initially be team maintenance goals, but if they can be integrated with task goals (by offering the team the satisfaction of achievement, recognition or reward) the cooperative drive can be turned to the organisation's advantage
- Competition with other groups: members of a group will act in unison if the group's existence or patterns of behaviour are threatened from outside.
- Positive leadership, supporting open communication, individual and team development, a trusting and co-operative team culture and so on.

3.13 Cohesion is partly the result of positive factors such as communication, agreement and mutual trust – but in the face of a 'common enemy' (**competition or crisis**) cohesion and performance will be even stronger. Within each competing or crisis-facing group, members close ranks and submerge their differences: loyalty and conformity are highly motivated. The climate changes from informal/sociable to task-focused, and individual needs are put aside. The group may accept a much more authoritarian style of leadership than normal, to mobilise its resources more efficiently. Meanwhile, the polarised sense of 'us and them' further reinforces cohesion.

3.14 Cohesion is broadly regarded as desirable in order to create committed, cooperative working, mutual loyalty and accountability, open information sharing, all of which may help to maximise the potential synergy of teamworking *and* individual social satisfaction. However, you should be aware that it is possible for groups to become *too* cohesive. *Handy* notes that 'ultra-cohesive groups can be dangerous because in the organisational context the group must serve the organisation, not itself'. If a group is completely absorbed with its own maintenance, members and priorities, it can divert energy and attention away from the task.

3.15 It can also become dangerously blinkered to outside information and feedback and may confidently forge ahead in a completely wrong direction! *I L Janis* described this as **'groupthink'**: 'the psychological drive for consensus at any cost, that suppresses dissent and appraisal of alternatives in cohesive decision-making groups'. Symptoms of groupthink include the following.

- A sense of invulnerability – blindness to the risk involved in 'pet' strategies
- Rationalisations for inconsistent information
- Moral blindness ('might is right')
- A tendency to stereotype all outsiders as 'enemies'
- Strong group pressure to quell dissent and 'rocking the boat'
- A perception of unanimity – filtering out or ignoring divergent views
- Mutual support and solidarity to guard the decision.

3.16 Since by definition a group suffering from groupthink is highly resistant to criticism, recognition of failure and unpalatable information, it is not easy to break such a group out of its vicious circle! It must, however, be encouraged to exercise self-criticism, to welcome outside ideas and evaluations and to respond positively to conflicting evidence.

Team decision-making

3.17 Decision-making is a key team process. Team decisions may be arrived at in various ways:

- The application of authority by the leader, perhaps after taking members' views into account
- The use of power or influence, eg by a team specialist or charismatic member
- Majority rule: by voting or the leader's getting a 'sense' of the view supported by the majority of team members
- By consensus: a process whereby divergent views are examined and persuasive arguments used until there is broad agreement among all members. This takes longer, but is often more effective in implementation, as all members of the group are able to 'own' the decision.

In less effectively functioning teams, this may be a negative process, where decisions are taken without input from team members; by minority (eg a dominant clique within the team); or by default (eg if the leader has abdicated his responsibility).

3.18 As discussed earlier, group decision-making tends to take longer (especially through consensus-seeking), but decisions are often better-evaluated and more representative (owing to the input of different viewpoints) and therefore implemented with more commitment. Perhaps the key task of the manager is to avoid the 'risky-shift' phenomenon, whereby groups tend to take greater risks than the same individuals on their own. As we have seen, this is aggravated in cohesive groups, due to groupthink, and must be combated by a rigorous insistence on hearing divergent viewpoints and evaluating options.

3.19 In an effectively functioning group, decision-making will become less leader-centred over time: processes for constructive problem-solving will be carried out with appropriate member involvement and information sharing (without degenerating into groupthink).

Team communication

3.20 Effectively functioning groups tend to move from a leader-centred, leader-initiated pattern of communication to one where interaction is multi-directional or 'all-channel': any member can communicate directly with any other member. Cliques and isolated individuals become included within this web of interaction over time.

3.21 Features of effective group communication therefore include:

- Open, honest communication – including the ability to deal with conflicts, issues and criticism openly, directly and fairly (without personal animosity or grudge-holding)
- Task-relevant information sharing (no withholding on a 'need to know' or 'knowledge is power' basis)

- All-member participation in meetings, discussions and decision-making. Equitable participation does not mean that all members will share *equally*, but that all members can get a fair hearing when they have something to say.
- Absence of artificial status barriers, so that senior and junior members communicate with ease
- Positive contributions (giving/seeking information, suggestions and opinions; encouraging and affirming others; being appropriately vulnerable; checking understanding; giving constructive feedback; summarising etc) outweigh negative contributions (attacking, being defensive, difficulty stating, fault finding, interrupting or overriding others and so on).

3.22 *Rackham & Morgan* suggest the technique of contribution profiling: analysing the number of contributions of different (positive and negative) types made by each member of a team during a meeting or discussion, to identify dysfunctional behaviours which can be fed back and adjusted or compensated for with positive leadership.

4 Team building

4.1 As we suggested above, one way in which teams can be built is by encouraging team identity: getting people to see themselves as part of the group. This may be done by naming the group; expressing the team's identity in slogans and mottos; building a team history in stories and jokes (especially heroic successes and failures); or giving the team distinctive 'badges' or symbols.

4.2 Another teambuilding technique is encouraging team solidarity: building loyalty to the group. This may be done by expressing solidarity ('one for all and all for one'); encouraging interpersonal relationships within the team; controlling intra-group conflict and competition in positive, affirming ways; and encouraging inter-group competition.

4.3 A third approach to teambuilding is to encourage commitment to shared objectives and to cooperative working to achieve them. This is likely to be a key tool for building virtual or multi-organisational supply chain teams, as well as conventional in-house teams. It will involve:

- Clear articulation of the team's individual and group objectives and their place in the organisation's (or supply chain's) activity as a whole
- Involving the team in setting specific targets and standards and agreeing methods of organising work
- Providing the resources the team requires to fulfil its objectives
- Giving regular feedback on progress and results via team briefings
- Inviting feedback and suggestions from team members, so that they can influence work methods and drive improvements, again via team briefings
- Positively reinforcing behaviour that demonstrates commitment to the task (through rewards, recognition and celebration).

5 What is an effective team?

What makes a team effective?

5.1 The task of the team leader is to build a 'successful' or 'effective' team. The criteria for team effectiveness, however, are both fulfilment of task and organisational goals and satisfaction of team members. According to the human relations school of management the one is not, in fact, possible without the other: satisfied team members are more likely to work in a committed and cooperative fashion towards task objectives – while the successful achievement of task objectives actively promotes satisfaction, in a 'virtuous' circle (as opposed to a 'vicious' circle).

What does an effective team look like?

5.2 There are a number of factors, both quantitative and qualitative, that might be assessed in order to decide whether or how far a team is operating effectively. Some factors cannot be taken as evidence on their own, but may suggest underlying problems in the team: accident rates, labour turnover and absenteeism, for example.

5.3 Signs of an effective team may include the following. (You might think through the opposite of each factor, for signs of team ineffectiveness.)

Quantifiable factors

- Low rate of labour turnover, accidents, absenteeism
- High output/productivity and quality performance
- Specific individual and team targets and standards are achieved
- Infrequent disruptions of work for problems, conflicts and so on

Qualitative factors

- High commitment to the achievement of targets and goals
- Clear understanding of team goals and role in organisational or supply chain activity (particularly customer care or quality)
- Clear understanding of the role of each member within the team
- Trust between members, reflected in free and open communication and the willingness to share tasks (trusting others to 'do their part')
- New idea generation and sharing of ideas
- Mutual support and facilitation by members of each other's work
- Open confrontation and investigation of problems and divergent views, with commitment to finding mutually satisfactory solutions
- Active interest and involvement in work decisions
- Seeking of opportunities for individual challenge, responsibility and development in the work

Key values in positive team relationships

5.4 The leader has a key role in modelling and promoting the cultural values that build co-operative and mutually enriching relationships within a team. Key values underpinning such relationships include the following.

- **Trust**: Encouraging open communication and information-sharing (particularly, owning up to problems and difficulties); and allowing every member to focus on their part of the task, knowing that the others will perform theirs.
- **Fairness**: ensuring that decisions which affect team members (such as the allocation of tasks and resources, arbitration of disputes and investigation of grievances) are made equitably and objectively; that discipline and rewards are applied consistently and without partiality; and so on.
- **Equal opportunity**: ensuring equal access to opportunities for training, promotion and rewards – regardless of gender, race, age, disability or other criteria.
- **Diversity**: supporting diverse cultures (eg encouraging discussion of represented cultures' values and norms); abilities (eg adapting the workplace for those with disabilities, or being aware of language issues in cross-cultural teams); and lifestyles (eg by offering flexible working hours, or broadening married-partner benefit schemes to same-sex partners).
- **Respect**: encouraging respect for individual differences (without harassment, prejudice or discrimination) and courtesy and respect in all inter-personal dealings, particularly in disagreement or conflict.
- **Ethical conduct**: practising and encouraging personal integrity, honesty, confidentiality of information, professional courtesy, support for colleagues – and whatever other ethical values the team collectively adopts (eg in regard to suppliers/customers, the environment or the community).

Diagnosing poor-functioning teams

5.5 We have focused on the attributes and dynamics of effectively maturing/functioning teams. You should be able to use the *opposite* factors to describe an ineffective or dysfunctional team. Drawing all that we've said together, the following is a brief checklist of some of the reasons identified for poor team performance.

- Lack of support, information or resources from management to fulfil the task (including lack of genuine decision-making authority and accountability)
- Unclear or unrealistic individual/team objectives
- Inappropriate team size or composition (gaps or lack of balance in team roles)
- Conflicts of interest, interpersonal hostility or status barriers blocking team development, co-operation and information-sharing
- Under-performing or under-motivated individuals holding back the team, and causing mistrust and resentment
- Poor team leadership, creating power conflicts and imbalances, lack of communication and uncertainty
- Unchecked team cohesion, diverting attention from the task and creating 'groupthink'

- Lack of leadership and teamworking skills to maintain team development and guide team processes (role allocation, decision-making, communication) in helpful ways
- Group norms undermining performance (eg restricting output, resisting leadership)

You can no doubt think of other factors – perhaps even from your own experience...

6 Motivation and performance

What is motivation?

6.1 The word 'motivation' is used in different contexts with different meanings.

- The mental process of choosing desired outcomes, deciding how to go about them, assessing whether the likelihood of success warrants the amount of effort that will be necessary, and setting in motion the required behaviours. Our 'motivation' to do something will depend on this calculation of the relationship between needs/goals, behaviour and outcome.
- The social process by which the behaviour of an individual is influenced by others. 'Motivation' in this sense usually applies to the attempts of organisations to get workers to put in more effort by offering them certain financial and non-financial rewards if they do so.

6.2 For a manger, motivation boils down to questions such as: how can we get people more excited about their work? How can we get them to achieve more? How can we recognise and reward achievements? What will make the work itself more meaningful, interesting and challenging for people? What can we do to help people grow and develop and take on more responsibility? What will the team/organisation gain from having committed, loyal people?

Motivation, job satisfaction and performance

6.3 You may be wondering whether motivation is really so important. It could be argued that if a person is employed to do a job, he will do that job – and no question of 'motivation' arises. If the person doesn't want to do the work, he can resign.

6.4 The point at issue, however, is *how* the job is done. It is suggested that if individuals can be 'motivated', by one means or another, they will work more efficiently (and productivity will rise) or they will produce a better quality of work, or will exercise their creativity and initiative in the service of organisational goals. They will work in a more committed fashion.

6.5 Job satisfaction is an even more controversial concept.

- It is often said that 'happy bees make more honey' – but this is difficult to measure and demonstrate in practice.
- Job satisfaction is difficult to define: it means different things to different people, and over time, according to needs and expectations.
- As *Huczynski and Buchanan* note, there is not so much talk about 'the quality of working life' when there is little work to be had!

6.6 On the other hand, low morale, dissatisfaction or demotivation can cause direct and indirect performance problems, through effects such as:

- Higher than usual (or higher than acceptable) labour turnover (resignations and transfers)
- Higher levels of absenteeism (whether through work avoidance or genuine stress-related illness)
- Deterioration in timekeeping and discipline
- Reduction in upward communication, proactive involvement (such as suggestions for quality improvements) and other benefits of employee commitment
- Higher incidence of employee disputes and grievances
- Restricted output quantity and/or quality (through lack of commitment or deliberate assertion of negative power).

6.7 You may gather that motivation is an art, not a science: it is a highly subjective phenomenon. Some models of motivation have highlighted the cultural dimension of motivational strategies. Managers will attempt to motivate their teams according to their own assumptions about what makes workers 'tick': what will encourage or force them to work better. We will begin by looking at some of these assumptions.

Theory X and Theory Y

6.8 Theory X and Theory Y (*Douglas McGregor*) are not 'types of people' but two extreme sets of managerial assumptions about what makes workers tick, at opposite ends of a continuum.

6.9 Theory X asserts that the average human being has an inherent dislike of work and will avoid it if he can. People must therefore be coerced, controlled, directed and/or bribed or threatened with punishment in order to get them to expend adequate effort towards the achievement of organisational goals. This is quite acceptable to the worker, who prefers to be directed, wishes to avoid responsibility, has relatively little ambition and wants security above all.

6.10 Theory Y asserts that the expenditure of physical and mental effort in work is as natural as play or rest. The average human being does not inherently dislike work, which can be a source of satisfaction. People can exercise self-direction and self-control to achieve objectives to which they are committed. Commitment to objectives is a result of rewards associated with the achievement: satisfaction of self-actualisation needs. The average human being learns, under proper conditions, not only to accept but to seek responsibility. The capacity to exercise a relatively high degree of imagination, ingenuity and creativity in the solution of organisational problems is widespread.

6.11 McGregor's point is that Theory X and Theory Y assumptions are, in essence, self-fulfilling prophecies. If employees are treated as if Theory X were true (using carrot-and-stick motivation systems, detailed rules and close supervision, low-discretion jobs and so on) they will begin to behave accordingly: it is negative experience at work that fosters lack of ambition, the need for security and intellectual stagnation. If employees are treated as if Theory Y were true (using empowered teamworking, employee involvement schemes and facilitative managerial styles) they will begin to behave accordingly and rise to the challenge.

Other theories of motivation

6.12 One way of grouping the major theories of motivation is by distinguishing between content theories and process theories.

- Content theories ask the question: '*What* are the *things* that motivate people?' They assume that human beings have a set of needs or desired outcomes that they pursue.
- Process theories ask the question: '*How* can people be motivated?' They explore the conscious or unconscious process of calculation by which individuals choose certain outcomes and the most advantageous or acceptable paths towards them.

6.13 We will now look at some of the major motivation theories. (They are not explicitly mentioned in the syllabus, but you may want to cite them in support of team motivation measures: this is what the study of organisational behaviour concepts is for!)

7 Key theories of motivation

7.1 According to content theories, motivated behaviour is aimed at reducing the tension experienced as a result of an unsatisfied need or drive. The managerial task is therefore to offer the means of satisfying the individuals' needs – or to create or awaken needs in the individual which the organisation is in a position to satisfy.

7.2 Needs vary between individuals and within the same individuals over time. It is, however, possible to identify various classes of need which are assumed to be innate: natural to all human beings. (Content theories are, in effect, need theories.)

Maslow's hierarchy of needs

7.3 *Abraham Maslow* described seven innate needs, arranged in a 'hierarchy of relative pre-potency' (summarised in Figure 10.1). Each level of need is dominant until it is satisfied (however incompletely): only then does the next level of need become the dominant motivating factor.

Figure 10.1 *Maslow's hierarchy of needs*

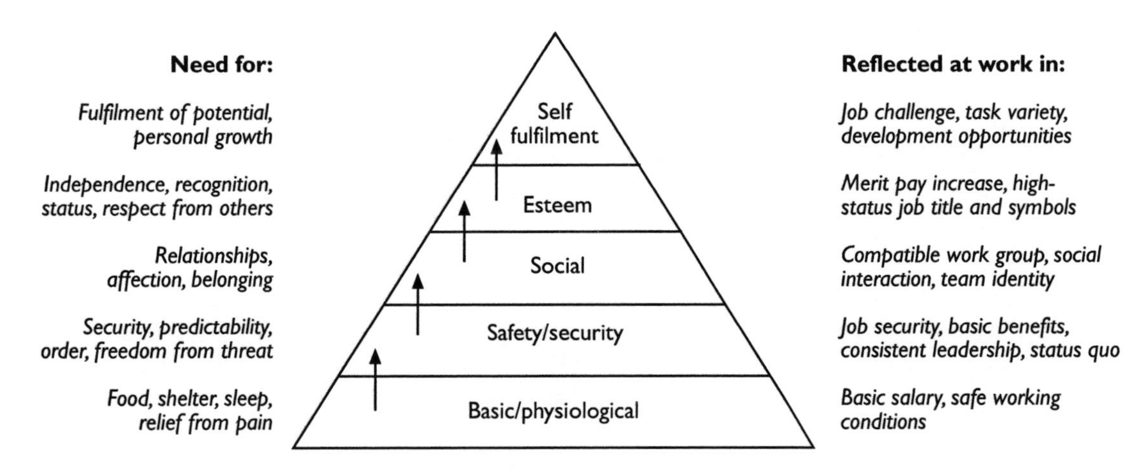

7.4 There is a certain intuitive appeal to Maslow's theory. After all, you are unlikely to be concerned with status or recognition while you are hungry or thirsty: primary survival needs will take precedence until they are satisfied.

7.5 However, it is difficult to use the hierarchy to predict employee behaviour. (Maslow did not intend it to be applied to the work context.) The boundaries between the needs are, in practice, indistinct and overlapping; different people emphasise different needs; and the same need may prompt different behaviours in different individuals. In some contexts, people are clearly able to suppress even their basic physiological and safety needs for the sake of a perceived 'higher cause' or for the sake of others.

7.6 In addition, *Huczynski and Buchanan* suggest that 'Maslow may simply have reflected American middle class values and the pursuit of the good life, and may not have hit on fundamental universal truths about human psychology.' Research studies indicate that cultural values affect work behaviour and the success of management techniques.

7.7 The role of pay is problematic, since it arguably acts as a 'stand in' for (or way of obtaining) other rewards. Self-actualisation is particularly hard to offer as an 'off the shelf' reward package, since it is highly subjective. However, the hierarchy of needs is a useful reminder to managers to adopt a contingency approach to motivating employees.

Herzberg's two-factor theory

7.8 In the 1950s, *Frederick Herzberg* interviewed Pittsburgh engineers and accountants to find out what 'critical incidents' had made them feel good or bad about their work. Analysis revealed two distinct sets of factors: those which created satisfaction (which Herzberg called 'motivator factors') and those which created dissatisfaction ('hygiene' or 'maintenance' factors).

7.9 Herzberg highlighted two basic needs of individuals:

- the need to avoid unpleasantness, satisfied by **hygiene** factors;
- the need for personal growth, satisfied at work by **motivator** factors only.

7.10 'When people are dissatisfied with their work it is usually because of discontent with environmental factors.' These include company policy, salary, style of supervision, interpersonal relations, working conditions and job security. Herzberg called them 'hygiene' factors because they are essentially preventative: they minimise dissatisfaction but do not give positive or long-lasting satisfaction, in the same way that sanitation minimises threats to health but does not give good health. An individual is much more likely to be dissatisfied with his pay, for example, than satisfied with it: he may temporarily be satisfied with a pay rise, but only until he begins to take it for granted or compare it to others' pay.

7.11 Motivator factors create job satisfaction and are effective in motivating an individual to superior performance and effort by offering personal growth and fulfilment. 'Satisfaction can only arise from the job', so motivator factors include: advancement, recognition, responsibility, challenging and interesting work, achievement and growth in the job.

7.12 Evidence that motivator factors increase productivity has proved hard to find. Also, the research is highly context-specific: the factors may reflect cultural, occupational and personal values which cannot necessarily be generalised to other contexts.

Nevertheless, Herzberg's work has been helpful in highlighting the concept of job satisfaction (the intrinsic rewards to be found in work itself) and thus contributing to job redesign (discussed in Chapter 5) and the 'quality of working life' movement.

Intrinsic and extrinsic rewards

7.13 Herzberg's two factors also highlighted the two types of reward that can be offered to individuals at work.

- **Intrinsic** rewards arise from the work itself, and (in a sense) from within the worker: challenge, interest, team identity, pride in the organisation, the satisfaction of achievement and so on.
- **Extrinsic** rewards do not arise from the work itself, but are within the power of others (typically, management) to award or withhold: wages or salary, bonuses, prizes, promotion, improved working conditions and so on.

Vroom's expectancy theory

7.14 Expectancy theory is a process theory of motivation, which basically states that the strength of an individual's motivation to do something will depend on the extent to which he expects the results of his efforts to contribute to his personal needs or goals.

7.15 *Victor Vroom* worked out a formula by which human motivation could be assessed and measured, based on expectancy theory. He suggested that the strength of an individual's motivation is the product of two factors.

- The strength of his preference for a certain outcome. Vroom called this 'valence': it can be represented as a positive or negative number, or zero – since outcomes may be desired, avoided or regarded with indifference.
- His expectation that the outcome will in fact result from a certain behaviour. Vroom called this 'subjective probability' or 'expectancy'. As a probability, it may be represented by any number between 0 (no chance) and 1 (certainty).

7.16 In its simplest form, the expectancy equation may be stated as follows.

$$F = V \times E$$

where:

F = the force or strength of the individual's motivation to behave in a particular way
V = valence: the strength of the individual's preference for a given outcome or reward
E = expectancy: the individual's perception that the behaviour will result in the outcome/reward.

7.17 In this equation, the lower the values of valence or expectation, the less the individual's motivation. An employee may have a high expectation that increased productivity will result in promotion (because of managerial promises, say), but if he is indifferent or negative towards the idea of promotion (because he dislikes responsibility), he will not be motivated to increase his productivity. The same would be true if promotion was very important to him, but he did not believe higher productivity would get him promoted (because he has been passed over before, perhaps).

7.18 Expectancy theory can be used to measure the likely strength of a worker's motivation to act in a desired way in response to a range of different rewards, to find the most effective motivational strategy.

Pay as a motivator

7.19 The objectives of pay from the organisation's point of view are: to attract and retain labour of a suitable type and quality; to fulfil perceived social responsibilities; and to motivate employees to achieve and maintain desired levels of performance.

7.20 Pay occupies a central – but ambiguous – role in motivation theory. In *Herzberg*'s theory, for example, pay is a hygiene rather than a motivator factor. *Drucker* noted that incentives such as pay, once regularly provided, come to be perceived as 'entitlements' and their capacity to create dissatisfaction, to become a deterrent to performance, outstrips their motivatory power. *Lawler*, moreover, suggested that in the absence of information about how much colleagues are earning, individuals guess their earnings and usually overestimate – and are then dissatisfied because they resent earning less than they *think* their colleagues are getting!

7.21 However, pay is the most important of the hygiene factors, according to Herzberg. It is valuable not only in its power to be converted into a wide range of other satisfactions but also as a consistent measure of worth or value, allowing employees to compare themselves and be compared with other individuals or occupational groups inside and outside the organisation.

7.22 Employees need income to live. The size of that income will affect their standard of living, but people tend not to be concerned to maximise their earnings. They may like to earn more, but are probably more concerned:

- to earn *enough* pay; and
- to know that their pay is *equitable* in relation to others and to the effort they are putting in.

7.23 Payment systems tread the awkward path between equity (an objective rate for the job, preserving pay differentials and so on) and incentive (offering rewards that will stimulate extra effort and attainment by particular individuals and groups).

7.24 *Goldthorpe, Lockwood et al* researched the supposed 'instrumental' orientation to work: the attitude that work is not an end in itself, but a means to other ends. In their 'Affluent Worker' research, the team found that highly-paid Luton car assembly workers experienced their work as routine and dead-end. They had in fact made a rational decision to enter employment offering high monetary reward rather than intrinsic satisfactions.

7.26 The Luton researchers did not, however, claim that *all* workers have an instrumental orientation to work, but suggested that a person will seek a comfortable balance of:

- the rewards which are important to him and
- the deprivations he feels able to put up with in order to earn those rewards.

7.27 Even those with an instrumental orientation to work have limits to their purely financial aspirations and will cease to be motivated by pay if the deprivations – in terms of long working hours, poor conditions, social isolation, boredom or whatever – become too great: in other words, if the price of pay is too high.

Problems with monetary incentives

7.28 There are a number of difficulties associated with incentive schemes based on monetary reward, or performance-related pay.

7.29 Increased earnings may, as we noted above, not be an incentive to all individuals. Moreover, workers are unlikely to be in complete control of results (especially a company's profitability). The link between effort and reward may be insufficient to act as a meaningful incentive – or may be a cause of frustration to workers, if they put in the effort and are not rewarded to the level of their expectation.

7.30 Even if employees are motivated by money, the effects may not be altogether desirable. An instrumental orientation may encourage self-interested performance at the expense of teamwork. It may encourage attention to output at the expense of quality, or the lowering of standards and targets to make bonuses more easily accessible. Workers often remain suspicious that if they achieve high levels of output and earnings, management will alter the basis of the incentive rates to reduce future earnings: work groups therefore tend to restrict output to a level that they feel is fair but achievable.

7.31 A range of **non-financial rewards** and incentives may be offered in addition to monetary incentives. These often include benefits such as: company car, health insurance, above-statutory holiday time; access to facilities (social, sports); canteen or luncheon vouchers; gift certificates and so on. There has been a trend in recent years towards flexible benefit schemes, allowing employees a choice from a 'menu' of potential benefits: the element of choice increasing the perceived value (valence) of the reward/incentive, and supporting the motivation of an increasingly diverse workforce.

8 The team leader as motivator

8.1 Reward and motivation systems such as pay, benefits, promotion and job design may be determined at a department- or organisation-wide level. However, the motivational theories we have discussed suggest several ways in which a team leader can contribute to the motivation of his team.

Leadership as a motivator

8.2 Clear goals and objectives are essential in order for individuals to calculate how much effort a task will require (and whether it is worth it, given the rewards on offer). They also provide yardsticks by which individuals can measure and feel good about their progress.

8.3 If team members can be involved in setting goals, and articulating values, they are more likely to own and pursue them in a committed way. A team 'charter' or contract may even be drawn up to clarify the team's commitment to each other: what the team wants to accomplish, why it is important, and how the team will work together to achieve results.

8.4 On-going formal and informal feedback on progress and results is essential for individuals to calculate what further effort is required; to build confidence and shared accountability; and to enable milestones to be celebrated.

8.5 Praise and recognition should not be underestimated as a reward and incentive to further effort: they are highly valued by employees – and yet they cost the manager nothing to give. Teamworking gurus like *Ken Blanchard* advocate 'Keeping the accent on the positive'.

- Looking for (and rewarding) positive behaviours that reflect the purpose and values of the team
- 'Catching people doing things right' (or even 'approximately right') instead of wrong
- Redirecting people towards the goal, when they get things wrong, instead of punishing them
- Linking all recognition and rewards back to the team's purpose and goals

Chapter summary

- A team is 'a small group of people with complementary skills who are committed to a common purpose, performance goals and approaches for which they hold themselves basically jointly accountable'. (Katzenbach and Smith)
- Teams have significant advantages for individual wellbeing, pooling and coordination of work, and interpersonal processes (including testing and ratifying decisions and generating ideas). However, there are also drawbacks in lengthier and riskier decision-making and the potential for group dynamics to subvert organisational goals.
- Teams develop over time. According to Tuckman, this takes place in four basic phases: forming, storming, norming and performing (with potential for dorming and mourning at later stages).
- The dynamics or processes within teams, which require management in order to support effective functioning and performance, include:
    - Team role adoption. (Process roles within a team can be classified using Belbin's nine role definitions, which you should be able to identify.)
    - Team cohesion or 'closeness'; solidarity, identity and shared commitment to goals. While this is a feature of high-performing teams, it can become dysfunctional if allowed to blinker the group ('groupthink').
    - Team decision-making, by authority, consensus or majority: less leader-centred as the team matures.
    - Team communication: less leader-centred as the team matures, ideally becoming open, positive and multi-directional.
- Team building describes a range of activities to increase team cohesion.
- Effective teams both fulfil task goals *and* satisfy individual and team belonging and development needs.
- Motivation is the process by which individuals decide that it is worthwhile putting effort into work in order to achieve goals which they value. The role of management is to offer satisfaction of worker needs and drives; to give goal and feedback information to support decision-making; and to positively reinforce desired behaviours with rewards, praise and recognition.

- Motivation theories include: McGregor's Theory X and Theory Y; Maslow's hierarchy of needs; Herzberg's two factor theory (focusing on job satisfaction); and Vroom's expectancy theory.
- Pay, monetary and non-monetary incentives and leadership style can all be used to motivate team members.

Self-test questions

Numbers in brackets refer to paragraphs where you can check your answers

1. What is the difference between a group and a team? (1.1, 1.6)
2. How does teamworking contribute to individual satisfaction? (1.8)
3. Describe the stages of team formation. (2.2–2.6)
4. List Belbin's nine process roles. (Table 10.1)
5. What is groupthink and how can it be overcome? (3.17, 3.18)
6. Evaluate the good and bad points of group decision-making. (3.20)
7. List the key values underpinning mutually satisfying team relationships. (5.4)
8. Why would a manager want to ensure high morale and job satisfaction in his team? (6.4, 6.6)
9. Distinguish between (a) Theory X and Theory Y, (b) hygiene factors and motivator factors and (c) valence and expectancy in motivation theory. (6.9, 6.10, 7.9, 7.15)
10. Are people always motivated by monetary rewards and services? (7.22, 7.24–7.30)

CHAPTER 11

Managing Conflict

Learning objectives and indicative content

4.3 Assess the sources of conflict which may arise within the purchasing function

- Disagreement about needs, goals, values, priorities and interests
- Poor communication
- Lack of trust in leadership
- Lack of direction
- Lack of clarity in role
- Scarcity of resources
- Interpersonal and hygiene issues

4.4 Explain how to build relationships and encourage integration with other parts of the business.

- Changing perceptions of purchasing (from process to advisory)
- Advocates for the profession/business
- Consultancy
- Adding value

4.5 Evaluate techniques to deal with conflict within teams and between individuals in the purchasing and supply functions

- Consultation
- Mediation
- Negotiation
- Arbitration
- Dispute resolution (including discipline and grievance)

Chapter headings

1 Different views of conflict

2 Causes and symptoms of conflict

3 Integrating purchasing within the organisation

4 Managing and resolving conflict

5 Conflict resolution mechanisms

Introduction

One of the key roles of management is to develop and maintain co-operative working in the organisation (and supply chain).

In an interpersonal sense, this involves a complex, ongoing process of managing diversity and difference. 'Diversity', because the organisation is made up of individuals and groups with potentially very different personalities, goals, attitudes, backgrounds and so on. 'Difference', because those areas of diversity will inevitably, from time to time, cause misunderstandings, disagreements, competition and perhaps hostility. This is the kind of difference we generally call 'conflict' – although conflict itself is a complex term which can be seen from a number of different points of view.

In this chapter, we discuss what conflict might mean in a work team, and whether it is a good or bad thing. We outline common causes (why conflict arises) and symptoms (how you can know it when you see it) and how it can be prevented, controlled and resolved.

1 Different views of conflict

Constructive and destructive conflict

1.1 Conflict can be highly desirable. It can energise relationships and clarify issues. *John Hunt* suggests that conflict is **constructive**, when its effect is to:

- Introduce different solutions to problems
- Define power relationships more clearly
- Encourage creativity and the testing of ideas
- Focus attention on individual contributions
- Bring emotions out into the open
- Provide opportunity for catharsis (the release of hostile feelings that might otherwise be repressed)

1.2 Conflict can also be **destructive,** negative and damaging to social systems (which the radical perspective still regards as positive and desirable). Hunt suggests that conflict of this kind may act in a group of individuals to:

- Distract attention from the task
- Polarise views and 'dislocate' the group
- Subvert objectives in favour of secondary goals
- Encourage defensive or 'spoiling' behaviour
- Result in disintegration of the group
- Stimulate emotional, win-lose conflicts, or hostility

1.3 *Robbins* suggests that a contemporary approach to conflict:

- Recognises the inevitability (even necessity) of conflict
- Explicitly encourages opposition and challenge to ideas and the *status quo*
- Defines conflict management to include stimulation as well as resolution of conflict
- Considers the management of conflict as a major responsibility of all managers.

2 Causes and symptoms of conflict

Causes of conflict

2.1 *Dessler* classifies four major sources of organisational conflict.

- Interdependence and shared resources. Conflict is most likely to occur where groups are dependent on each other to achieve their goals and use shared resources in pursuit of these goals.
- Differences in goals, values and perceptions. Groups are distinctive social units and will have special interests, particular views of what is important and what is not, and will tend to see the world in a way which supports the maintenance and success of the group. (Overlapping membership – eg if a team member is also a trade-union member – may cause conflict within the individual, as well as within the group.)
- Authority imbalance. Where a group has too little authority compared to its responsibilities or prestige, it will aggressively seek more (in competition with other groups): if it has too much, it will be a target of others who attempt to enhance their own authority or prestige. If group contributions are equivalent or substitutable, political conflict may escalate as groups by-pass or replace one another.
- Ambiguity. Where a group's responsibilities are ambiguous or unclear, power vacuums arise: competition to fill the vacuum ensues. Similarly, uncertainty about *other* groups' purpose or motives leads to mistrust and political game-playing.

Inter-group conflict

2.2 Various forms of inter-group conflict are therefore common in organisations.

- Institutionalised conflict, such as that between trade unions and management.
- Hierarchy-based conflict, caused by inequalities of positional power.
- Functional conflict, caused by clashing goals and competition for power and resources between different organisational functions.
- Line/staff conflict, such as that between production and sales functions and 'advisory' functions such as the HR department, Accounts and so on: the power of staff functions is often resented and resisted by line managers as interference, and staff functions have to reassert their authority (often by negative means, such as red-tape and rule enforcement).
- Formal/informal conflict, where the unwritten rules, communication channels and power structures of the informal organisation clash with those of the formal organisation.
- Status conflict, where groups compete for status and prestige.
- Resource conflict, where groups compete for finance, staff, space and other resources. This is often the basis of adversarial negotiations: 'win/lose' competition where one party can gain only at another's expense.
- Political conflict, where 'individuals or interest groups exercise whatever power they can amass to influence the goals, criteria or processes used in organisational decision-making to advance their own interests'. (*Miles*)

Conflict within the team

2.3 In addition, conflict may arise within a team due to everyday factors such as the following.

- Disagreement about needs, goals, values, priorities and interests (since individuals may have different 'agendas' – or different perceptions about the team's goals and purposes). This will be made worse by:
  - Lack of direction (from the organisation or team leader) as to what the team's purpose and goals are.
  - Lack of clarity in the roles assigned to team members, leading to stressful role ambiguity (where individuals don't know clearly what they are expected to contribute) and/or frustration and loss of co-ordination, as roles are duplicated or left vacant.
- Poor communication, which is a cause (as well as a symptom) of conflict. The less people communicate, the more potential there is for negative assumptions, stereotypes and misunderstandings. Withholding of information may also escalate conflict, as it is perceived to be a hostile political 'game'.
- Competition for scarce resources, which also operates at the team level. Individuals may compete for power, office space, team-based rewards, the manager's recognition/attention, machine time (or other resources) and so on.
- Interpersonal issues, such as 'personality clashes', aggression or domination by strong individuals, argumentative or manipulative communication styles and so on.
- 'Hygiene' issues (in the technical sense used by Herzberg): dissatisfactions with the leadership, working conditions or pay, say, which can cause grievance against the organisation (or leader) and/or spill over into interpersonal conflict in the team (eg if some members feel others are being paid more).

Symptoms of organisational conflict

2.4 According to *Handy*, the observable symptoms of conflict in an organisation will be:

- Intra-personal struggles, where an individual has conflicting goals
- Poor communication (upward, downward and/or lateral)
- Interpersonal friction
- Inter-group rivalry and jealousy
- Low morale and frustration
- The proliferation of rules, norms and myths
- Widespread use of arbitration, appeals to higher authority and grievances
- Inflexible attitudes towards change
- Poor co-ordination between hostile, non-communicating groups, resulting in work delays (and possibly customer complaints).

3 Integrating purchasing within the organisation

What kind of authority?

3.1 It is common to distinguish three kinds of authority in organisations.

- **Line** authority is the direct flow of authority down the vertical chain (or line) of command: for example, the authority a manager has over a subordinate. This confers the right to set objectives, make decisions and issue instructions and expect to see them carried out.
- **Staff** authority is the authority one manager or department may have to give specialist advice or guidance to others. This does not include the right to make or influence decisions. Whether the advice is taken depends on how much power the department has – and this in turn depends on its credibility, the persuasive quality of its advice, and the perceptions of other departments that its expertise is valuable and necessary.
- **Functional** authority is a mix of line and staff authority, whereby a manager or department has the authority, in certain circumstances, to direct, design or control the activities or procedures of another department.

3.2 A manager in the purchasing and supply function therefore has direct line authority over his own staff, and over any subordinate departments or sections within the function.

3.3 In relation to other departments in the organisation, the purchasing manager may exercise functional authority in some areas: from day-to-day purchase requisition and authorisation procedures to policy guidelines on environmental/ethical sourcing or quality management. In other areas, his role may be purely advisory: recommending suppliers, prices or order quantities to project purchasing officers, say, or advising product designers on materials, specifications and quality issues.

3.4 Areas of ambiguity can become a cause of conflict. It is common for 'strategic' functions (such as production or finance) to resist what may be perceived as ignorance, interference or empire building by 'support' functions. Where support functions are excluded from any strategic role, they tend to become preoccupied with their own specialisms and status – so that their priorities may genuinely diverge from (or be irrelevant to) the strategic objectives of the organisation.

3.5 These issues of lack of integration and negative perception within the organisation must be addressed by purchasing and supply managers. They place a high premium on a manager's networking, relationship-building and negotiation skills!

4 Managing and resolving conflict

4.1 There are many approaches to the management of conflict and the suitability of any given approach must be judged according to its relevance to a particular situation. There is no 'right way'. In some situations, the best outcome may be achieved by compromise; in others, imposition of a win-lose solution may be required; in others, the process of seeking a win-win solution, whatever the eventual outcome, may be helpful.

4.2 *Robbins* provides the following classification of possible strategies for resolving conflict.

- Problem-solving: the parties are brought together to find a solution to the particular issue
- Superordinate goals: the parties are encouraged to see the bigger picture and identify shared goals that override their differences
- Expansion of resources: resources are freed and mobilised to meet both parties' needs, eliminating the need for competition
- Avoidance: one or both parties withdraws from the conflict or denies/conceals the incompatibility
- Smoothing: one or both parties plays down the differences and 'papers over the cracks'
- Compromise: bargaining, negotiating and conciliating, so that each party makes some concessions in order to obtain some gains
- Authoritative command: an arbitrator with authority over both parties makes a decisive judgement
- Altering the human variable: effort is made to change the attitudes, beliefs and perceptions underlying the conflict
- Altering the structural variable: effort is made to re-organise work relationships in order to minimise the potential for conflict

A model of conflict styles

4.3 *Thomas* (1976) suggested that individuals' conflict-handling styles could be mapped on two dimensions, according to the intentions of the parties involved: their assertiveness (the extent to which they try to satisfy their own concerns) and their co-operativeness (the extent to which they try to satisfy the other party's concerns). The five extreme points on this map can be shown as follows: Figure 11.1.

Figure 11.1 *Model of conflict-handling styles*

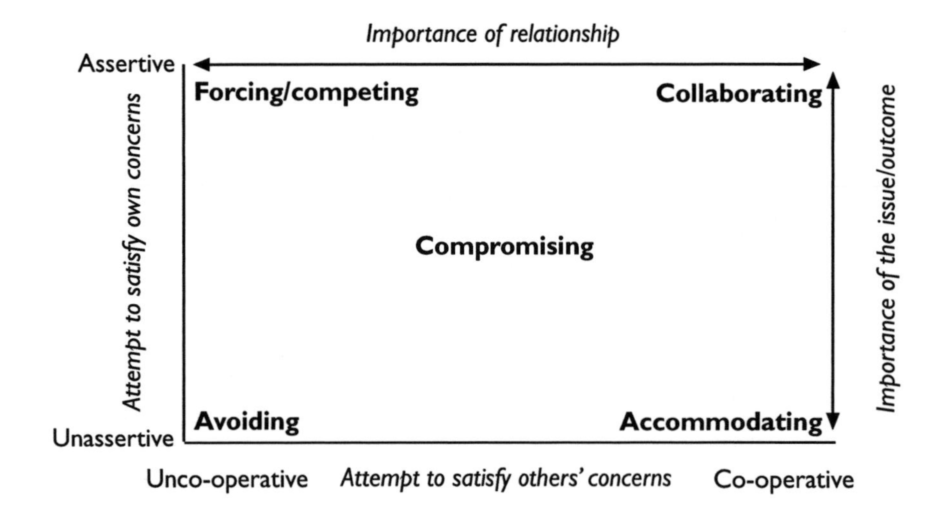

4.4 The five styles can be compared as follows.

- **Avoiding**: you withdraw from the conflict or attempt to sweep it under the carpet. This allows you to avoid dealing with conflict, and avoids immediate tensions: it may be appropriate if the issue is genuinely trivial, or you need a 'cooling off' period, or someone else is better placed to deal with the conflict. However, underlying problems don't get resolved: long-term frustrations and resentments may emerge in other ways.
- **Forcing/competing**: you impose your solution on the problem. This allows you to get your way, and may be appropriate for issues that need winning: breaking down the inflexibility of others or implementing unpopular measures quickly in a crisis, say. However, the other party is likely to feel defeated and demeaned, and this can damage ongoing collaboration and trust.
- **Accommodating**: you concede the issue without a fight, to preserve harmony. This avoids upsetting people, and may be appropriate where maintaining the relationship is more important than the issue (or if you realise you are wrong!). However, you are giving permission for the other person to take advantage of the situation, and your authority may be undermined.
- **Compromising**: you use bargaining or negotiation, so that each party trades some concessions for some gains. This reaches an agreement that both parties can live with, and enables you to get on with work: it may be necessary where power is evenly balanced and there is genuine conflict of interest. However, the solution is often more expedient than effective, and may leave both parties unsatisfied.
- **Collaborating**: you work together to try and find an outcome which meets the clearly stated needs of both parties as far as possible: a problem-solving or 'win-win' approach. This assumes that both positions are important, even if they are not necessarily equally valid. It takes time, but at the end of the process, both parties should be committed to the solution and satisfied that they have been treated fairly. This facilitates learning, generates more creative options and encourages trust. (We examine the 'win-win' approach in more detail below.)

Note that there is still no 'one best' style: managers need behavioural flexibility!

The win-win approach to conflict resolution

4.5 Another useful model for conflict resolution is 'win-win'. *Cornelius and Faire* suggest that there are three basic ways in which a conflict or disagreement can be worked out.

- Win-lose: one party gets what he wants at the expense of the other party. However well justified such a solution is, there is often lingering resentment on the part of the 'losing' party, which may begin to damage working relationships.
- Lose-lose: neither party gets what he really wants. Compromise comes into this category. However logical such a solution is, there is often resentment and dissatisfaction on both sides: even positive compromises only result in half-satisfied needs.
- Win-win: both parties get as close as possible to what they really want. Whether or not the outcome is possible, the approach generates more options, more creative problem-solving, more open communication, and enhanced cooperation, as well as preserving working relationships.

4.6 Cornelius and Faire outline a win-win approach as follows.

Step 1 Find out why each party needs what they say they want. Getting to the other party's fears and needs in the situation facilitates meaningful problem-solving. It also encourages communication, supports other people's values, and separates the problem from the personalities involved.

Step 2 Find out where the differences dovetail. Diverging needs may seem like the cause of conflict – but they also offer potential for problem-solving, since the different needs may not be mutually exclusive, but may dovetail at some point.

Step 3 Design new options, where everyone gets more of what they need. Techniques include: brainstorming; chunking (breaking a big problem down into manageable chunks and seeking solutions to those); and devising usable 'currencies' (suggestions and concessions which are easy or low-cost for both parties, and can be traded). The aim is mutual gain.

Step 4 Co-operate. Treat the other person as a partner, not an opponent.

4.7 The example given is of two men fighting over an orange. The win-win approach would ask each man why he needs the orange. One may want to make orange juice, while the other wants the skin of the orange to make candied peel: the conflict disappears. If they both want the juice, other options will be explored: sharing the juice; getting more oranges; diluting the juice; buying one man some bottled orange juice and so on. Even if compromise is settled on, the outcome will be a win-win, because both parties will have been fully assertive and willingly cooperative, enhancing the relationship between them (which adds to the 'win' outcome).

5 Conflict resolution mechanisms

5.1 Formal mechanisms are often set up in organisations to prevent or resolve conflict.

- Disciplinary procedures
- Grievance procedures
- Consultation mechanisms
- Negotiatory mechanisms
- Dispute resolution

Disciplinary procedures

5.2 Disciplinary procedures reflect the attempt of the organisation to enforce its rules and standards of acceptable behaviour. The organisation should have written rules and standards, and a written procedure by which managers can pursue disciplinary action in cases where an employee breaches those rules or expectations.

5.3 Many enterprises base their disciplinary procedures on the idea of progressive discipline: sanctions of increasing severity for each repetition or exacerbation of an offence. The following is a standard progression.

- **Informal talk**. The manager draws the individual's attention to the offence and the standards of behaviour expected by the organisation. This may be sufficient to clear up minor or one-off situations.
- **Oral warning or reprimand**. The manager issues a spoken warning that repeated offences will lead to formal disciplinary proceedings.
- **Formal written warning**. Such a warning enters the employee's personnel record and may be used as evidence to justify further action (such as later dismissal). The advice given in the ACAS Code of Practice applies from this point on, for the protection of employees' rights to fair treatment.
- **Disciplinary sanctions** (eg demotion, loss of pay, lay-off or suspension). A range of sanctions may be used, depending on the seriousness of the offence, the anticipated effect on the morale of the offender and the rest of the work team, and the effectiveness of the action as a reformative or deterrent measure.
- **Dismissal** is a last resort – or first resort only in the most serious circumstances. The threat may be a sufficient deterrent. Ultimately, however, the only solution to maintaining discipline may be the removal of a persistent offender.

5.4 In addition to progressive discipline, which leaves plenty of room for warnings and reformative measures, there are some general principles for conducting fair and effective disciplinary action.

5.5 All employees should be informed in advance (ideally from recruitment and induction) of what the rules, regulations and behavioural standards of the organisation are. This will help to encourage self-discipline – and no-one will be able to complain that they committed offences unknowingly.

5.6 Disciplinary action should be consistent and impersonal. Inconsistency encourages uncertainty, unfairness and loss of respect for discipline. Mitigating circumstances may be taken flexibly into account in determining penalties, but rules (and the consequences of breaking them) should apply equally to all employees and on every occasion: it should not seem as if managers turn a blind eye to some offenders and not others, or punish, warn or let people off with no apparent logic. It should be emphasised that rule-breaking has consequences: it is nothing personal. Managers should not victimise particular offenders, or hold grudges, on the basis of personal differences.

5.7 The Employment Act 2002 established a **statutory procedure**, setting out minimum requirements for internal disciplinary (and grievance) procedures, which came into force in October 2004. The requirements are for a basic three-step procedure: the complaint must be set out in writing; there should be a meeting with the employee to discuss the complaint; and there must be a right of appeal. Unfortunately, a 2007 review has found these measures ineffective (increasing rather than decreasing the number of disputes) and has recommended that they be repealed: watch this space...

Grievance procedures

5.8 Grievance is often confused with discipline: in effect, they are two sides of the same coin. Discipline is applied when an employee 'does wrong'. Grievance is applied when an employee is (or feels he has been) 'wronged'. An individual may institute informal or formal grievance proceedings when he feels he has been wrongly treated, victimised, unfairly appraised or passed over for development opportunities, discriminated against, harassed and so on.

5.9 Some grievances may require informal conflict resolution between the individuals concerned, mediated by their manager. However, there may be situations where the grievance is more serious, or where the manager himself is the subject of the complaint. In such circumstances, it is important to have systematic formal grievance procedures in place.

5.10 The advantages of having a formal grievance procedure are as follows.

- To allow objective grievance handling – including 'cooling off' periods and independent case investigation and arbitration
- To protect employees from victimisation – particularly where a grievance involves their immediate superiors
- To provide legal protection for both parties, in the event of a dispute resulting in claims before an employment tribunal
- To encourage the airing of grievances – which is an important source of feedback to management on employee problems and dissatisfactions
- To require full and fair investigation of grievances, enabling the employer–employee relationship to be respected and preserved, despite problems

5.11 Many of the issues in successful grievance-handling are similar to those in disciplinary proceedings. The most important thing is that the issue should be (and be seen to be) fairly dealt with.

5.12 A typical progressive procedure for pursuing a grievance includes the following stages.

- Informal discussion with a staff/union representative, colleague or manager (subject to confidentiality). This may be sufficient to 'clear the air' or initiate informal conflict resolution or remedial action.
- Grievance interview with the immediate superior. If the immediate superior is the subject of the complaint, this may be referred to the next level up.
- Grievance interview with a higher authority. If the first interview fails to satisfy the employee, the matter may be referred upwards.
- HR department mediation. Cases referred upwards should also be reported to the HR department: specialist mediation and/or arbitration may be required. In the case of an employee who feels unfairly passed over for promotion, for example, the employee may be entitled to claim a review of his annual appraisal by the HR department, or an interview with a special promotion appeals board.

Consultation mechanisms

5.13 Consultation is a form of 'issues' management, in which potential causes of conflict are discussed, and stakeholders have an opportunity to give their input, before the problem arises (or as soon as possible, once it has arisen).

5.14 Some formal non-negotiatory consultation with employee representatives is required as part of EU employee involvement provisions. Works councils, for example, are currently being introduced into the UK. Their purpose is to inform and consult employee representatives about decisions that are likely to have a significant effect on employees' interests (such as redundancies or changes in work organisation).

5.15 Less formal consultation may take place in team briefings, discussion forums – and day-to-day team communication.

Negotiatory mechanisms

5.16 Negotiation is a useful approach to conflict resolution at any level.

- As a style of communication, it may be used by managers or teams to resolve issues between them. Each party puts forward its position persuasively, and then seeks constructive compromise, through bargaining (trade-offs) or common ground (as seen in the 'win-win' approach above), so that both parties come to a solution they can agree to.
- As an official mechanism, it is often used in industrial relations: the resolution of collective disputes (between employees and their employer), the negotiation of pay agreements and so on. '**Collective bargaining**' is the process whereby employers and employee representatives negotiate agreements by which terms and conditions of employment (and related matters) are determined for groups of represented employees. This is generally carried out at a series of formal meetings, specifically convened for the purpose.

Dispute resolution

5.17 **Conciliation** is a process where conflicts or grievances are aired in a discussion facilitated by an impartial conciliator. His role is to provide information, to manage the process (eg by laying down ground rules and keeping participants to them) and to make constructive suggestions: *not* to make judgements for one side.

5.18 A typical conciliation process would involve the following steps.

- Fact-finding, to explore the cause of the dispute (perhaps in individual meetings with the mediator)
- Joint meetings, in which each side explains its position. Where discussion gets 'stuck' on an issue, the mediator may have side meetings with each party, to discuss potential areas of movement towards settlement (which parties may not wish to consider in front of their 'opponents' at first).
- Negotiation towards a mutually acceptable position, if possible.

5.19 **Mediation** may follow conciliation, if a voluntary settlement has not been reached. It involves the appointment of an independent person (or panel) who will:

- Consider the case of both sides (set out in writing)
- Hear their evidence and arguments at a mediation hearing
- Make a formal proposal or recommendation (not binding on either party) as a basis for settlement of the dispute.

5.20 **Arbitration** may follow unsuccessful mediation, if both parties agree (or if organisational policy requires it). It involves the appointment of an independent person (or panel) who will follow a similar procedure to mediation – except that, at the end of the process, the arbitrator delivers a decision or judgement which is binding on both parties.

5.21 Industrial relations arbitrations are based on defined terms of reference, setting limits to the arbitrator's powers and to the issues that will be considered. There are two basic approaches.

- In traditional arbitration, the arbitrator draws from both sides of the argument (following unsuccessful negotiation) and makes a decision that reflects the 'middle ground'. (This sometimes encourages parties to exaggerate their initial positions, knowing that they will eventually 'split the difference'.)
- In pendulum arbitration, the arbitrator chooses the final negotiating position of one side or the other (eg the employer's final pay offer, or the employees' final claim). This encourages parties to moderate their final positions and to attempt to settle in good faith.

5.22 In the UK, ACAS (The Advisory, Conciliation and Arbitration Service) have been formed to 'promote the improvement of industrial relations'. It may be brought in to individual or collective disputes between employees and employers, for the purposes of conciliation, mediation and/or arbitration.

Chapter summary

- Conflict can be seen as constructive as well as destructive or dysfunctional. A contemporary approach to conflict explicitly encourages challenge and disagreement, while resolving relationship-damaging conflicts.
- There are four major underlying causes of conflict in organisations: interdependence and shared resources; differences in goals, values and perceptions; authority imbalance; and ambiguity.
- From these roots, both inter-group and inter-personal conflict can develop in different forms; heretical or functional conflict; line-staff conflict; resource competition; political conflict; personality clashes and so on.
- Thomas introduced a two-dimensional model of conflict styles (avoiding, accommodating, forcing/competing, compromising, and collaborating). While any style may be appropriate in given circumstances, the ideal approach is regarded as a collaborative or 'win-win' approach.
- Conflict resolution mechanisms include:
  - Disciplinary procedures, to resolve performance/conduct conflicts through a system of warnings and sanctions
  - Grievance procedures, to resolve disputes between individual employees (or at a group level, between workers and management) through a system of investigations and appeals
  - Consultation mechanisms, to manage potential issues of conflict or concern through information and discussion with employee representatives
  - Negotiating mechanisms, to resolve conflicts of interest through formal or informal bargaining
  - Conciliation, mediation and arbitration, in which the services of a facilitator are used in conflict resolution processes.

Self-test questions

Numbers in brackets refer to paragraphs where you can check your answers

1 In what circumstances may conflict be positive? (1.1)

2 Explain the four underlying causes of conflict. (2.1)

3 What is (a) line/staff conflict, (b) resource conflict and (c) political conflict? (2.2)

4 What factors may cause conflict within a team? (2.3)

5 List five symptoms of organisational conflict. (2.4)

6 What are (a) avoiding and (b) accommodating and when might they be appropriate styles for handling conflict? (4.4)

7 Why is collaborating (or 'win-win') a valuable strategy? (4.4, 4.5)

8 What is 'progressive discipline'? (5.3)

9 What are the advantages of having a formal grievance procedure? (5.10)

10 Distinguish between conciliation, mediation and arbitration. (5.17, 5.19, 5.20)

CHAPTER 12

Human Resource Management

Learning objectives and indicative content

4.6 Assess the benefits of a systematic approach to recruitment, appraisal, training and development

- High calibre of staff
- Recognition of achievement
- Conducting appraisals/personal development reviews (PDRs)
- Identification of development needs
- Providing appropriate training to meet individuals' role needs
- Retention
- Contented workforce
- Maintaining high levels of performance

Chapter headings

Introduction

Organisations are made up of people – as are the markets from which they source labour and supplies and to which they offer products and services. Most organisational functions depend on human knowledge, relationships, decisions or activity. Human beings are therefore, arguably, one of the key resources of any organisation.

Like other resources, labour must be managed. It needs to be sourced, controlled, utilised and developed with a view to key strategic objectives such as added value, distinctive competences, organisational learning/flexibility and competitive advantage. This is what human resource planning (HRP) and human resource management (HRM) are all about: a systematic approach to ensuring that the organisation has the right human resources available in the right place at the right time.

In this chapter, we will look at the role of HRM and personnel policy in meeting the current and future needs of the organisation. We will then look at systematic approaches to some of the key HR tasks – human resource planning, recruitment and selection, appraisal, and training and development – and why they are important.

1 Benefits of systematic HRM

1.1 As we noted in our introduction to this chapter, organisations are made up of people. The day-to-day management of people involves a number of task- and teamwork-related roles and functions: articulating goals, giving instructions, controlling conflict and so on. We have discussed many of these aspects of management in this Course Book.

1.2 However, there is another aspect to the management of people, arising from the broader relationship between an employer and its employees, and the 'employment lifecycle' from recruitment to exit. People are sought by the organisation; they enter into a contractual relationship with it; they are required to function within it according to certain policies and procedures; they are deployed, appraised, trained, developed, disciplined and rewarded in such a way as to meet their own changing needs and those of the organisation; and (sooner or later) they leave.

1.3 *Someone* in an organisation will have to be responsible for these matters. Traditionally, that has meant a specialised personnel function. However, 'personnel management' may also refer to those aspects of a line manager's job – in any department – which deal with the management of the employment relationship and lifecycle.

What is 'human resource management (HRM) – and why is it important?

1.4 Personnel practitioners have long argued that people are the key to an organisation's success, added value and the bottom line. *Peters and Waterman* suggested that this viewpoint was a key characteristic of excellent companies: they called it, simply, 'success through people'.

1.5 Research findings appear to back them up. 'The acquisition and development of skills (via selection, induction, training and appraisal) and job design are significant predictors of changes in both profitability and productivity. More broadly, the study concludes that – compared with, say, research and development, quality, technology and strategy – by far the most powerful indicators of future business performance are [personnel] practices.' (*People Management*, 1998)

1.6 Employees are increasingly being regarded not as a cost to be controlled, but as an asset to be nurtured and developed over time.

1.7 At the same time, the growing complexity of the social and business environment has placed HR issues at the centre of organisational objectives and concerns: quality; social responsibility; the management of change; workforce diversity; the need for flexibility; the expectations of an increasingly sophisticated marketplace. HR issues have had to be more closely integrated into the strategic plans of the organisation.

1.8 Organisations have also come to recognise the human issues of employment. Employees have not only a legal contract with their employing organisation, but a **psychological contract**. The psychological contract of employment is an unwritten set of expectations that the employer and employee have of each other: the organisation expects individuals to fulfil certain requirements in return for the rewards it offers; the individual expects to derive certain benefits from the organisation in return for his contribution. These 'terms and conditions' may never be formally or explicitly stated, but they influence the employment relationship and behaviour.

1.9 Economic recession, increased competition, automation and other factors have led to a shift in the psychological contract in recent decades.

- With the erosion of job security, promotional ladders and (in some cases) financial rewards, organisations have had to make explicit a new set of expectations and rewards: offering development/empowerment opportunities, say, in return for gains in flexibility and productivity.
- The recognition of the added value of commitment over mere compliance has led to a shift from calculative contracts (based on a transaction or exchange of effort/contribution for identifiable rewards) to cooperative contracts (where managers attempt to get employees to identify with the organisation and its goals, so they actively seek to contribute as a 'win-win' outcome).

1.10 The term 'human resource management' (HRM) reflects this new approach. *Michael Armstrong* has defined it as: 'a strategic and coherent approach to the management of an organisation's most valued assets: the people working there who individually and collectively contribute to the achievement of its objectives.'

Advantages of a strategic/systematic approach to HRM

1.11 We will look at the importance of systematic approaches to key HRM activities in the following sections of this chapter. However, the following summary should indicate the benefits of planned (rather than '*ad hoc*') personnel practices.

1.12 The general benefits of a systematic approach to HRM, based on well-defined policies and procedures, are as follows.

- It ensures **compliance** with employment legislation and regulation – on equal opportunity, health and safety, employment protection, employee involvement and so on.
- It also supports **ethical values** such as fairness and equity in dealing with people: ensuring (as far as possible) objectivity, impersonality and equal treatment in matters such as selection, pay awards and discipline and grievance handling.
- It communicates and supports the desired **culture** of the organisation. Consistent, integrated HR systems can be used to bring suitable values/attributes into the organisation (through selection), and to reinforce them (through appraisal, training and reward).
- It enables the organisation to meet its **human resource needs**, both currently and in the future – in the light of its own plans, and forecast changes and challenges in its environment. The role of human resource planning (HRP) is to ensure that the organisation has plans in place to source (from outside) and/or develop and retain (from within) the skills it needs to pursue its objectives.
- It supports the **motivation, commitment and retention** of staff, offering structured opportunities for recognition and reward (through appraisal), job satisfaction (through job design) and personal growth (through training and development). It also minimises 'hygiene' factors, which might otherwise cause dissatisfaction: ensuring fair treatment (through grievance and disciplinary procedures), fair pay (through job evaluation) and so on.
- Its core purpose is to **improve the performance** of individuals, teams and the organisation as a whole, by:

- Acquiring or developing high-calibre, job-relevant skills and competences
- Ensuring that employees are informed, involved and empowered to pursue team/organisational objectives
- Encouraging labour flexibility and versatility
- Facilitating continuous organisational learning and development, for innovation and adaptability in response to changing demands.

1.13 We will now go on to look at key HRM activities: what a systematic approach to them might look like – and what their specific benefits are.

2 Human resource planning

What is HRP – and what is it for?

2.1 The aim of human resource planning (also known as 'manpower planning') is to ensure the availability of the right quantity of the right skills at the right price and at the right time to meet the organisation's requirements. It has been defined as: 'a strategy for the acquisition, utilisation, improvement and retention of the human resources required by the enterprise in pursuit of its objectives'.

2.2 You may think this sounds unnecessarily complicated, particularly for a small or medium-sized organisation, or for an individual department such as purchasing. After all, if someone leaves – creating a 'vacancy' – you replace him. If you find you have a staff shortage, or new skill requirements arise (from the introduction of technology or legislation, say) you hire or train someone to do the job. In fact, the process is rarely so simple, particularly at the level of the organisation.

2.3 *Livy* suggested that 'Manpower planning has maintained its imperative for several reasons: (i) a growing awareness of the need to look into the future; (ii) a desire to exercise control over as many variables as possible which influence business success or failure; and (iii) the development of techniques which make such planning possible'.

2.4 Human resource planning can be seen as a form of supply management. As with any other resource, the flow of people into and through the organisation must be planned and controlled so as to meet requirements efficiently and effectively.

2.5 The scarcity of the labour resource (particularly in terms of specific skill shortages) is one of the strongest arguments for advance manpower planning. Forecasting labour requirements gives the organisation the lead time it needs to acquire skills from the labour pool (by recruitment) or to retain and develop them internally (by motivation, training, redeployment or promotion). The more complex the organisation and the job, the more difficult it may be to add or replace staff.

2.6 Likewise, if skill requirements are declining (because of new technology or business contraction, say), advance manpower planning allows the organisation the lead time it needs to retrain and redeploy people, to shed surplus labour by voluntary means (natural wastage, including retirement and staff turnover) or to give adequate notice of redundancies, as required by law and the organisation's desired image as a socially responsible employer.

2.7 The advance planning of labour supply and demand has never been an exact science – and it is, arguably, becoming increasingly difficult. Manpower planners' assumptions are constantly undermined by changes affecting labour turnover (such as the rise of temporary, part-time and freelance working), changes in the sources of labour (such as the opening of a pan-European labour market) and changes affecting skill requirements (such as the emergence of new technologies and markets).

2.8 According to *Cuming*, these are not reasons to abandon manpower planning, but to perform it flexibly. 'The environment, then, is uncertain, and so are the people whose activities are being planned. Manpower plans must therefore be accepted as being continuous, under constant review and ever-changing.'

A systematic approach to HRP

2.9 The process of HRP may be outlined as follows.

- Forecast the likely **demand** for labour (staff skills/competencies, grades, numbers). This will take into account factors such as: the objectives of the organisation; proposed expansion, contraction or diversification; current labour utilisation (ie productivity); and environmental influences which will affect demand (technology, economic recession, competition and so on).
- Forecast the likely **supply** of labour. This will take into account factors such as: the actual and potential skills and productivity of the existing workforce; likely changes in the structure and size of the existing workforce due to labour turnover (by resignation or retirement), promotion or transfer; the flexibility of the existing workforce; and the likely supply of relevant skilled labour in the external labour market (given competitor activity, demographic changes, educational trends, market rates of pay and so on).
- Prepare plans to **close the gap between demand and supply** by meeting a labour shortfall (eg by recruitment, training, retention, redeployment/flexibility, productivity or outsourcing) or reducing a labour surplus (eg by freezing recruitment, supporting labour turnover, banning overtime, redeployment or redundancy).

2.10 The outcome of human resource planning will – naturally enough – be a human resource (or manpower) plan. This should include integrated tactical plans for recruitment, training, flexible working, promotion (or management succession), productivity, retention, redundancies and so on.

2.11 Human resource decisions at the departmental level, taken within the constraints and guidelines of these plans, will therefore support the strategic requirements of the organisation as a whole. A purchasing manager will not, for example, be advertising exciting new career opportunities in his department at a time when the organisation is planning to downsize. Or watching half the department retire just as the organisation is taking on a new project. Or training staff in technology and methods which will be unsuited to organisational requirements within three years.

3 Recruitment and selection

Recruitment

3.1 Recruitment is the process by which an employer reaches out to the labour market in order to inform potential employees of opportunities in the organisation, with a view to generating interest and/or applications.

3.2 The objectives of recruitment are basically fourfold.

- To target the market in which the relevant labour resources can be found
- To attract interest in the organisation and the job, in the form of enquiries or applications
- To provide sufficient and relevant information about the organisation and the job to aid applicants in the decision of whether and how to apply
- To project a positive image of the organisation to the outside world

3.3 Recruitment may be identified as necessary in the following situations.

- The human resource plan sets out specific requirements for the recruitment of a given number and type of people (or skills) within a given timeframe.
- Labour or skills have been lost (or are expected to be lost) through retirement, resignation, temporary absence, promotion or transfer. The fulfilment of departmental objectives and the human resource plan requires that they be replaced.
- Task requirements have changed (or are expected to change) in such a way as to require a new job or job skills, as set out in the human resource plan. (Examples include the introduction of new technology, processes and organisational structures.)

In each case, note that the requirements of departmental objectives and the human resource plan should be observed: not every departing team member will automatically create a 'vacancy', for example.

3.4 There may also be alternative sources for the required skills, and these should be evaluated according to their relative benefits and costs, as well as relevant organisational policy. For example, if the required skills are available (or potentially available) in the existing workforce, internal transfer, training and/or promotion may be preferred, where possible, to external recruitment. Organisational flexibility may, on the other hand, give priority to the use of temporary, freelance or agency staff over the recruitment of permanent labour.

Selection

3.5 Selection is the process by which an employer chooses between applications, weeding out those who are unlikely to suit the job or the organisation and evaluating potentially suitable candidates in order to fulfil the required criteria.

3.6 Effective selection procedures have three main benefits for organisations.

- They make it more likely that the organisation will obtain the right skills, experience, values and attributes for the job or role. (We saw how jobs and roles were defined for this purpose, in Chapter 5.)
- They increase the likelihood that employees will stay in the job (retention) because they find a good 'fit' with job requirements and organisational culture.
- They ensure that all potential candidates are treated fairly and courteously, in line with equal opportunity law, the organisation's ethical values and its desired 'employer brand' (or reputation in the labour market).

A systematic approach to recruitment and selection

3.7 A systematic approach to this process would include the following stages.

- Human resource planning, defining the organisation's human resource requirements
- Job analysis, so that for any given job there is a job description (a concise statement of the tasks, duties, objectives and conditions of the job) and a person specification (a reworking of the job description in terms of the kind of person needed to perform the job competently)
- The identification of vacancies (from the requirements of the HR plan, the need to replace an outgoing team member, or the emergence of new task requirements)
- The authorisation and initiation of recruitment activity (perhaps using a job requisition form)
- The evaluation of alternative sources of labour: the internal and/or external labour markets; standard and/or non-standard contract labour (part-time, temporary, freelance and so on)
- The evaluation of alternative media and methods for advertising vacancies: recruitment consultancies and agencies; advertising at source (eg in schools); media advertising; the internet; informal word-of-mouth networks and so on
- Job advertisement: preparing and issuing information about vacancies and inviting applications
- The processing of applications: screening responses at the end of the application period, notifying candidates of the initial result or progress of their application, planning the selection process
- The assessment of candidates: short-listing potential candidates, conducting interviews and/or various forms of selection testing, checking references
- Follow-up: the offer of employment, notification of unsuccessful short-listed candidates, planning the induction of new recruits
- Evaluation of the whole process, to ascertain whether it has been effective (resulting in the employment of the right people and the fostering of the desired employer brand) and efficient (in a timely and cost-effective manner).

4 Appraisal

4.1 Appraisal may be defined as: 'the regular and systematic review of performance and the assessment of potential, with the aim of producing action programmes to develop both work and individuals.' Appraisals are sometimes referred to as **personal development reviews** (PDRs).

4.2 In all organisations, the performance of each employee is assessed by someone. Often this is a subjective, *ad hoc* activity carried out by the individual's immediate superior in the course of day-to-day operations. Increasingly, however, organisations are choosing to formalise the assessment and feedback process and use it in a proactive attempt to improve business performance and manage the potential of employees for ongoing skill and career development.

Purposes of appraisal

4.3 Different organisations use performance appraisal for different purposes, but the following are some of its potential uses.

- To generate and exchange feedback on individual and team performance, as information for management and to provide feedback for the learning and motivation of the employee
- To appraise past performance in relation to relevant standards in order to determine merit pay awards, or (more generally) to set salary levels for the following period
- To identify potential in the employee for career development, and the planning of management succession in the organisation
- To identify the training and development needs of the individual or team, in order to plan and subsequently evaluate appropriate programmes
- To provide a context for counselling and problem-solving, to resolve any barriers to employee performance
- To aid continuous learning, quality/service improvement and innovation: providing a context for open discussion of performance issues, and encouraging upward communication to harness employee 'front line' knowledge and commitment

4.4 Note that systematic appraisal has key advantages both for the organisation and for its management (information for performance management, development, succession planning and so on) *and* for individual employees (clarity of goals and targets, feedback for learning, reinforcement/reward for motivation, the opportunity to discuss work problems and development needs).

A systematic approach to appraisal

4.5 A typical performance appraisal system would therefore involve the following stages.

- Identification (or review) of criteria for assessment

- Preparation of an appraisal report by the appraisee's manager (and others, where appropriate eg in the case of upward, peer or 360° feedback), giving feedback on the appraisee's performance in relation to relevant assessment criteria
- An appraisal interview, allowing an exchange of views about the results of the assessment, problem solving, target-setting for improvement and so on
- Provision for review of (or appeal against) the appraisal, if required to establish the fairness of the procedure
- Preparation, agreement and implementation of action plans
- Follow-up monitoring of progress

This assessment would typically take place on an annual or six-monthly cycle.

4.6 A systematic approach to appraisal is thus a classic control system, incorporating planning, measurement of performance, comparison of performance against plan, and adjustment of performance or plan in an ongoing cycle (illustrated in Figure 12.1).

Figure 12.1 *Formal appraisal as a control cycle*

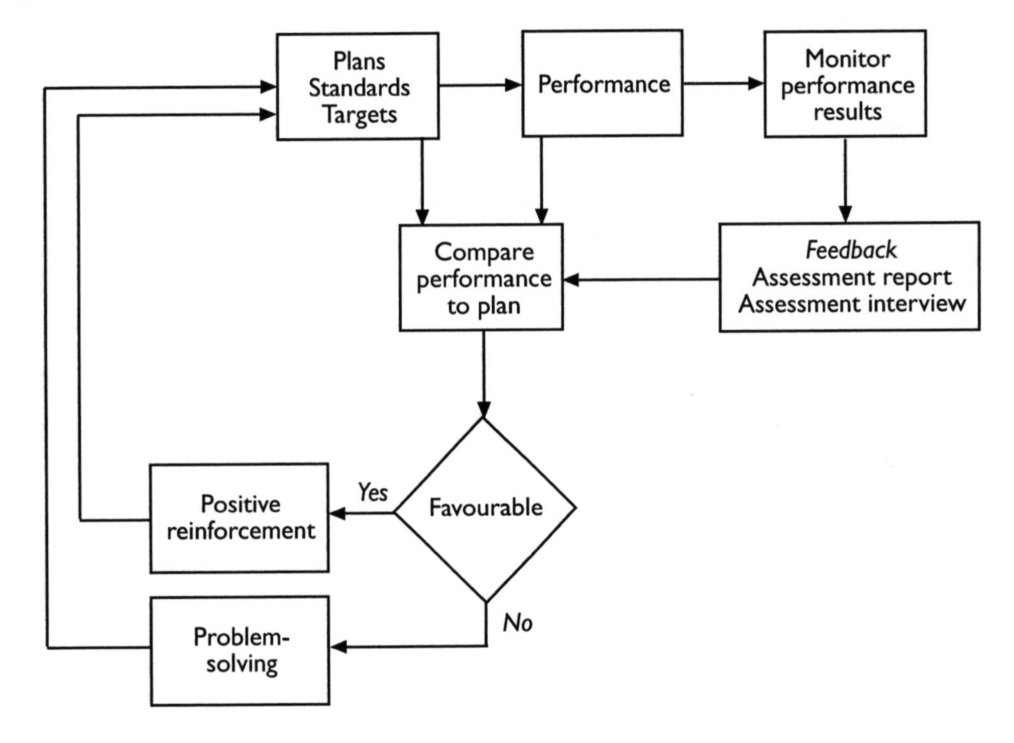

Performance management

4.7 *Connock* notes that 'In the late 1980s, the emphasis moved from performance appraisal to performance management. Whilst setting clear and measurable objectives was always a major part of earlier schemes, the emphasis was more on the appraisal of past performance. Under performance management, there is a dual emphasis: on setting key accountabilities, objectives, measures, priorities and time scales for the following review period and on appraising performance at the end of the period.'

4.8 *Armstrong* provides a useful overview of the performance management process.

'Performance management is a continuous and flexible process which involves managers and those whom they manage acting as partners within a framework which sets out how they can best work together to achieve the required results. It focuses on future performance planning and improvement rather than retrospective performance appraisal. It provides the basis for regular and frequent dialogues between managers and individuals or teams about performance and development needs.'

4.9 There are four key activities in performance management.

- Preparation of performance agreements (also known as performance contracts). These set out the individual's or team's objectives, how performance will be measured, the competencies needed to achieve the objectives and the organisation's core values.
- Preparation of performance and development plans. These set out identified performance and personal development needs in order for performance agreements to be met.
- Management of performance throughout the year. This involves the continuous process of providing feedback on performance, conducting informal progress reviews and dealing with performance problems as necessary.
- Performance reviews: taking a view of an individual's progress to date and reaching an agreement about what should be done in the future. These should be discussions, not interviews.

4.10 There are a number of advantages to a performance management orientation to appraisal. Objective-setting gives employees the security and satisfaction of both understanding their jobs and knowing exactly what is expected of them. If they are encouraged to participate in objective-setting, they are more likely to accept and 'own' (or commit to) change and improvement targets.

Giving feedback

4.11 In addition to (and as part of) these formal performance management approaches, managers have a key role in giving ongoing performance feedback to team members. Feedback may be of two broad types.

- **Motivational** feedback (praise, encouragement) is given to acknowledge, reward and encourage positive behaviour or performance by the team member. Its aim is to boost the team member's confidence.
- **Developmental** feedback (constructive criticism, coaching or counselling) is given when an area of the team member's performance requires improvement, helping the individual to identify the problem and plan for change. Its aim is to increase the team member's competence.

4.12 Some guidelines for giving constructive (developmental) feedback are as follows.

- Investigate and check your facts before offering criticism: be prepared to coach for improvement.
- Choose an appropriate time and place to give feedback; as close as possible after the event being criticised/praised; when the team member will be receptive; and ideally in private, to avoid possible embarrassment.
- Clearly explain the positive, development purpose of the feedback.
- Start with positives, where possible.
- Focus on specific behaviours, actions and results – not generalisations, exaggerations ('you always...') or personality factors: your aim is to facilitate change.
- Gain the team member's cooperation: ask him how effectively he thinks he handled a situation, and invite him to work with you to solve the problem.
- Don't tackle large issues or lots of issues all at once: facilitate 'kaizen' (continuous small-step improvements).
- Close with positive encouragement and support.

5 *Training and development*

5.1 According to the Department of Employment, training is 'the systematic development of the attitude/knowledge/skill/behaviour pattern required by an individual in order to perform adequately a given task or job'.

5.2 *Livy* suggests that 'Training is to some extent a management reaction to change (eg changes in equipment and design, methods of work, new tools and machines, control systems, or in response to changes dictated by new products, services or markets). On the other hand, training also induces change. A capable workforce will bring about new initiatives, developments and improvements – in an organic way, and of its own accord. Training is both a cause and an effect of change'.

5.3 The modern approach to human resource development can be defined as 'the process of achieving outstanding organisational performance through empowering people to achieve and give of their best'.

Purposes and benefits of effective training

5.4 There are a number of benefits of training, both to the employing organisation and to the trainee, as shown in Table 12.1.

Table 12.1 *Benefits of training*

Benefits for the trainee
• Enhanced skills/competence, offering: psychological benefits (self-esteem, security, achievement) and financial benefits (opportunities for increased performance-related rewards)
• Opportunities for career development, job enlargement, job enrichment (and potentially job satisfaction)
• Opportunities to extend own interests, skills and social contacts: meet own developmental needs and enhance employability (value in job market)
Benefits for the organisation
• Increased skills, knowledge, competence, awareness, ethics etc in workforce, offering: enhanced job performance; added value to human assets; enhanced employee commitment and contribution
• Enhanced workforce versatility and flexibility, offering: more efficient labour utilisation; better adaptation to change; more innovation
• Less need for supervision, freeing management for proactive roles (or delayering)
• Greater awareness of quality; harnessing of knowledge for improvement
• Enhanced employer brand (eg as Investors in People) to attract quality labour
• Foundation for continuous learning and improvement for competitive advantage

A systematic approach to training

5.5 Figure 12.2 depicts a systematic approach to designing training programmes.

Figure 12.2 *A systematic approach to training*

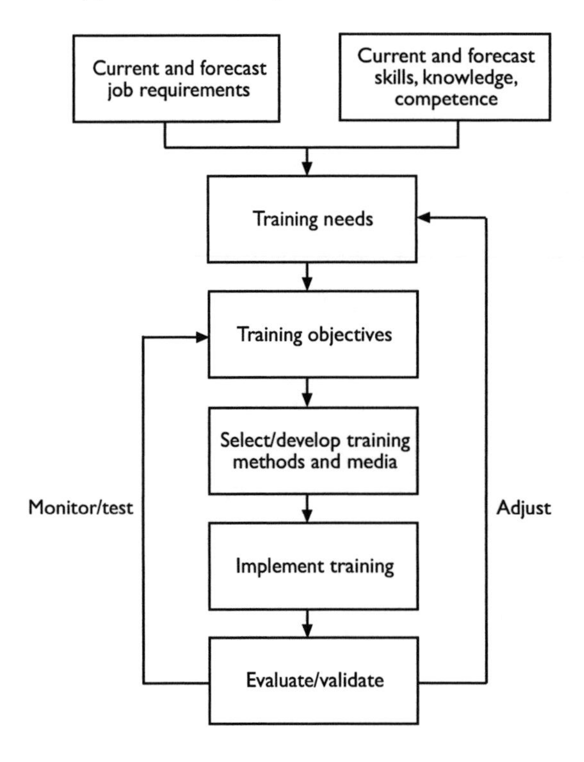

Training plans

5.6 We discussed the analysis of training needs in Chapter 5. To summarise:

- What are the skill/knowledge requirements of the project/unit plan?
- What are the current skills/knowledge of the team?
- What gaps (training or learning needs) can be identified. (Note that some performance gaps may *not* be best met by training: systems, technology, leadership resources may be the problem ...)
- What type of training will best fill the identified gaps?

5.7 A typical training plan for a business unit or function might include: the training objective (expressed as a specific, measurable, time-bounded outcome); the number of people requiring the training; the timescale or schedule for training; the method(s) chosen; resources (people, machines, space, materials) and support (authorisation, time off) required; the training budget; and how learning will be measured and assessed (post-training tests, observation/sampling of work, impact on results and so on).

Training methods

5.8 A wide variety of training methods and media are available: on-the-job (such as job instruction, coaching or job rotation) and off-the-job (such as taught classes, use of case studies and role plays, open/distance learning, visits and tours, video- or computer-based training and e-learning); formal (such as courses, planned coaching and so on) and informal (such as picking up information from reading, watching how others perform activities, or getting informal advice and feedback from co-workers or managers).

5.9 On-the-job training in the workplace is very common, especially where the work involved is not complex. Various methods may be used.

5.10 '**Sitting with Nellie**' is an approach whereby the trainee is placed beside an experienced worker (Nellie) and learns by observing her work and imitating her operations and methods, under supervision, working with the actual materials and equipment involved in the job.

5.11 **Coaching** is one element of the 'sitting with Nellie' approach, but may be used flexibly in a wide range of training situations and on an ongoing basis. Coaching is on-the-job guidance, advice, correction and teaching with a view to improving performance: it is a process of collaboration between the coach and trainee.

5.12 **Mentoring** by more senior staff includes personal and career development guidance, as well as job training. A mentor may occupy a role as the trainee's teacher/coach, counsellor, role model, supporter/sponsor in the organisation, critic and encourager, as appropriate to the situation as the trainee develops over time. A mentor should help the trainee achieve greater self-awareness; encourage him to formulate and clarify career and personal development goals; and support him in taking responsibility for his self-development.

5.13 **Experiencing different roles** may be accomplished by a number of methods.

- Job rotation or 'work shadowing': the trainee is given different jobs in succession, in order to gain wider experience.
- Temporary promotion: an individual is promoted into a superior's position while the superior is absent.
- 'Assistant to' positions: an individual with management potential may be appointed to assist or shadow a manager.
- Project or committee work: trainees might be co-opted to project teams or committees to gain experience of relevant areas of the organisation's activities, as well as multi-functional team processes and problem-solving.

5.14 The most appropriate method should be selected according to the following criteria.

- The nature of the skills/competences/knowledge to be developed (requiring theoretical knowledge or hands-on practice, say)
- The benefits of learning outside the job context (less risk; less distraction; standardisation; suits theoretical/reflective learners) or within it (relevance to the job, team and environment; better application/transfer of learning; suits 'hands-on' learners)
- The abilities and learning preferences (or 'styles') of the trainees: Honey and Mumford classify learners as theorists, reflectors, activists and pragmatists, for example
- The availability and cost-effectiveness of alternative methods.

Evaluation of training

5.15 It is important that training activities be evaluated in order to ascertain:

- whether specific training objectives have been met (and therefore whether the processes of planning and delivering training have been effective);
- whether the training intervention was 'worthwhile', representing a return on the organisation's investment;
- what improvements are required – or possible – for the future.

5.16 This process needs to be carried out at various stages of the training process: before training (to check that plans are feasible and cost-effective); during training (so that shortcomings in the plan or its delivery can be adjusted in 'real time' to improve the outcomes); and after training (to appraise its effectiveness and adjust future plans, where required).

5.17 There are a number of different criteria for evaluating training.

- Trainee reactions to the experience can be measured, using feedback forms and attitude surveys to ask trainees whether the training programme was relevant to their work and whether they found it useful. This form of monitoring is inexact and does not allow the training department to measure results for comparison against specific training objectives. However, it may help to assess more qualitative aspects of training.

- Trainee learning can be measured, using post-training competence assessment or testing, against specific training objectives.
- Changes in trainees' job behaviour or performance can also be monitored, using observation or work sampling, to measure how far learning has been transferred or applied to on-the-job tasks.
- Performance can also be monitored (at unit and organisational level) to assess the impact of training on results. Training may change attitudes to learning, mistakes, quality, ethics and so on. It may also show a knock-on influence on labour turnover, accident rates and other HR indicators.
- The costs of training should be compared to the benefits obtained. Costs will include the training establishment, training materials, the time (usually with pay) of the staff attending the training courses, their travelling expenses, the salaries or fees of training staff and so on. Benefits might be measured in terms of quicker working (reductions in overtime or staff numbers); greater accuracy of work; more extensive skills and versatility, offering labour flexibility; and enhanced job satisfaction resulting in reduced labour turnover.

Development

5.18 In every organisation, there should be a system of staff development, by which:

- Staff gain experience, which will enable them to take on more responsibility with time
- Staff are given guidance, support and counselling to help them to formulate personal and career development goals
- Staff are given suitable education, training and informal learning opportunities to develop their skills and knowledge
- Staff are facilitated in planning their future and identifying opportunities open to them in the organisation.

Chapter summary

- Human resource management is an orientation that recognises the importance of the human resource and the influence of the psychological contract between employer and employees. It is 'a strategic and coherent approach to the management of ... people'.
- A systematic approach to HRM ensures compliance; supports ethical values; creates culture; enables the organisation to meet its human resource needs; supports motivation, commitment and retention of staff; and improves the performance of individuals, teams and the organisation through effective skilling, deployment, flexibility and learning.
- Human resource planning (HRP) involves planning to close the gap between the demand for, and available supply of, skills. It includes tactical plans for recruitment, training, flexible working, succession, productivity, retention, downsizing and so on.
- Recruitment and selection are concerned with reaching and identifying the right people for organisational needs.
- Appraisal is 'the regular and systematic review of performance and the assessment of potential, with the aim of producing action programmes to develop both work and individuals'. This is typically done through annual performance review and feedback. A more proactive approach is performance management, which includes collaborative goal-setting, the agreement of performance and development plans, and on-going feedback – as well as annual reviews.
- Training is 'the systematic development of the attitudes, skills, knowledge and behaviours required by an individual to perform competently in a job'. Training (and the wider process of skill, personal and career development) offers significant benefits to the organisation and individual. A systematic approach embraces training needs analysis; selection of appropriate (on- and off-the-job, formal and informal) methods of learning; implementation of learning/training plans; and evaluation of learning.

Self-test questions

Numbers in brackets refer to paragraphs where you can check your answers

1. What is a psychological contract? (1.8)
2. How can systematic HRM improve organisation performance? (1.12)
3. Outline the process of human resource planning (HRP). (2.9)
4. Distinguish between recruitment and selection. (3.1, 3.5)
5. Outline a systematic approach to recruitment and selection. (3.7)
6. List three purposes of appraisal. (4.3)
7. Distinguish between motivational and developmental feedback. (4.11)
8. List benefits of training (a) for the individual, (b) for the organisation. (Table 12.1)
9. List three factors to be taken into account in selecting training methods. (5.14)
10. List three on-the-job and three off-the-job learning methods. (5.8)

CHAPTER 13

Managing Change

Learning objectives and indicative content

5.1 Evaluate the causes of organisational change and analyse their potential impact on the organisation

[For full indicative content, please see page xii]

5.2 Differentiate between the need for fundamental and incremental change in organisations

[For full indicative content, please see page xiii]

5.3 Formulate plans to overcome human resistance to change and to implement change successfully within the purchasing and supply function

[For full indicative content, please see page xiii]

5.6 Identify ways to monitor and control the impact of the change process on the performance of the supply chain and assess their effectiveness

[For full indicative content, please see page xiv]

5.7 Assess the importance of managing continuity of performance whilst implementing change and explain how to do this

[For full indicative content, please see page xiv]

Chapter headings

1 The nature of change

2 Causes of organisational change

3 Responses to change

4 Managing change and resistance to change

5 Models of change management

6 Monitoring the impact of change on supply chain performance

7 Managing continuity of performance through change

Introduction

We have already seen something of how changes of various kinds affect organisational structures and processes, and how management has sought to build adaptability and flexibility into organisation structures and cultures.

In this chapter, we look at the kinds of change that affect organisations – and how organisations and individuals typically respond to those changes.

We then go on to discuss how change can be effectively managed at an organisational level (by altering structures, systems and cultures) and at a personal level (by supporting employees through change).

Finally, we look at some of the models and tools that help managers to understand and manage the change process.

1 The nature of change

1.1 For some people in some organisations, change is a positive and energising thing, as the title of Tom Peter's well-known book, *Thriving on Chaos*, suggests. For others, it means loss of security, loss of competence – perhaps loss of livelihood. As someone once said: 'We're all for progress – we just don't like change'.

1.2 The fact is that in today's fast-moving business and social environment – with its technological innovation, ever-increasing competition and demographic shifts – change within organisations is inevitable.

1.3 The purchasing function, for example, has been affected by change in various ways. New production technologies and globalised markets, coupled with shorter product lifecycles, have called for corresponding changes in supply chain management. Purchasing staff have been required to adopt a more proactive stance, in which planning and liaison with other functions are key activities. Strategic concerns have largely taken over from efficient performance of administrative tasks as key performance criteria. At the same time, emphasis on processes has diminished the strength of functional boundaries: HR strategies such as horizontal and output-focused structures, empowerment and flexibility have changed the role of purchasing (along with other functions).

1.4 Some commentators have argued that change is out of control and that people are suffering from the increased pace of life and its accompanying transient relationships. Others argue that change is being introduced too slowly and that organisations, particularly in the UK, are left behind by their major competitors who embrace continuous and transformational change.

Fundamental and incremental change

1.5 *Buckly and Perkins* make a distinction between change (or incremental change) and transformation (or fundamental change). 'Change' is gradual, incremental and small, while 'transformation' is change at a fundamental level and on a significant scale.

- Organisational transformation includes major changes in job definitions, reporting lines and work structures: for example, the introduction of multi-disciplinary horizontal structures.
- Transformation in the way the system operates involves major changes in communication patterns, working relationships and processes: for example, the introduction of empowered teamworking, partnership relations with suppliers or lean supply philosophies.
- Transformation in employee consciousness involves major changes in the way that things are viewed, involving shifts in attitudes, beliefs and myths: for example, the adoption of the internal customer concept or a culture of continuous improvement (*kaizen*).

1.6 Other authors use the terminology 'evolutionary' for incremental change and 'revolutionary' for fundamental change or transformation.

1.7 **Evolutionary change** is often used as a proactive approach, building on the existing situation (the *status quo*) in small steps over a long period of time. This is the basis of business improvement strategies such as *kaizen* (continuous improvement) and total quality management: because it requires only realistic, small operational improvements, it can be implemented from the 'bottom up', involving employees through suggestion schemes, quality circles and self-improvement plans.

1.8 This makes it a particularly effective approach for building up organisational learning and core competencies: building the organisation's general responsiveness to change (such as shifting patterns of customer demand, sector dynamics and cultural change).

1.9 **Revolutionary change** is often a reactive approach, responding to 'disruptive' change, crisis or the need for a completely new paradigm. It seeks to overthrow (or throw out) the *status quo* and introduce radical transformation in a relatively short period of time. This is the basis of business improvement strategies such as Business Process Re-engineering (BPR): because it requires discontinuous and sweeping change across organisational structures and systems, it can only be implemented from the 'top down', with top management vision and leadership. Although it requires heavy investment, and some risk, it can achieve transformative improvements.

1.10 This makes it a particularly effective approach where the *status quo* has become dysfunctional for organisational survival or growth, and where sudden challenges require a radical response (such as the introduction of new technology, re-alignment of processes in response to competitive pressure, or re-structuring in response to take-overs or mergers).

1.11 *Johnson, Scholes and Whittington* also distinguish between:

- **Emergent change**: which is allowed to develop naturally, often from the bottom up, in response to environmental influences. This is a 'fluid', ongoing approach, which by definition stays 'up to date' with current developments. This approach focuses on continuous learning and responsiveness, and is suitable for organisations in fast-changing, dynamic environments.

- **Planned change**: which involves deliberately-formulated strategies and programmes for implementing change. This is said to be a 'frozen' approach, as it locks goals and plans into place for defined planning periods: while it is proactive (dealing with a forward period), it runs the risk of plans being overtaken by fast-changing events. It is primarily 'top down', driven by change sponsors and agents in the organisation. This approach is necessary for operational changes such as new product development, in order to co-ordinate all the resources and activities required.

2 Causes of organisational change

Internal triggers for change

2.1 Internal triggers for change are those factors that cause organisational disequilibrium: in order for equilibrium to be re-established, some element of the system will have to change. They may include any of the following.

- The questioning of authority, possibly leading to intra-organisational conflicts
- Poor performance: the pressure to become competitive or cut costs may stimulate a move away from old processes and procedures and towards new strategic directions
- The presence of entrepreneurs, new senior management or other innovators who act as evangelists for more modern approaches
- Changes in, or re-ordering of, organisational goals, processes and structures. Changes in the activities of the organisation may take the form of growth (organic or by acquisition), downsizing or divestment, a strategy of diversification (new products, new markets) business process re-engineering and so on.
- Favourable changes experienced in the past
- Changes in knowledge, enabling the adoption of different processes and technologies (this includes the process of learning to learn, to support continuous improvement.)

External forces for change

2.2 These internal triggers may, or may not, be related to external forces operating within the organisation's competitive ('micro') and wider ('macro') environments. Such external forces might include any of the following.

- Economic opportunities and threats, such as the opening up of new markets, economic recession or new initiatives by competitors (which must be kept pace with), and the general shift from agricultural to manufacturing to service economies.
- Changes in the demographic, psychographic, ideological or cultural characteristics of the population. These may give rise to demand for new products, or changes in customers' and employees' expectations of organisations.
- Ecological/environmental considerations, including increasing scarcity of resources and changes in consumer perceptions. These may lead a purchasing function to change its attitudes to sustainable sourcing, eco-friendly materials, pollution and waste management, for example.

- Technological developments: supporting new products and business processes, while rendering others obsolete. (We will look at these factors in detail in Chapter 15.)
- The move from a national to an international and ultimately (perhaps) to a global economy, changing corporate structures, marketing and supply chain strategies.
- Constant amendments and additions to law and regulation of business activities by the EU, national governments and other agencies and regulatory bodies. (We will look at these factors in detail in Chapter 14.)

2.3 **Globalisation** is one of the major trends in the external environment (alongside technological development, which will be discussed in Chapter 15). It has been driven by factors such as the following.

- Improvements in transport technology, creating the 'shrinking' of distance for logistics
- Improvements in ICT (including the e-commerce potential of the internet), abolishing distance for communication
- Reduction in trade barriers (eg through trading blocs and agreements), facilitating direct investment and the movement of goods and labour (eg within the European Economic Area)
- Increasing numbers of multi-national corporations (no longer necessarily large, and no longer necessarily US-based) through joint ventures and foreign direct investment
- Convergence in cultural values and consumer tastes (due to increased travel and global media), creating the potential for more global brands
- The business benefits of larger markets, economies of scale, outsourcing to low-cost-labour economies, moving beyond intense domestic competition, extending product lifecycles by introducing products to new markets and so on.

Environmental analysis

2.4 One of Mintzberg's key roles of managers (as we saw in Chapter 1) is that of 'Monitor': scanning the environment for information about changes, trends, threats and opportunities. This is one of the reasons for networking within your profession (other people are a great source of information), as well as reading and searching the internet with your eyes open!

2.5 Organisations also carry out systematic environmental monitoring and analysis, continually gathering and analysing environmental intelligence from sources such as professional/industry/trade journals and their websites; conferences and exhibitions; published reports and online databases (such as Mintel); and statistical sources such as Social Trends and the Economic & Labour Market Review (formed in 2007 from the merger of Labour Market Trends and Economic Trends); and so on. (If you are interested, you might like to browse National Statistics Online, at www.statistics.gov.uk.)

2.6 The organisation may also retain specialist consultants or advisers who have knowledge, experience and contacts relevant to a particular aspect of the environment – such as technology, law or social trends.

PESTLE and SWOT

2.7 PESTLE analysis simply involves the classification of factors in the external environment as Political, Economic, Socio-cultural, Technological, Legal and Ecological factors, as a helpful way of organising environmental data. We covered the basic principles briefly in Chapter 7: Table 13.1 draws out some of the implications for change management.

Table 13.1 *PESTLE ANALYSIS*

Factor	Description	Change management question
Political	Government influence on your industry.	What are the likely implications of changes in government policy?
Economic	Growth trends; patterns of employment, income, interest/exchange/tax rates etc.	What are the implications of changes for future demand for your products/services; future supply and cost of resources/labour?
Socio-cultural	Changing composition, attitudes, values, consumption patterns and educational standards of the population	What are the implications of changes for customer demands and expectations, and labour availability?
Techno-logical	Changing tools for design/manufacturing, information and communications etc.	What opportunities for development – or risks of obsolescence – are implied by new technologies?
Legal	Law and regulation on business, employment, information etc.	How will the organisation need to adapt its policies and practices in order to comply with forthcoming measures?
Ecological	The natural environment: resources, ecology/ sustainability, impact management, weather, 'green' pressures	Which environmental factors will impact on the industry/business, through availability of resources, logistical problems or compliance issues?

2.8 SWOT analysis is one commonly-used technique for applying environmental data to strategic planning and change management. External factors/changes are identified as potential opportunities and threats for the organisation. At the same time, internal factors are audited and analysed to identify the organisation's strengths and weaknesses – which will enable them to exploit opportunities and meet threats (and adapt to change) more or less effectively. We discussed SWOT analysis in Chapter 7, as a tool of decision-making.

3 Responses to change

Individual attitudes to change

3.1 Changes may affect individuals in many different ways: physically (eg different shift patterns or work methods); circumstantially (eg relocations, re-establishing work relationships with a new team); and psychologically (eg the requirement to learn new skills). Change may create feelings of disorientation, insecurity, fear of loss of competence and so on.

Conditions favouring change in organisations

3.2 We most often hear about 'resistance to change' (and we will consider, below, how it can be overcome), but organisations can also create conditions that are favourable to the acceptance – or even welcoming – of change.

- Financial viability and stability: insecurity is a prime source of resistance. (However, it may also be argued that change is more readily complied with when it is perceived to be a necessity for survival.)
- Adaptable (or 'organic') organisation structures: task- or output-focused (rather than process or job-description focused); flexible (eg temporary, multi-skilled); and 'horizontal' (eg networked and team-based, facilitating co-operation and communication across 'vertical' barriers of departments and specialisms).
- Good multi-directional communication systems, and systems for formal and informal negotiation and consultation.
- Vision, leadership and support from senior management: setting clear goals for, and benefits of, change – and modelling the flexibility of attitude and practice required to achieve it.
- Supporting HR systems and procedures: selection, training, appraisal and reward systems which reinforce flexibility and willingness to change as a cultural value.
- Supportive culture and attitudes: trust between management and staff; receptivity to new ideas, learning and information-sharing; tolerance of mistakes and shortfalls in the process of learning; and flexibility. These attributes are all broadly characteristic of a 'learning organisation'.

Resistance to change

3.3 Organisations often talk about 'resistance to change', but resistance may be directed more against the change strategy (the method of introducing and implementing the change) or the change agent (the person charged with introducing the change) than against the change itself.

3.4 Resistance (like other forms of conflict discussed in Chapter 11) may be welcomed as a form of feedback from those affected by change to those managing it: it can be used constructively to modify the change strategy.

Sources of resistance to change

3.5 *Arthur Bedeian* cites four common sources of resistance to change.

- Parochial self-interest: individuals or groups have a vested interest in maintaining the *status quo*. They may feel that there is a threat to established ways of working (and therefore to their sense of competence); to existing social arrangements and relationships (eg breaking up a work team); to health and safety (eg introducing new machinery, or shift working); or to earnings (eg changes to the way in which bonuses are calculated). In the extreme case, they may fear that their role may disappear.
- Misunderstanding and lack of trust: people do not understand the reasons for change, or its likely consequences, and therefore resist to minimise the perceived risks.

- Contradictory assessments: people's perceptions of the nature and likely consequences of change differ from the information being given by change agents or supports. This may be aggravated where change is imposed. (Bedeian points out that contradictory assessment, in particular, can lead to constructive criticism and improved proposals for change.)
- Low tolerance of change: individuals feel insecure in the face of uncertainty. This may take the form of self-doubt ('Will I be able to cope with the changes?'), overwhelm (if change is introduced too quickly) or exhaustion (if change is constant, without time to consolidate and regroup) even where the benefits of change in general are recognised. Low tolerance of change also exists in organisation cultures: eg bureaucracies are highly resistant to change, as they depend on roles and rules and attract security-seeking kinds of people.

The coping cycle

3.6 An influential approach to understanding how people cope with change is based on *Elizabeth Kubler-Ross's* theory of how we respond to grief and loss: all change involves 'mourning' a *status quo* that is passing away, and learning to live with a new set of circumstances. Kubler-Ross suggested that we typically move through a number of stages.

- Denial: unwillingness to recognise or confront the reality of the loss or change
- Anger: blaming the people or circumstances perceived to be responsible
- Bargaining: attempting to negotiate to reverse or mitigate the loss or change
- Depression: experiencing the sadness of the reality
- Acceptance: coming to terms with the new situation and its implications, in order to move on.

3.7 The stages of the coping cycle can be plotted on a **transition (or change) curve**, depicting the highs and lows of emotional energy and/or competence development (as in a learning curve) through the period of transition: Figure 13.1.

Figure 13.1 *Transition curve*

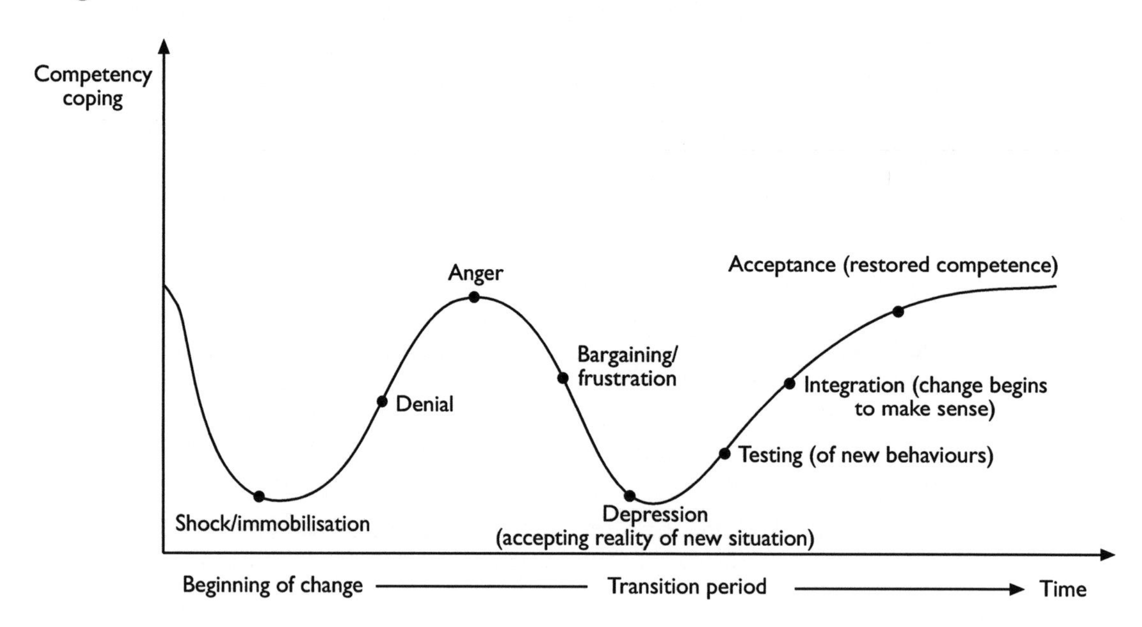

3.8 This is a general model. Individuals may get 'stuck' at different stages of the cycle, spend more time in some stages than others, and skip or revisit stages. The model is useful, however, in helping managers to understand responses to change – and to facilitate passage through the stages.

The dynamics of change

3.9 Another influential approach to understanding the dynamics of change is *Kurt Lewin*'s **force field analysis**. This model recognises that at any time in an organisation there exist both forces for change (pushing towards a preferred state) and forces for maintaining the *status quo* (pushing back towards the way things are). It is the interplay of these forces that determines the current state of the organisation and the pace and direction of change at any given moment.

3.10 Force field analysis suggests a method of visualising or mapping the forces for and against change using directional arrows, the thickness of which represent the strength of each force. As an example of this, consider an organisation seeking to introduce a system of performance review: Figure 13.2.

Figure 13.2 *Force field analysis*

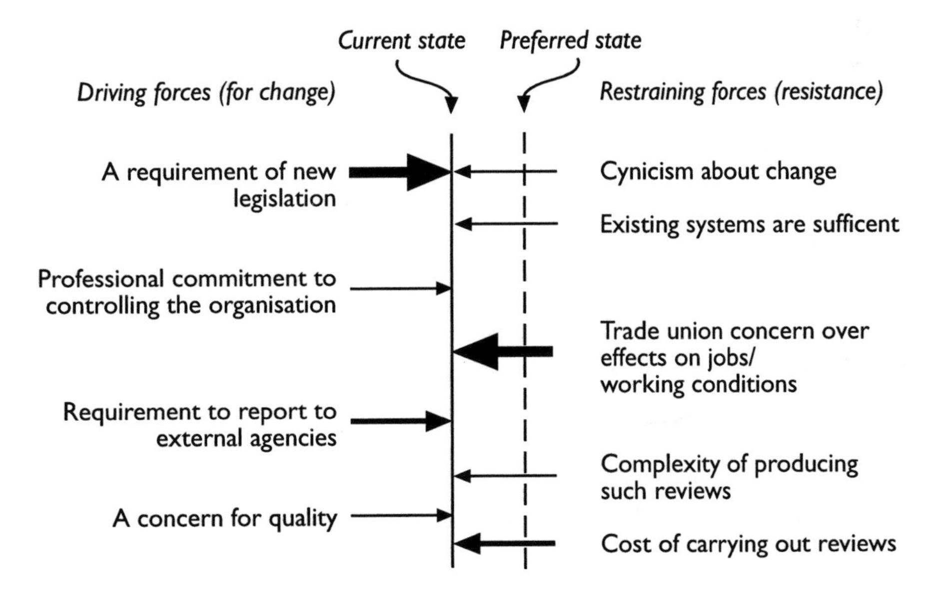

3.11 The force field model suggests that to implement change, managers should first understand the forces for and against change, and the strength of each: they should then concentrate either on strengthening the forces for change, or weakening the forces opposed to change, or both.

- Driving forces can be strengthened, for example, by co-opting people associated with them to educate their opponents.
- Restraining forces can be weakened by participation (involving resistors in diagnosing and solving the problem), education and communication (persuading resistors of the need for change), coercion (applying power to silence resistors) or negotiation (offering concessions to buy resistors off).

4 Managing change and resistance to change

4.1 While change can never be fully planned, many organisations are recognising the need to adopt a positive and proactive attitude to change. Part of the impetus behind moves towards more flexible organisational structures and cultures is the desire to minimise the trauma of change and to embrace its competitive advantages.

4.2 There are five widely-recognised change management strategies (*Kotter and Schlesinger*).

- Participation
- Education and communication
- Facilitation and support
- Power/coercion
- Negotiation

We will look at each of these in turn.

Participation

4.3 Employees are considered more likely to support changes if they are encouraged to 'own' them through having participated in the decision-making process. Quite apart from the advantages of enhanced commitment to change, participation may allow better quality decision-making by taking advantage of employees' expertise and knowledge in relevant areas.

4.4 Classic studies by *Coch and French* demonstrated the effectiveness of a participative approach in overcoming resistance to change. Changes were introduced in three production groups in a pyjama factory which had been experiencing resistance due to perceived loss of status and earnings.

- The non-participative group was informed about the change but not involved in the decision making. Resistance was immediate: conflict flared, efficiency remained low, and some members left.
- The representative group was given a hand in the change to the extent that after a preliminary meeting of explanation, representatives were given appropriate training and subsequently trained fellow members. The group was cooperative and submissive, and efficiency rose rapidly.
- The total participation group also had a preliminary meeting, but all members then took part in the design and standard setting for the new job. The group recovered its efficiency rating very rapidly, and then increased it to a level much higher than before the change, without conflict or resignations.

4.5 There are, however, some recognised drawbacks to a participative approach. It can be a lengthy process, particularly if consensus is sought, and a strong relationship of trust must exist between management and workforce if participation is to be genuine and effective. Where participation is genuine, management may be unacceptably constrained by resistance due to the contradictory assessment of change by workers.

Education and communication

4.6 This strategy relies on the belief that communication about the need for change, and its benefits, can be used to persuade employees to accept the change programme. Management's viewpoint may need support from a perceivedly neutral source (eg external consultants) in order to be persuasive, and this may be time-consuming. However, the benefits of clear communication are that it dispels unnecessary fears, gives employees some sense of control (reducing insecurity), and reduces the potential for demotivating rumours.

Facilitation and support

4.7 The change manager reassures those affected that they will be helped to develop the necessary skills and will be given the necessary resources to achieve the change.

- **Facilitation** involves assisting employees to change (with training, coaching, resources or extra staffing, say).
- **Support** involves helping employees to come to terms with the change psychologically – eg through counselling about change issues and help with coping (eg in the case of redundancy or relocation).

4.8 Although this process can be time-consuming and costly, it reduces fears of loss of competence and security, and demonstrates management's commitment to supporting employees through the change – and it may also be necessary to enable the change itself (eg through retraining employees). It is important that reassurances are actually followed through, otherwise it will be perceived as attempted manipulation.

Power/coercion

4.9 This strategy involves the application of power, according to the managerial prerogative, to enforce change. Despite the prevalence of more 'enlightened' HR approaches, coercion may be effective in certain contexts, such as:

- traditional command-and-control organisation cultures, where participation and consultation are not expected;
- situations of crisis change, where employees expect management to show 'strong leadership' swiftly in response to threats to the organisation's survival;
- labour markets characterised by high unemployment, in which the managerial prerogative is supported by the desire for job security;
- highly automated and programmed work, where compliance is sufficient to secure adequate performance, without seeking employee commitment.

4.10 The advantage of such an approach is that change decisions can be made and implemented with speed, as may be required by a crisis situation. Its disadvantages are that coercive changes may (at best) secure mere compliance, where commitment has greater power to harness the positive energies and efforts of the human resource. A coercive approach basically fails to address resistance, and makes employees feel powerless in the face of potentially threatening changes. Even if they are unable directly to prevent the implementation of changes, resistance and negative power may emerge in low morale, employee absenteeism or turnover, work-to-rules, industrial disputes, sabotage and so on.

Negotiation

4.11 A negotiation strategy may be required where resistance groups have considerable power: for example, where the workforce is represented by recognised trade unions. Opposing interest groups bargain towards an agreement based on compromise. Negotiation may be based on adversarial/win-lose or partnership/win-win bargaining strategies (discussed as an approach to conflict management in Chapter 11): this will obviously influence the approach to change.

4.12 The main advantage of a negotiation strategy is that (ideally) it allows conflicts of interest to be acknowledged and taken into account in a systematic fashion. If a win-win outcome can be reached, this may encourage commitment and enhance morale. The main disadvantage is that negotiation can polarise opposing positions, in order to allow for eventual compromise: this may be unnecessarily time-consuming and adversarial in style.

Attributes of a successful change agent

4.13 In addition to organisational and cultural conditions supporting change, the success of a change programme depends to a large extent on the attributes and skills of the change agent or champion. The key attributes of a successful change agent may, in part, be identified with the key attributes of 'leaders', since modern models of leadership emphasise their role as drivers of change (eg *Kotter, Burns*).

- **Vision**. Change agents must be able to visualise where the organisation needs to be, and what it needs to look like, in order to be able to articulate the vision and goals to other stakeholders in a concrete and inspiring way.
- **Team building and management skills**. Change programmes cannot be driven or completed single-handed. If only in order to co-opt key stakeholders and influencers into the process, the change agent will need to be able to select, build and manage teams for planning and implementing change. This includes a range of interpersonal skills, for managing team relationships and communication, but also managerial skills – for example in order to delegate effectively.
- **Interpersonal skills**. Successful change management requires extensive interpersonal communication and skills in areas such as articulating goals and values, in order to motivate change; influencing, persuading and negotiating, in order to change attitudes; assertiveness and conflict resolution, in order to confront resistance and opposition; supportive communication and counselling, in order to address fears and insecurities.
- **Personal flexibility**. Change managers must themselves be open to challenge, uncertainty, ambiguity and risk, in order to set an example and convince others of the benefits of change. Innovative approaches may be required as part of the change programme. Setbacks and mistakes, inevitable in the early stages of change, should be regarded as learning opportunities and useful feedback – not as 'failures', either by the change agent or by the affected employees.
- **Commitment, perseverance and stamina**. A change programme is typically a long-term project, and the energy must be kept up throughout. Setbacks must be overcome and not allowed to derail the process. A positive outlook, and deep commitment to the organisation's future, are required to maintain focus and momentum.

5 Models of change management

The three-stage ('unfreeze-refreeze') model

5.1 *Lewin and Schein* further developed the force field model, to draw up a three-step model for changing human behaviour: Figure 13.3.

Figure 13.3: *The three-step model of change*

5.2 **Unfreeze** is the most difficult (and in many cases neglected) stage of the process, concerned mainly with 'selling' and motivating the change. It involves addressing and responding to resistance; communicating the need for, and the benefits and feasibility of, change; and offering incentives and rewards for compliance or co-operation. If the need for change is immediate, clear and perceived to be associated with the survival of the individual or group (for example, change in reaction to an organisational crisis) the unfreeze stage will be greatly accelerated.

5.3 **Change** is the second stage, mainly concerned with identifying what the new, desirable behaviour or norm should be, communicating it and encouraging individuals and groups to 'own' the new attitude or behaviour. To be successful, the new ideas must be shown to be workable and effective.

5.4 **Refreeze** is the final stage, implying consolidation or reinforcement of the new behaviour. Positive and/or negative reinforcement may be used, together with coaching and training, and the alteration of policies and procedures.

5.5 It is worth noting that this model is less applicable in fast-changing or turbulent business environments, where 'freezing' may be seen as counter-productive, hampering flexibility and responsiveness. Writers such as *Tom Peters* suggest that organisations must exist in a constant state of unfreezing and changing, without 'rehardening' policies, procedures and practices.

N-step change models

5.6 There are a number of change management approaches based on the concept of a phased project management structure: 'n' sequential steps or phases to implement change. Change guru *John Kotter* (1995), for example, proposes an eight step model for major or transformational change (cited in *Huczynski & Buchanan*).

Step 1 Establish a sense of urgency
Step 2 Form a guiding coalition
Step 3 Create a vision for change
Step 4 Communicate the vision
Step 5 Empower people to act on the vision
Step 6 Create 'short-term wins'
Step 7 Consolidate improvements to produce further change
Step 8 Institutionalise new approaches (embed in culture, procedures, HR systems)

6 Monitoring the impact of change on supply chain performance

Assessing impact: a multi-level framework

6.1 Table 13.2 provides a useful framework for looking at the **evaluation of change**.

Table 13.2 *A framework for assessing the impact of change*

Level	Evaluation of ...	Monitoring/measurement methodologies
1	***Reactions*** How far are stakeholders satisfied with the programme?	Employee (and other stakeholder) attitude surveys; focus groups; feedback gathering
2	***Outcomes*** Have programme objectives and targets been met?	Budgets and budgetary control; project measurements
3	***Behaviour*** Have people changed their behaviours as a result of the programme?	Observation; feedback; work sampling
4	***Results*** Is the change reflected in unit or business performance and results (and wider stakeholder benefits)?	Benchmarking; auditing

6.2 We will look at some of these **control mechanisms** in turn.

Employee and stakeholder feedback

6.3 Feedback can be sought on employee and other stakeholder reactions to change, using various mechanisms.

- Formal attitude surveys may be distributed (or accessed online) to measure responses.
- Individual and group feedback may be sought using discussion forums such as focus groups, change/quality circles, team meetings and so on.
- Specific feedback/appraisal forms or interviews may be used for a given change project. (Structural change may involve downsizing, for example, in which case exit interviews with redundant staff might be used to gauge attitudes to the handling of the change. Employee performance appraisals and developmental discussions might be used for the same purpose.)
- Informal feedback may be gathered in the course of networking, communication and business dealings with stakeholders.

Budgetary control

6.4 A budget is a plan expressed in monetary terms. It is prepared and approved prior to the budget period and may show income, expenditure and the capital to be employed.

6.5 Budgets are plans expressed in financial and/or quantitative terms either for the whole of a business or for the various parts of a business for a specified period of time in the future. The budgets are prepared within the framework of objectives and policies that have been determined by senior management as part of its own planning activities.

6.6 In general, budgets are set for specific periods of time in the future, for example the budget for the coming year. Sometimes budgets are constructed for specific projects that are to be undertaken, but again these can be analysed into the periods of time that the projects are expected to last. Thus, if a project is planned to last two years, the total budget for it can be split into that relating to the first year and that relating to the second year.

6.7 Essentially the budgetary control process consists of two distinct elements.

- Planning. This involves setting the various budgets for the appropriate future period. Managers at the various levels in an organisation should be involved in the budgetary planning stage for their own areas of responsibility. In many medium and large businesses this activity can take a considerable amount of time. There is a need to coordinate the budgets of the various parts of a business to ensure that they are vertically and horizontally aligned.
- Control. This involves comparison of the budget with the actual results achieved for the appropriate period. Significant divergences between the budgeted and the actual results should be reported to the appropriate managers so that the necessary action can be taken.

6.8 The benefits of budgetary control for change projects are numerous.

- Budgetary control provides a formal framework for planning: problems are anticipated and steps taken to avoid or reduce them. Knowing what the change programme aims to achieve in terms of costs and revenues, management has a formal set of objectives to work towards: a form of management by objectives.
- Approval of the master budget explicitly authorises the policy represented by the budget. This enables the responsibility for carrying out the policy to be delegated to participants.
- The budget represents a target against which the performance of change managers can be assessed.
- Preparing budgets involves communication between stakeholders and participating functions, which may have other benefits for problem-solving and relationship-building.
- Budgetary control focuses managerial attention where it is most needed: eg where there are major differences between budgeted and actual performance. Areas of the change programme which are proceeding according to plan need not be subjected to unnecessary scrutiny.

Project control measures

6.9 Project management includes a structure of reports and meetings for measuring progress and securing stakeholder agreement: the project initiation meeting, end stage assessments, highlight reports, checkpoints and so on.

6.10 Techniques such as project budgets, Gantt charts and network analysis (or critical path analysis, CPA) can be used to monitor progress against specific cost and schedule criteria. Complex project management software (such as Microsoft Project) may be used to co-ordinate planning, track progress and report data.

6.11 There are further opportunities for feedback gathering and reporting at the end of each project or programme of change. The project manager should produce a completion report, summarising the project objectives and outcomes achieved; budget and schedule variances; and any ongoing issues or unfinished business (and how these will be followed up).

Audits

6.12 A post-completion audit is often used as a formal review of a change programme or project, in order to assess its impact and ensure that any lessons arising from it are acknowledged and learned. Such an audit may be carried out using a survey questionnaire of all project team members and key stakeholders, or meetings to discuss what went well and what didn't. The focus of a post-completion audit (and resulting audit report) is:

- Assessing whether and how far the project outcomes met the expectations of the sponsor and other stakeholders: were the deliverables up to standard, were they achieved on time and within budget and so on?
- Assessing the effectiveness of the management of the process: the effectiveness of the plans and structures set up for the project; the performance of individuals and teams; what problems (communication lapses, conflicts, errors, delays) might affect similar projects in future, and how they can be avoided.

6.13 In addition, an audit may be carried out to measure purchasing performance, and compare key performance indicators against previous measures, to assess the impact of the change. Some common quantifiable performance metrics for purchasing are shown in Table 13.3 (repeated for convenience from Chapter 8): you might like to think through how each would be a relevant measure for a particular change project.

Table 13.3 *Performance metrics for purchasing*

Efficiency metrics	
Cost	Procurement cost as a % of spend
Staffing	Staff per £million of spend; labour cost per employee
Productivity	Purchase orders/material receipts per employee Cost per purchase order/receipt
Technology leverage	Technology cost as a % of procurement cost % of purchase orders, RFIs/RFPs/RFQs communicated electronically
Cycle time	Hours required to complete a requisition and purchase order
Standardisation	Use of company-wide policies, commodity codes

Effectiveness metrics	
Cost savings	Annual cost savings as a % of spend
Supplier leverage	Number of suppliers per £x of spend % of suppliers providing 80% or more of the annual spend % of purchases made from preferred suppliers
Error rates	% of transactions requiring correction after process
Customer satisfaction	% of deliveries received in full and on time (IFOT)
Partnering	Procurement control over material/goods spend Cross-functional teams in supplier development, sourcing, negotiation Use of scoring models for suppliers
Strategic alignment	Visibility of a formal documented procurement strategy Percentage of objectives linked to business strategy % of procurement time spent on global/enterprise-wide focus

6.14 *Van Weele* also points out that different performance measures will be used, depending on the role of the purchasing function in the organisation. If its role is perceived as primarily administrative, measures such as lead times, productivity and error rates may be used. If its role is primarily commercial, cost savings will be a priority. At a more strategic level, from a supply chain perspective, emphasis will shift to higher measures such as strategic alignment, partnering, supplier leverage and so on.

Benchmarking

6.15 Benchmarking is a continuous process of measuring products, services and practices against models of best practice and/or competitor practice. It encourages organisations and units continually to define and emulate best practice in their field, but can also be used as a yardstick for measuring progress *towards* best practice objectives, as part of the process of controlling change programmes.

6.16 *Bendell, Boulter and Kelly* distinguish four types of benchmarking.

- Internal benchmarking: comparison with high-performing units in the same organisation. For example, a divisional purchasing function might be benchmarked against the purchasing function in another division, to lift standards and consistency within the organisation.
- Competitor benchmarking: direct comparison with high-performing competitors in key areas which impact on performance (eg Xerox comparing its product reliability, delivery lead times or time-to-market of innovations with Canon's).
- Functional benchmarking: comparison with a similar function in another, high-performing (but not directly competing) organisation. For example, an electronics manufacturer might benchmark its purchasing function against that of a construction company which is known for effective materials management.
- Generic benchmarking: comparison of business processes across functional boundaries and industries. For example, benchmarking against 'excellent' companies, learning organisations – or exemplars of whatever attribute the organisation is interested in pursuing.

6.17 Benchmarking allows the impacts of change to be measured using a set of objective, systematic and performance-relevant criteria. It sets performance targets and quality standards which are realistic (since other organisations have achieved them) yet challenging (since the benchmarking organisation has not yet achieved them): the most effective combination for maintaining motivation.

6.18 At the same time, benchmarking helpfully stimulates more research and feedback-seeking into customer needs and wants. Even if no specific areas for improvement are identified from the direct comparison, this may lead to useful insights for learning and innovation. Benchmarking also generates new ideas and insights outside the box of the organisation's accustomed ways of thinking and doing things. Proponents of the learning organisation identify benchmarking as an important technique which they identify as SIS: 'steal ideas shamelessly!'

6.19 The process of benchmarking has not always been easy, because of the restricted information available about organisational processes and practices (particularly among competitors). However, as the increase in inter-organisational networks (such as supply chains) has developed, considerable resources have developed to support benchmarking, including online clubs and networks.

Stakeholder communication programmes

6.20 In general, the change leader will need to set up appropriate programmes for communication with relevant primary and secondary stakeholders. Changes in purchasing policy and practice, for example, will have to be communicated not only to those directly involved in the change (such as suppliers, outsource companies, logistics providers, product designers or production planners), but also to third parties affected by them: cost analysts, line managers with responsibility for purchasing in their units, marketing staff, accountants, legal advisers – and so on. (They in turn may have responsibility for communicating the relevant implications of the changes to customers, government bodies, interest groups and other external stakeholders.)

7 *Managing continuity of performance through change*

The importance of maintaining business as usual

7.1 The key responsibility of the purchasing and supply function is to maintain continuity of supply: reliable flow of the right materials at the right price to the right place at the right time. It should be obvious that continuity and reliability of supply takes precedence over the implementation of change: there should be no 'interruption to normal services' while a new computer system suffers teething troubles or staff undergo training, or in the transfer of business from one supplier to another.

Internal handovers

7.2 At a certain point, a change project must become business as usual for its stakeholders. There will be a handover from the change/project team to the operational team which will use and apply the new strategy, system or procedures. This process will be easier if representatives of user groups have been involved in the planning and implementation stages, through stakeholder communication and involvement.

7.3 Additional measures to ensure a smooth transition may include the following.

- Clear lines of responsibility for implementing and following up the change: the change agent should work closely with the operational manager who will assume responsibility for bedding in the change
- Briefing for all relevant staff on the changes to be implemented
- Comprehensive documentation of new policies, systems and procedures: user manuals, policy statements, procedure flow charts and so on. Ideally, these should be developed in collaboration with users, so that questions can be addressed and documentation designed for ease of user understanding.
- Initial education and training of users. Training needs are likely to be significant in the case of new systems or major changes to job specifications and skill requirements.
- Acceptance testing. Users should, if possible, be given the chance to operate the new system, and to report on how far it meets their needs and how its results compare with old methods and with the stated deliverables of the change project. The system can then be adjusted, if necessary, prior to acceptance and full implementation.
- Mechanisms for follow-up, support and assistance, where needed: for example, project team members may mentor, coach or 'buddy' with users; technical support services may be available on an ongoing basis (eg for the introduction of new IT systems) or during the initial period.

7.4 For some change projects (such as the introduction of new technology or systems), there may also be plans for phased implementation, to minimise the risks of teething troubles and to allow time to embed and adjust the system.

- **Direct changeover** is a comparatively simple, but risky, approach, where an old system is completely replaced by a new system in one step. It may be the appropriate solution where two systems are very different. New systems are often introduced during down time – such as a bank holiday weekend or business closure – to minimise disruption.
- A less risky approach is to use **phased (or incremental) implementation**, where one discrete change (or part of the overall change programme) is made and bedded in before moving on to the next: changes may be made to one process, product category or supplier at a time, say.
- **Parallel running** allows old and new systems to be run in parallel for a period of time. Results can be cross checked, to evaluate the new system, and the risks of disruption are minimised, as the old system provides a back-up. Parallel running will have to be carefully planned to avoid confusion and inefficiency.
- **Pilot programmes** may be used in selected units of the organisation, or for selected suppliers, so that the new systems can be tested live (or online) while limiting the risk of disruption in the event of problems. This allows bugs to be ironed out and gives users practice in the new system: staff involved in the pilot programme can then be used to coach others.

Supplier implementation programmes

7.5 The adoption of a new supplier, or the replacement of one supplier with another, represents a significant change where the product or service supplied is important to the buying organisation or where the supply contract represents significant expenditure. There are a number of key issues, which should be familiar to you from your studies in *Developing Contracts* and other modules.

- Negotiation and preparation of product/service specifications, service level agreements and supply contracts, so that there is clear understanding of the expectations of both parties and how the relationship between them will be managed (in terms of communication and collaboration, quality and performance management, dispute resolution and so on).
- The contract should include a negotiated transition plan, detailing the risks and responsibilities of both parties in the changeover process, including the identification and ironing out of unforeseen problems or issues. There should also be provision for **acceptance testing** (measuring the quality/service provided against requirements specifications) prior to adoption of the contract, perhaps during a trial period or pilot programme.
- Readiness of stakeholders, systems and infrastructure for the implementation of the new contract. Buying and supplying organisations must have plans, controls, systems and resources in place to handle the logistics, inventory, quality and other operational implications of the contract. Staff in both organisations need to be aware of the new relationship and their responsibilities within it. Customers may need to be made aware of any implications for quality or delivery.
- Different changeover approaches may be used. A trial period or pilot programme, for example, allows buyer and supplier organisations to test their readiness, identify issues and iron out problems prior to acceptance or full implementation. Direct or phased implementation may be used, depending on whether there are discrete sub-sets of the service that can be phased in incrementally. Some variation of parallel running may be used, where the outgoing supplier's activity is progressively reduced or 'ramped down' while the incoming supplier's is 'ramped up'. A ramp-up/ramp-down phase gives all parties a chance to adjust with minimal disruption (and the chance to measure the new supplier's performance against the old).
- Contract management and review, to ensure that: co-operative working relationships are built with the new supplier; shortfalls on agreed specifications or service levels are followed up; any changes to contract terms are systematically documented and managed; and continuous improvements are built into supplier performance over time. (This will be particularly important for outsourced services, in order to retain control over the activity.)

Maintaining performance from 'outgoing' suppliers

7.6 In any change of supplier, there is a risk that the current supplier may attempt to disrupt the transfer of business to new suppliers for a new contract period, or may simply lose motivation to provide the required service levels.

7.7 Constructive relationship management should underpin any change in supplier. The buying organisation may offer the outgoing supplier helpful feedback on the reasons for non-renewal (enabling it to plan improvements). Where possible, the door should be left open for renewal of the relationship in future: the contract may be revisited at the end of the contract period, for example, or there may be new contracts for which the supplier will be invited to bid.

7.8 Additional incentives may be used, in the form of loyalty or performance-related bonuses or positive supplier rating, to motivate the supplier to provide quality service right to the end of the existing contract.

7.9 Where necessary, however, sanctions may be applied to enforce the terms of the contract and service level agreement for the full duration of the contract. Model contracts often include clauses to ensure smooth transition, so that any disruption caused by the outgoing supplier is interpreted as breach of contract, opening them to legal damages. An example of such a clause may be as follows.

The Supplier shall co-operate fully with the Buyer during the handover arising from the completion or earlier termination of the Contract. This co-operation, during the setting up operations period of the new Supplier, shall extend to allowing full access to, and providing copies of, all documents, reports, summaries and other information necessary in order to achieve effective transition without disruption to routine operations.

Chapter summary

- Change is a feature of organisational life. It may be planned (deliberate goal-oriented programmes for change) or emergent (responding at need to environmental pressures). It may be incremental/evolutionary (continuous, small-step, bottom up) or transformational/revolutionary (radical, discontinuous, fundamental, large-scale).
- Organisation change may be driven by internal triggers (causing disequilibrium or challenges) and/or external forces in the environment (which can be analysed using a PESTLE framework). They include competition, growth/diversification strategies, performance problems, globalisation, technological and legal developments and so on.
- A culture and conditions supportive of change can be created through: leadership vision; trust; organisational learning; adaptable/flexible structures; multi-directional communication; and adequate resourcing.
- Resistance to change can be classified under four general causes: self-interest (resistance to loss of or threat to the benefits of the *status quo*); misunderstanding or lack of trust; contradictory assessment of the need for change; and low tolerance/flexibility.
- Models for understanding the dynamics of change include: Kubler Ross's coping cycle and the transition/change curve; and Lewin's force field analysis (driving forces and restraining forces).
- Models for managing change include: five strategies (participation, education/communication, facilitation/support, power/coercion and negotiation); Lewin and Schein's three step ('unfreeze-change-refreeze') model; and Kotter's eight step major change model.
- The impact of change programmes can be monitored at various levels including: stakeholder satisfaction (using attitude surveys and other feedback mechanisms); outcomes (measured against target deliverables, eg by budgetary control and project measurements); behaviour and results (using benchmarking and auditing of appropriate performance measures).
- The key responsibility of the purchasing function is to maintain continuity of supply: the implementation of change must be planned to minimise risks and disruptions.
- In internal handover from the change/project team to the operational team, transitional arrangements may include: leader coaching, team briefing, training, documentation, acceptance testing and support/assistance.
- Various transitional approaches may be used, including: direct changeover, phased (or incremental) implementation, parallel running and pilot/trial programmes.
- The adoption of a new supplier represents a significant change where the product/service is important to the buying organisation or where the supply contract represents significant expenditure. Supplier implementation programmes require detailed attention to: contract development; transition planning; acceptance testing; systems/staff/stakeholder readiness (eg using trial/pilot periods or ramp-up/ramp-down phases); and contract management and review.
- Outgoing suppliers may need to be carefully managed and motivated (using positive incentives and negative sanctions) to fulfil their contract obligations.

Self-test questions

Numbers in brackets refer to paragraphs where you can check your answers

1 Distinguish between evolutionary and revolutionary change. (1.7, 1.9)

2 What is 'emergent' change and why may it be a beneficial approach? (1.11)

3 List three internal and three external drivers of change. (2.1, 2.2)

4 What factors have contributed to globalisation? (2.3)

5 What kinds of organisation structure support change? (3.2)

6 How can self-interest cause resistance to change? (3.5)

7 Explain the coping cycle. (3.6)

8 Distinguish between driving forces and restraining forces. (3.9)

9 Distinguish between facilitation and support. (4.7)

10 Explain the 'unfreeze' and 'refreeze' stages of change. (5.2, 5.4)

11 Identify three ways in which stakeholder feedback may be gathered in order to monitor the impact of change. (6.3)

12 Explain the process of budgetary control. (6.7)

13 List ten performance measures for purchasing. (Table 13.3)

14 Explain the four different types of benchmarking. (6.16)

15 Outline a process for internal handover of a change project to operational users. (7.3)

16 What is (a) phased implementation and (b) parallel running? (7.4)

17 What is the role of (a) acceptance testing and (b) contract management in supplier implementation? (7.5)

18 List three measures that may be taken to ensure that outgoing suppliers maintain performance for the duration of their contract. (7.7–7.9)

CHAPTER 14

Legislative Change

Learning objectives and indicative content

5.4 Identify and analyse the current legislation relating to employment and equality of opportunity in organisations.

- The Equal Pay Act 1970 (as amended)
- Employment Act 2002 and Dispute Resolution Regulations (2004)
- Health and Safety at Work Act 1974
- EU Employment Directives, TUPE, equal treatment, working time, young people
- Disability Discrimination Acts 1995 & 2005
- Employment Equality (Age) Regulations 2006 and Amendment Regulations 2008
- Sex Discrimination Act 1975 and Amendment Regulations 2008

Chapter headings

1 The legal environment

2 Equal opportunities and diversity

3 Equal pay

4 Health and safety at work

5 Other legislative changes

Introduction

In this chapter we look at the various laws and regulations which affect the relationship between employers and their employees. (Of course, there are many other legal aspects to purchasing and supply management, but they are beyond the scope of this syllabus.)

There are increasing legal/political constraints on managerial decision-making in these areas, aimed at: protecting employees from bias, discrimination and exploitation in accessing and retaining employment opportunities; protecting employees from health and safety risks at work; and so on. In recent years, the social policy of the European Union has added momentum to this trend: European Directives are still being enacted into the law of member states in the areas of equal opportunities, industrial democracy and employment rights. Some issues are very current: there is brand new legislation in areas such as sex discrimination and age discrimination, for example. You will need to keep an eye out for regular updates on the CIPS student website, as the requirements change.

In this chapter, we consider why the legal environment is particularly important for change management. We then look at recent and forthcoming legislation in the areas specifically mentioned in the syllabus.

1 The legal environment

1.1 The legal environment consists of legislation, regulations, voluntary codes of practice and other requirements formulated by governments (by enacting legislation or statutes), courts (by setting legal 'precedents' or case law) and regulatory bodies.

1.2 This is a particularly important area for environmental monitoring and change management because:

- The organisation's response is not 'optional' or left to managerial discretion: compliance is required and enforced by various sanctions and penalties
- The requirements are constantly changing, as courts and tribunals define them through their decisions, and as legislators and regulatory bodies issue new provisions and amendments.

1.3 Legal provisions affect businesses in many areas: fair trading and competition; contracts; data protection and privacy; copyright and intellectual property; incorporation and corporate governance; financial reporting; and so on. However, this syllabus focuses on recent developments in **employment law**: laws and regulations on equal pay, equal opportunities and diversity, health and safety at work, working hours and conditions, employment protection rights and so on.

1.4 In the following sections, we focus on legislation specifically mentioned in the syllabus. This may seem like a bit of a 'pick and mix' approach, since the laws mentioned cover a range of topics and dates. However, it should serve to alert you to the sheer variety of areas in which requirements may affect managerial activity; the frequency with which legislation changes; and the impact of long-term cultural and policy shifts on business practice.

2 Equal opportunities and diversity

2.1 'Equal opportunity' in an employment context means that everyone has a fair chance of getting a job, accessing training and benefits and competing for promotion, regardless of individual differences or minority status. It is, effectively, non- or anti-discrimination.

Discrimination on grounds of sex

2.2 Only in recent decades has there been a widespread challenge to discrimination and segregation in employment on the grounds of sex. Reports show that women continue to be excluded from senior executive positions and are clustered in gender-segregated occupations (regarded as 'women's work') such as textiles, footwear and clothing, hotel and catering, retail distribution and repairs, professional and scientific services and health services. A significant percentage of the women employed in these categories work part-time (creating sex discrimination issues in the treatment of part-time workers in general).

2.3 In the UK, the **Sex Discrimination Act** 1975 (and subsequent amendments) prohibits certain types of discrimination in employment against women (and men) by reason of sex, marital status (eg if an employer believes that a single man will be able to devote more time to the job), and change of sex or gender reassignment. The Employment Equality (Sexual Orientation) Regulations 2003 also outlaw discrimination on the grounds of sexual orientation.

2.4 There are three basic types of unlawful discrimination under the legislation.

- Direct discrimination is where one group is treated less favourably than other (except for specifically exempted cases, such as 'genuine occupational qualifications').
- Indirect discrimination (in employment and vocational training) is where an employer applies a provision, criterion or practice to men and women equally, but this has the effect of putting one sex at a particular disadvantage, without justification (eg changing shift patterns to include early morning starts, as this would disadvantage women responsible for child care). This is a new definition under the Employment Equality (Sex Discrimination) Regulations 2006. Previously, the treatment had to be to the detriment of a large proportion of members of one sex to be construed as discriminatory: now, it merely has to put women at a particular disadvantage when compared to men (or *vice versa*).
- Harassment is defined (in the 2006 regulations, bringing sex into line with race, disability, sexual orientation and religion/belief protections) as unwanted conduct which violates a person's dignity, or creates an intimidating, hostile, degrading, humiliating or offensive environment for a person, on the grounds of his or her sex (eg placing vital objects on a high shelf, where women are less likely to be able to reach). It also includes verbal, non-verbal or physical conduct of a sexual nature (eg degrading jokes or offensive comments about appearance or dress).

2.5 Sexual harassment has always been unlawful (as a form of direct discrimination), but the new regulations are an example of legislative changes which clarify the law and stimulate amendments to policies, guidelines and training for management and staff. Other areas related to sex discrimination include issues such as employee rights during pregnancy and maternity leave, and equal treatment of part-time workers (a high proportion of whom are women).

2.6 The obligation not to discriminate applies to all aspects of employment including job advertising, recruitment and selection procedures, access to training and promotion, terms and conditions of work, access to benefits, the application of disciplinary procedures, selection for redundancy and company-determined retirement ages.

Discrimination on grounds of race

2.7 As with discrimination against women, race discrimination occurs partly because people from ethnic minorities are comparatively recent entries to the workforce and have historically suffered discrimination. They tend to be concentrated in particular industrial sectors and occupations which are contracting (like manufacturing) or of low status, and they have not had access to occupational skills and qualifications training. In addition, of course, there has been direct racial discrimination.

2.8 In the UK, the **Race Relations Act** 1976 (amended 1996, 2000 and 2003 – which gives you some idea of the need to keep up to date!) covers discrimination on grounds of colour, race, nationality, and ethnic or national origin. The Employment Equality Regulations 2003 also prohibit discrimination on the grounds of religion or belief.

2.9 The Race Relations Act generally follows the wording of the Sex Discrimination Act in relevant areas: direct and indirect discrimination and victimisation are unlawful across a range of employment practices.

2.10 In January 1995, the Commission for Racial Equality launched a benchmarking standard for employers, *Racial Equality Means Business*. This aimed to move the issue beyond compliance and ethics, to a recognition of the business benefits of equality. Companies which have implemented practical policies and action plans on racial equality (including Littlewoods and W H Smith) claim to have found measurable benefits in terms of staff morale and performance, and customer loyalty.

Discrimination on grounds of disability

2.11 The **Disability Discrimination Act 1995** (and subsequent amendments, including the Disability Discrimination Act 2005) made it unlawful for an employer (with more than 20 employees) to discriminate against a disabled person in deciding whom to interview or employ, or in the terms of the employment offer; in the terms of employment and the opportunities for promotion, transfer, training or other benefits; in decisions relating to redundancy and dismissal.

2.12 In addition, the employer has a duty to make reasonable adjustments to working arrangements or to the physical features of premises where these constitute a disadvantage to a particular disabled employee. According to the supporting Code of Practice, this may include altering working hours, adapting equipment, reallocating some duties, providing special supervision or training, ensuring access to facilities and premises and providing special services (eg a reader or interpreter).

2.13 A disabled person is defined as a person who has a physical or mental impairment that has a substantial and long-term (more than 12 months) adverse effect on his ability to carry out normal day-to-day activities. This may include impairment of hearing, sight, memory, mobility, coordination or speech. Severe disfigurement is included, as are progressive conditions such as HIV even though the current effect may not be substantial.

Age discrimination

2.14 Age discrimination (or 'ageism') has not so far been illegal in the UK, although it has been the subject of a voluntary Code of Practice on Age Diversity in Employment since 1999. The Employment Equality (Age) Regulations 2006 came into force in the UK in October 2006, outlawing direct discrimination (for example, not providing medical insurance to employees aged 50 or older), indirect discrimination (for example, requiring all new recruits to take a health and fitness test which older people may find more difficult to pass) and harassment on grounds of age.

2.15 The new legislation (and subsequent amendments, including the Amendment Regulations 2008) effectively bans discrimination in terms of recruitment, promotion, access to training and rights to claim unfair dismissal or receive redundancy payments. It also bans companies from setting compulsory retirement ages below 65 (unless this can be objectively justified), and introduces the right for employees to request working beyond retirement age (which must be considered by employers, although not necessarily granted). Employers must give employees at least six months notice of their intended retirement date, to enable them to plan for retirement (and be confident that 'retirement' is not being used as a cover for unfair dismissal).

2.16 This is a major new piece of legislation, illustrating improvements in rights and protections for groups previously suffering discrimination; moves to widen the labour/skill pool to match demographic changes; and the need for organisations to prepare for legislative change by adapting policies and practices. (Think how many recruitment advertisements you see asking for 'dynamic recent graduates', for example...)

The Equality and Human Rights Commission

2.17 The Equal Opportunities Commission, Commission for Racial Equality and Disability Rights Commission have been dissolved under the Equality Act 2006. From October 2007, it is the responsibility of the new Commission for Equality and Human Rights (CEHR) to promote equality and tackle discrimination in the areas of sex, race, disability and age, religion/belief and sexual orientation.

2.18 In addition, the 2007 Equalities Review and Discrimination Law Review are now complete. As a result, at the time of writing (September 2009) the UK government has announced a new Equality Bill which will, when enacted, harmonise all the existing discrimination legislation.

3 *Equal pay*

3.1 The **Equal Pay Act** 1970 was the first major attempt 'to prevent discrimination as regards the terms and conditions of employment between men and women'. (Note that it does not cover other grounds of discrimination.)

3.2 The **Equal Pay (Amendment) Regulations** 1984 (implementing the European Equal Pay Directive) established the right to claim equal pay and conditions for work of equal 'value'. A woman (for example) no longer had to compare her terms to those of a man in a similar job, but to those of a man doing a job of *similar value* in the organisation. This 'value' could most objectively be assessed by job evaluation: a systematic approach to analysing, valuing and ranking jobs according to their skill requirements, importance and other factors. If job evaluation was not used in the organisation, the employee could apply to an Industrial Tribunal: this process has recently been facilitated by the introduction of an 'equal pay questionnaire' (Employment Act 2002).

3.3 'Equal pay and conditions' includes overtime, bonuses, employment-related benefits (such as sick pay), welfare provisions (such as holiday or parental leave) and pension rights.

4 *Health and safety at work*

4.1 In 1972, the Royal Commission on Safety and Health at Work reported that unnecessarily large numbers of days were being lost each year through industrial accidents, injuries and diseases, because of the 'attitudes, capabilities and performance of people and the efficiency of the organisational systems within which they work'.

4.2 Since then, major legislation has been brought into effect in the UK, most notably:

- The Health and Safety at Work Act 1974
- Smoke Free Regulations 2006 (workplace smoking ban, under the Health Act 2006)
- Regulations implementing EU directives on health and safety, including:
  - The Manual Handling Operations Regulations 1992
  - The Workplace (Health, Safety and Welfare) Regulations 1992
  - The Provision and Use of Work Equipment Regulations 1992
  - The Health and Safety (Display Screen Equipment) Regulations 1992
  - The Personal Protective Equipment at Work Regulations 1992
  - The Control of Substances Hazardous to Health Regulations 1994
  - The Reporting of Injuries, Diseases and Dangerous Occurrences Regulations (RIDDOR) 1995
  - The Fire Precautions (Workplace) Regulations 1997
  - The Management of Health and Safety at Work Regulations 1999

4.3 We will not be able to cover their provisions in detail here. Just be aware that the framework for HR policy in the area of health and safety is extensive, detailed – and constantly changing!

4.4 Wider attention has been given to health and safety issues, with consumer demand for social responsibility by organisations (underpinned by the competitive need to attract and retain quality labour) and widespread exposure of abuses through disasters such as the Bhopal chemical plant and Piper Alpha oil rig explosions. So why should organisations plan for health and safety at work?

- To protect people from pain and suffering (obviously, we hope)
- To comply with relevant legal/policy standards
- To minimise the costs of accidents and ill-health (including disruption to work, sickness benefits, repairs, replacement staff, legal claims etc)
- To enhance their ability to attract and retain quality staff
- To avoid negative PR and enhance their employer brand and reputation for corporate social responsibility.

The management of health and safety

4.5 Under the Health and Safety at Work Act 1974, every employer has a general duty to ensure the health, safety and welfare at work of all employees, so far as is reasonably practicable. Various aspects of this responsibility, included in the Act and subsequent Regulations, are set out in Table 14.1.

Table 14.1 *Employer and employee duties in managing health and safety*

Employee's duties	Employer's duties
HEALTH AND SAFETY AT WORK ACT 1974	
• To take reasonable care of himself and others affected by his acts or omissions at work • To cooperate with the employer in carrying out his duties (including enforcing safety rules) • Not to interfere intentionally or recklessly with any machinery or equipment provided in the interests of health and safety	• To provide safe systems (work practices) • To provide a safe and healthy work environment (well-lit, warm, ventilated, hygienic and so on) • To maintain all plant and equipment to a necessary standard of safety • To support safe working practices with information, instruction, training and supervision • To consult with safety representatives appointed by a recognised trade union • To appoint a safety committee to monitor safety policy if asked to do so • To communicate safety policy and measures to all staff, clearly and in writing
THE MANAGEMENT OF HEALTH AND SAFETY AT WORK REGULATIONS 1992	
• To inform the employer of any situation which may pose a danger	• To carry out risk assessment, generally in writing, of all work hazards, on a continuous basis • To introduce controls to reduce risks • To assess the risks to anyone else affected by their work activities • To share hazard and risk information with other employers, including those on adjoining premises, other site occupiers and all subcontractors entering the premises • To initiate or revise safety policies in the light of the above • To identify employees who are especially at risk (other legislation cites pregnant women, young workers, shift-workers and part-time workers) • To provide fresh and appropriate training in safety matters • To provide information to employees (including temporary workers) about health and safety • To employ competent safety and health advisers.
HEALTH AND SAFETY (CONSULTATION WITH EMPLOYEES) REGULATIONS 1996	
	• To consult all employees on health and safety matters (such as the planning of health and safety training, changes in equipment or procedures which may substantially affect health and safety at work, or the health and safety consequences of introducing new technology)

4.6 Other regulations cover particular safety and health risks in the workplace, and in particular industries: guidelines are available from the Health and Safety Executive. You will also encounter particular measures (eg in relation to manual handling and dangerous substances) in your studies for subjects such as *Storage and Distribution*.

Working hours

4.7 The Working Time Regulations require that workers cannot be required to work more than 48 hours per week on average (the average being calculated over a 17-week period). The Regulations also give rights to paid holiday, rest breaks and limits on night work.

4.8 There are special rules for some workers, such as young workers, trainee doctors and mobile workers in the transport industry.

4.9 For young workers (ie those over school leaving age, but under 18), the Regulations require that they cannot be made to work more than eight hours per day or 40 hours per week. These limits apply to every day and every week, ie they are not calculated by means of an average over a longer period. There are limited exceptions to the rules.

4.10 An employee who wishes to work in excess of these rules may opt to do so, but this must be voluntary and in writing. Young workers are not allowed to do this even if they wish to do so. A worker who does agree to work longer hours may later change his mind and opt back in to the Regulations.

5 Other legislative changes

Employment Act 2002

5.1 The Employment Act 2002 (and subsequent amendments including the Dispute Resolution Regulations 2004) is a wide-ranging package, covering a number of issues which may be relevant to managers. The main provisions are listed in Table 14.2.

Employment Relations Act 2004

5.2 The Employment Relations Act 2004 came into force in stages between October 2004 and 2005. It is another broad-ranging package of provisions in regard to collective labour law and trade union rights (amending the ERA 1999: a useful reminder that legislation is constantly being reviewed and updated...), including:

- Measures to improve the statutory union recognition procedure: clarifying 'topics' for collective bargaining; providing for earlier communication between unions and workers; and protecting workers from intimidation during ballots for recognition or derecognition
- Extending the protection against dismissal of employees taking official, lawfully organised industrial action
- Measures to improve some individual employment rights (eg clarifying the role of the 'companion' in grievance and disciplinary hearings).

Table 14.2: *Employment Act 2002*

Support for working parents (and enabling businesses to retain their skills)	• The right of parents of children under six (or of disabled children under 19) to request flexible working, and to have their request 'seriously considered' by employers. • A new right for fathers and adoptive parents to paternity and adoption leave and pay – as well as improved maternity rights and pay.
Dispute resolution in the workplace	• Encouraging internal resolution of workplace disputes, by introducing minimum internal disciplinary and grievance procedures, and encouraging employees to raise grievances with their employer before applying to an employment tribunal. • Requiring information about disciplinary and grievance procedures to be included in written particulars of employment • Altering the way unfair dismissals are judged, so that – provided the dismissal is otherwise fair – minor procedural shortcomings by the employer will not be penalised. • Providing for more efficient delivery of employment tribunal services.
Fixed-term workers (supporting flexible working)	• The right of fixed-term employees to get at least the same pay and conditions as similar permanent employees working for the same employer – unless the employer can justify different treatment. • Limits on the use of successive fixed-term contracts (ie really a permanent job)

Transfer of Undertakings (Protection of Employment) Regulations 2006

5.3 The TUPE Regulations 2006 (a revision of 1981 Regulations) came into force in April 2006. They are intended to preserve employees' rights to employment protection, terms and conditions:

- when a business or undertaking, or part of one, is transferred to a new employer (as under the old Regulations) *or*
- when a 'service provision change' takes place. This is a major change from the 1981 regulations, including cases where services are outsourced, insourced or re-assigned by a client from one contractor to another.

5.4 The regulations have the effect that employees employed when the undertaking is transferred or changes hands automatically become employees of the new employer, on the same terms and conditions.

5.5 The new employers must take over the contracts of employment of all employees: they cannot pick and choose. They cannot dismiss employees because of the transfer *unless* there is a sound economic, technical or organisational (ETO) reason entailing changes in the workforce: in this case, dismissal would be defined as redundancy, and the usual rights and procedures would apply. Otherwise, the dismissal will be deemed unfair by an Employment Tribunal.

5.6 The new employers take over all rights and obligations arising from the employment contracts, except some provisions for old age and invalidity. They also take over any collective agreements made on behalf of the employees, which were in force before the transfer.

5.7 Representatives of any employees affected by the transfer (eg their recognised trade unions) have the right to be informed about the transfer, and consulted about any proposed measures concerning the employees. In addition, the revised Regulations place a duty on the old employer to provide information to the new employer about the transferring workforce: this is called 'employee liability information'.

5.8 Be aware that this is part of a much broader body of employment rights and protection law. Dismissals, redundancies and trade union consultations are complex matters – and beyond the scope of this syllabus. If in doubt, a purchasing manager should consult the HR or legal department of the organisation before taking any action.

Freedom of Information Act 2000

5.9 The Freedom of Information Act came into force in January 2005. It gives members of the public the right to access:

- recorded information (such as e-mails, the minutes of meetings, research or reports)
- held by public authorities (central government and government departments; local authorities; hospitals and medical services; state schools, colleges and universities; and police forces and prison services)
- *unless* it is determined that the public interest in withholding the information is greater than the public interest in disclosing it: the 'public interest test'. (This is already established, for example, in the case of personal information, or disclosures that would result in an actionable breach of confidence.)

5.10 Public authorities must respond promptly (within 20 days) to requests, although they have 'reasonable time' to consider whether the disclosure would be in the public interest. If they decide not to disclose the information requested, they must explain why they consider it exempt. Complaints and disputes are arbitrated by the Information Commissioner's Office.

EU Employment Directives

5.11 There is a wide range of EU employment-related directives, for which the Department of Trade and Industry has UK responsibility. These are still in the process of being enacted into the law of member states, including the UK – so this in an area worth continual monitoring. Some of the key directives are summarised below: Table 14.3 (drawn from the DTI's website).

Table 14.3: *EU employment directives*

Subject	Implemented in UK?	Relevant UK legislation
Safeguarding employees' rights in transfers of undertakings and businesses	1979	Transfer of Undertakings (Protection of Employment) Regulations 1981 [TUPE]
Employer's obligation to inform employees of conditions relevant to the contract or employment relationship	1993	Employment Rights Act 1996
Organisation of working time	1996	Working Time Regulations 1998
Establishment of European Works Councils or procedures for informing and consulting employees	1999	Transnational Information and Consultation of Employees Regulations (1999)
Parental leave	1999	Maternity and Parental Leave etc Regulations 1999
Part-time work	2000	Part-time Workers (Prevention of Less Favourable Treatment) Regulations 2000
Equal treatment in employment and occupation	2006	Various Employment Equality Regulations (but watch this space for a possible Single Equality Bill)

Chapter summary

- The legal environment is a particularly important area for environmental monitoring and change management, because: the requirements are constantly changing; and the organisation's response is not optional!
- Equal opportunity in employment means that people have a fair chance of getting a job, accessing training and benefits and competing for promotion, regardless of performance-irrelevant individual differences, minority status or discrimination.
- Equal opportunities legislation in the UK prohibits discrimination on the basis of: sex, marital status and sex change (Sex Discrimination Act); race, colour, nationality and origin (Race Relations Act); sexual orientation and religious belief (Employment Equality Regulations); disability (Disability Discrimination Act); and age (from October 2006).
- Equal pay legislation establishes the right for a woman to claim equal pay and conditions of work for work of equal value (as established by job evaluation).
- The Health and Safety at Work Act 1974 (and subsequent regulations) imposes duties on employers and employees in areas such as: reasonable care; co-operation; safe systems, work practices and environment; consultation and involvement; risk assessment; and education and training.
- Other employment rights have recently been amended by legislation including the Employment Act 2002, the TUPE Regulations 2006 and the Freedom of Information Act. EU Employment Directives continue to be enacted into the law of member states.

Self-test questions

Numbers in brackets refer to paragraphs where you can check your answers

1. Who is responsible for formulating employment law and regulation? (1.1)
2. Distinguish between direct and indirect discrimination. (2.4)
3. Define sexual harassment. (2.4)
4. What piece of legislation prohibits 'colour prejudice'? (2.8)
5. What might an employer do to facilitate work for (a) disabled and (b) mature-age employees? (2.12, 2.15)
6. What is job evaluation? (3.2)
7. List five reasons why employers should manage health and safety. (4.4)
8. List five duties an employer has under the HSWA 1974. (Table 14.1)
9. What are workers' new rights on (a) flexible working, (b) fixed-term contracts, and (c) service provision change? (Table 14.2, 5.3)

Further reading

The best way to keep up to date with this rapidly changing topic area is via the internet. Here are some sites you may like to check out:

- The Information Commissioner http://www.ico.gov.uk
- The Women & Equality Unit http://www.womenandequalityunit.gov.uk
- The Health and Safety Executive http://www.hse.gov.uk
- ACAS http://www.acas.org.uk
- Age Positive http://www.agepositive.gov.uk

CHAPTER 15

Technological Change

Learning objectives and indicative content

5.5 Evaluate the impact of e-commerce and technology on the management of organisations and people, and in particular the benefit to the purchasing function

- Intranet
- Knowledge management systems
- Management information systems (MIS)/marketing information systems (MkIS)
- Flexible working arrangements
- Telecommunications
- E-sourcing
- E-procurement

Chapter headings

1 The impact of information technology
2 IT and purchasing
3 Management information
4 Intranet and extranet
5 Flexible working
6 The internet and e-commerce

Introduction

'Purchasing is an information function. It needs good information to function well, and it is an important provider of strategic and operational information.' (DTI: *Supplying the Challenge*)

In this chapter, we look at the impact of information technology on management of organisations and on the purchasing function.

We consider how the evolution of the purchasing function, management functions (such as decision making) and organisational trends (such as flexible working) have been supported by technological developments.

We then look at the impact of e-commerce and the internet, and some of its applications in e-purchasing and the management of supply chain relationships.

1 The impact of information technology

What is information technology?

1.1 The term 'information technology' was introduced to describe computerisation. However, related technologies are now used in a very wide range of applications, particularly in the field of communications. Many developments in communications media and tools (whether for mail, telephony or meetings) involve information technology applications. Hence the term information and communication technology (ICT).

Trends in information technology development

1.2 Broadly speaking, IT has changed the way people do business through the following means.

- Dramatically increasing the speed of communication and information processing. This also supports more genuine interactivity in information-gathering and transaction processing. Real-time answers to enquiries, updating of information, processing of transactions and conversations can be conducted via a computer network or the internet. Faster communication supports more efficient transaction processing, greater coordination (by keeping off-site staff and supply chain contacts in touch and up to date), and improved customer service (through swift response to queries and orders).
- Offering wider access to knowledge and information (especially from global sources). The internet offers unrestricted, constant access to formal information resources (in the form of websites, databases, libraries, expert agencies and so on) and informal resources in the form of network contacts.
- Facilitating 24-hour, 7-day, global business. The internet and e-mail allow companies to offer service and maintain communication across office hours, international time zones and geographical distances. Many processes do not require immediate human intervention (although distance and time may become a factor again, where goods have to be physically transported to the customer).
- Supporting paperless and transitless communications (eg electronic mail messages), business transactions (eg online ordering and payment) and service delivery (eg online ticket reservations, information/education services and so on).
- Creating 'virtual' relationships, teams and organisations, by making location irrelevant to the process of data-sharing, communication and collaboration.

Information technology as a strategic tool

1.3 Information technology can be used as a strategic tool in a number of ways.

- For competitive advantage, by improving and streamlining customer service and delivery, facilitating 24/7 customer access, allowing online credit card transactions and so on.

- To improve productivity and performance, eg through the use of computer-aided design and manufacturing (CAD/CAM) or JIT systems; speeding up communication using e-mail; reducing the need for expediting, using integrated information systems.
- To increase choice, innovation and organisational learning, with ever-increasing access to global information. For purchasing applications, this includes information on:
  - a wider range of small and overseas suppliers and products
  - global best practice and competitor activity for benchmarking and imitation. (A key tool of organisational learning is what *Pedler et al* refer to as SIS: 'steal ideas shamelessly'.)
- To develop new businesses. Examples include new information/knowledge services (online databases, training and education, search engines); marketing services (online shopping, booking, market research); and entertainment services (online games, music and video streaming).
- To streamline the organisational and management structure, enabling outsourcing, teleworking, downsizing, flexible working and co-ordinated decentralisation.
- To stimulate (and support) ongoing attention to the recruitment, retention, training and development of high-quality, technologically skilled employees – which will have long-term advantages for organisational flexibility and competitiveness.
- To develop loyal, mutually beneficial supplier and customer relationships, by:
  - Providing real-time information for transaction processing, delivery tracking and other value-adding services
  - Streamlining procurement and delivery processes for higher levels of customer service
  - Supporting the customisation of products/services and the personalisation of contacts for supplier or customer relationship management
  - Creating knowledge communities – sharing information via extranets, for example
  - Facilitating the coordination of collaborative activities.

1.4 We will see how some of these benefits can be achieved as we examine specific technologies throughout this chapter.

2 *IT and purchasing*

The evolution of purchasing

2.1 *Baily et al* describe the historical development of the purchasing function in terms of its information systems technology.

- **Infant stage**: a simple manual clerical system, supporting operational decision-making within the purchasing department.

- **Awakening stage**: improvement of the manual system, and exploration of early standalone computer processing, in response to the recognition of the importance of information to support purchasing decisions.
- **Developing stage**: beginning to link purchasing IT systems with those of other functions, to support more integrated materials planning and management (eg materials requirements planning or MRP).
- **Mature stage**: full computerisation of purchasing information processing within the firm, with an integrated purchasing database supporting coordinated materials planning and management (eg manufacturing resources planning or MRPII).
- **Advanced stage**: direct EDI link of internal purchasing database to the external supply chain (key customers and suppliers), for full integration of supply processes, efficiency of transaction processing and enhancement of supply chain relationships.

Computerisation of purchasing systems

2.2 Computerised information systems have transformed administrative work in all areas. They offer the following key benefits for purchasing.

- Routine and repetitive clerical tasks are automated, requiring less time and effort from buyers, who are free to spend more time on the creative, strategic and relational aspects of their roles.
- Information storage and retrieval is less wasteful of physical space and resources, and of clerical time. Computer disks and CD-ROMs can store massive amounts of information safely, cleanly and in a very small physical space. Records can be interactively interrogated, updated and transmitted without generating extra paper products.
- Data can be manipulated faster and more flexibly, for a range of transaction and decision-support functions.

2.3 The consequences of computerising purchasing systems can be dramatic. The DTI's booklet *Supplying the Challenge* described the process at Mars, the confectionery company. 'Buyers have replaced paper and files with electronic information and links to company operational data: now the company is reaping the rewards through more coordinated – increasingly pan-European – buying, better scheduled deliveries, and more information available more quickly to "customers" throughout the organisation. Everyone creating a requisition does so on a computer screen. Buying authorisations are registered on-screen and buyers create priced orders from the information brought together by the system. This alone saves huge amounts of time and money. Perhaps more important, the system helps Mars plan further ahead and control its purchasing better.'

2.4 An article in *Supply Management* also cited the example of supermarket giant Sainsbury's, which in the last five years has completely re-engineered its supply chain. Among other changes (involving the structure of the distribution system), Sainsbury's has fully automated two of its warehouses, in order to minimise human error and implement zero defect order fulfilment. It has also introduced real-time information and collaborative commerce across the extended supply chain. This includes:

- computerised inventory management, to enhance Sainsbury's control over the supplier-to-store replenishment network;
- data-mining applications, gathering information at point of sale, measuring on-shelf availability on an hour-by-hour basis, and facilitating real-time reordering.

2.5 You should be aware of computerised applications through your studies of purchasing procedures and processes: materials and inventory management, purchase requisitions and orders, order expediting and delivery tracking, electronic payments, budgetary control and other management reports.

Example: electronic data interchange (EDI)

2.6 One of the most important developments in IT from the purchasing viewpoint has been the introduction and widespread adoption of electronic data interchange (EDI) – the direct exchange of structured data between two or more computers. Instead of exchanging paper-based documents, inter-organisational enquiries and transactions are sent via cable or telecommunications links, via computer terminals, directly from one information system to the other.

2.7 EDI can be used for:

- query handling: sending marketing, transaction and technical information such as product and price details, technical product or process specifications, terms and conditions of trade, etc.
- transaction handling: generating quotes, purchase orders, delivery instructions, receipt acknowledgements, invoices, etc.
- funds transfer: electronic payments to supplier (or employee) accounts, using direct transfer or credit card.

Example: Radio frequency identification (RFID)

2.8 Electronic point of sale (EPOS) systems connect point-of-sale terminals to IT systems, including database information and data-processing applications. Point-of-sale data includes: product pricing, stock availability and location; product/line performance; and customer buying patterns. EPOS systems can be connected to inventory management systems (for automatic stock replenishment), payment systems (eg via electronic funds transfer) and management information systems (for sales analysis, demand forecasting and inventory).

2.9 EPOS systems (and inventory control systems) have for some years used barcoding as the main technology for automatic data capture. Barcodes are code numbers printed as optical bars and read using a scanner. Data is input direct to an information system and linked to related database records and applications. This allows accurate counting and recording of materials and finished items moving into and out of stock, or in transit.

2.10 More recently, radio frequency technologies have developed to allow radio frequency identification (RFID). An RFID tag (transponder) is attached to or placed inside items, and its micro-electronic circuits store data for transmission to a remote RFID reader. This offers significant advantages, compared to conventional optical barcode technology.

- The tag doesn't have to be scanned or 'seen' by the reader: it can be used for updating inventory of moving and 'hidden' items in complex storage/transport environments. The costs of manual scanning (or conveyor-systems) can be saved. Dust/abrasion and other problems for barcode reading do not apply.
- Data can be flexibly interrogated and updated for stock control, document generation, re-order triggering etc. Multiple tags can be read/written at once.
- A *CIPS Practice Guide* argues that, despite the newness (and vulnerability) of the technology: 'At a strategic level, the use of RFID technology in the supply chain enables value creation and helps deliver the following business objectives: increased revenue; reduced operating costs; optimised employment of assets; and enhanced safety and quality control.

  At an operational level, the benefits generated have included: increased product availability; improved utilisation of capital; lower total operating costs; and enhanced safety, security and quality control.'

3 Management information

Knowledge management

3.1 Knowledge management is the organisation, creation, sharing and flow of knowledge within organisations. Knowledge could be described as information that has a use or purpose. Where information can be placed onto a computer, knowledge exists in the heads of people. Knowledge is information to which intent has been added (see *www.wikipedia.org*).

3.2 A definition of knowledge management is given on the Virtual Library on Knowledge Management website:

'Knowledge management caters to the critical issues of organisational adaptation, survival, and competence in face of increasingly discontinuous environmental change. Essentially, it embodies organisational processes that seek synergistic combination of data and information processing capacity of information technologies, and the creative and innovative capacity of human beings.' (www.kmnetwork.com)

3.3 The objective of knowledge management is to optimise the knowledge that is available in an organisation, creating new knowledge, increasing awareness and understanding in the process.

3.4 Knowledge management is closely linked to organisational learning. It recognises that learning and doing are important to organisational success and that knowledge gained in developing products, developing processes, tightening supply chains etc should not be lost to the organisation. This knowledge, if shared, can give an organisation a competitive edge and innovation.

Management information systems (MIS)

3.5 Management information systems (MIS) are systems that take information captured by transaction processing systems (such as electronic point of sale, EPOS) and produce reports that management needs for planning and control. An information system consists of all the components that collect, manipulate, and disseminate data or information. The system includes hardware, software, people, communicating systems such as telephone lines, and the data itself.

3.6 The MIS system involves collecting, recording, storing, and processing data. Information systems support business processes and operations in a number of ways.

- Recording and storing sales, purchase, investment, payroll data and other relevant accounting records, and processing these accounting records into balance sheets, income statements and other forms of financial information.
- Recording and storing inventory, work-in-progress, equipment repair and maintenance and supply chain data, and other production/operations records and processing these operations records into production schedules, inventory systems and production monitoring systems.
- Recording and storing personnel data such as employment histories, personnel and salary data and processing these into employee performance and other human resource reports.
- Recording and storing market data, customer profiles, customer purchase histories, marketing research data, and other marketing records, and processing these into marketing plans, sales reports etc.
- Recording and storing business intelligence data, competitor analysis data and other strategic records, and processing these into industry trend reports, portfolio models, market share reports etc.
- Use of all of the above to implement, control and monitor plans, strategies, tactics, new products, new business models or new business ventures.

3.7 The MIS system underpins much of the decision making process by providing relevant and current material that managers can use to base their decisions on.

Decision support systems

3.8 The business support function of the MIS system is an integral part of decision-making. It allows users the ability to consider contingency planning scenarios, ie the 'what if?' questions. What if inflation increases? What if the value of sterling drops against the US dollar?, etc. The system is then able to predict possible outcomes based on the information held.

Marketing information systems (MkIS)

3.9 The marketing information system of an organisation is specifically designed to support marketing planning. It comprises the following elements.

- Marketing research information, drawn from primary research (questionnaires, surveys, interviews, focus groups) and secondary research (using published sources). This includes data about products, product positioning and new product development; sales patterns and trends; customer behaviour, motivation and feedback; pricing factors and effects; promotion; and other areas of marketing activity.
- Marketing intelligence on the macroenvironment (PESTLE factors and so on)
- The organisation's accounting system, which contains information on all current customers (including discounts, credit terms and payment schedules), budgets and inventory
- An analytical system that takes data from all database components of the MkIS and processes, statistically analyses and models it, in order to guide marketers in decision-making.

Databases

3.10 A database is a centralised collection of structured data, organised in such a way that:

- relevant, accurate and up-to-date information is held within the system and can be regularly monitored and amended to maintain its quality;
- different users are able to access and interrogate it according to their information needs;
- the right of different users to update or amend records is controlled and coordinated (to avoid confusion).

3.11 The same data can be used for many different applications. Supplier details, for example, will be relevant to buyers (to support purchase decisions), purchasing staff (for generating orders), accounts personnel (for checking terms and conditions), and so on. A buyer might be interested in the prices charged for a particular stock item by various suppliers, and will want to access all invoices which include that item; an accountant may want to inspect the history of dealings with a particular customer (because of credit control problems, say), and will want to access all invoices which include that customer.

3.12 An internal supply database may include a range of data about:

- Suppliers: products/materials available, prices, terms and conditions, quotations and contracts, delivery and quality performance (based on historical transactions), plant and management, contact details.
- Market variables: availability of materials, prices, trends (periodic shortages, price instability).
- Inventory: stocks, usage rates, locations, value, etc.
- Transactions: orders in progress, historical orders.

3.13 Databases can be interrogated, and the data analysed (using a process called 'datamining') for applications such as:

- identifying the 'best' suppliers (for purchase decisions) or customers (for targeted marketing effort or key account status).
- developing the supplier or customer base by identifying potentially valuable contacts and relationships to pursue.

- relationship/loyalty management, by using known information to personalise, target and streamline communications and transactions. (This use of databases is a particularly important trend in customer relationship marketing.)
- continuity of knowledge/service/relationship. People move on, and have limited memory capacity; databases allow historical data about supplier performance and customer preferences to be stored and retrieved as needed.

4 Intranet and extranet

4.1 The Internet and the world wide web are an accepted framework for implementing and delivering information system applications – as we will see later in this chapter. The internet is a global collection of telecommunications-linked computer networks, which has revolutionised global communication through tools such as e-mail. However, the same network protocols can be used more locally as a tool for employee and supply chain communication.

Intranet

4.2 An intranet is a set of networked and/or internet-linked computers. This private network is usually only accessible to registered users, within the same organisation or work group. Access is restricted by passwords and user group accounts, for example.

4.3 Intranets are used in employee communication: only employees are able to access relevant web pages and internal e-mail facilities (as well as having access to the wider internet). Intranets may provide employees with access to a wide range of internal information: performance databases and reporting systems; induction and employment information (online policy and procedure manuals, job vacancies and training opportunities); noticeboards (for posting messages, announcements and bulletins); internal e-mail facilities; mailings of employee newsletters and work updates; internal training software; and so on.

4.4 Intranets offer significant advantages for integrating internal communications. They support multi-directional communication and data-sharing; link remote sites and workers in 'virtual' teams; give employees wider access to corporate information for personal identification, ideas-swapping and culture-creation; encourage more frequent (because convenient) use of reference sources and updating of information; and save on the costs of producing and distributing the equivalent printed documents and messages.

Extranet

4.5 An extranet is an intranet that has been extended to give selected outside users authorised access (by password) to particular areas or levels of the organisation's web site or information network. Examples include the registered-user-only pages of corporate websites (encouraging customers to sign up for permission–based and personalised marketing contacts), and the member-only pages of professional bodies' websites (like the CIPS).

4.6 Extranets are particularly useful tools for relationship marketing and inter-organisational partnerships. Business partners, for example, can share data and information systems for more efficient transaction processing or to provide added value to customers.

4.7 An extranet may be used to publish news updates and technical briefings which may be of use to clients or supply chain partners; provide shared services (sharing data and systems to enable partners to cross-sell each others' products and services, say, to offer customers 'one-stop' shopping); exchange transaction data (orders, payments, delivery tracking and so on); share training and development resources as part of collaborative quality management; provide online presentations and promotions to business partners (while excluding competitors); and publicise trade or consumer promotions, conference attendance, loyalty schemes and other marketing tools.

5 *Flexible working*

5.1 As we noted at the beginning of this chapter, one of the key strategic impacts of IT is the streamlining of organisational and management structures. Improved communication, data-sharing and work monitoring has supported looser, flatter and more flexible organisation structures: outsourcing, and teleworking (and other forms of co-ordinated de-centralisation, downsizing and flexible working).

Flexible working

5.2 Flexibility has been recognised as the key to organisational survival. Various models and mechanisms for flexible working have become popular, including: flexible working hours (eg part-time working and flexitime); flexible working weeks (eg job sharing); flexible working years (eg annual hours); flexible contracts (eg temporary working and subcontracting); and – most clearly supported by technological developments – flexible places of work (eg teleworking, virtual teamworking and mobile telecommunications).

5.3 **Teleworking** (or tele-commuting) implies working from home, or from a satellite office, with the aid of networked or internet-linked computers and other ICT applications (such as fax). It may take various forms.

- Homeworking: traditional 'outworkers' such as home typists and tele-sales workers
- Freelancing: working on a self-employed basis for a number of clients, from a home office, or using client offices
- Mobile working: using laptop computers, the internet and mobile phones to work 'on the road' (eg for field sales and transport staff)
- Call-centre working: working in specialist centres providing tele-sales, marketing research, help-line services, data entry and so on. (This is a major boom in off-shore, outsourced service provision: sales, research and service staff in India, say, deal with customers in the UK and Europe as if they were in local offices.)

5.4 The benefits claimed by employers for teleworking include: savings on overheads (particularly the cost of maintaining office premises); and the ability to attract and retain the skills of people alienated by traditional working practices (eg single parents, working mothers, the disabled).

5.5 The benefits claimed by employees include: elimination of commuting (with associated reductions in travel costs and stress – and also traffic and pollution); and better work-life balance. Teleworking is not for everyone, however: it requires self-discipline, self-motivation and a tolerance for social isolation. Employers should select teleworkers carefully, and have a 'revolving door' policy to allow workers to return to full-time office work, or rotation, as their needs and circumstances change.

5.6 As with outsourcing, there are risks attached to allowing people to work relatively unsupervised. Employers need to define clear targets and standards, and monitor performance (electronically, where possible), in order to 'manage by results'. They need to develop good channels of communication, with visits by supervisors, regular meetings and gatherings, conference calls and so on. HR policies will have to be developed with the needs of teleworkers in mind, as well as policies to cover operational issues such as health and safety, confidentiality and so on.

Virtual teamworking

5.7 We discussed the concept of 'virtual organisations' in Chapter 4. Virtual teams are interconnected groups of people who may not be present in the same office or organisation (and may even be in different areas of the world), but who:

- share information and tasks (eg technical support provided by a supplier)
- make joint decisions (eg on quality assurance or staff training)
- fulfil the collaborative (working together) functions of a team.

5.8 Information and communications technology (ICT) has facilitated this kind of collaboration, simulating the dynamics of teamworking via teleconferencing, video-conferencing, networked computers and the internet.

5.9 Partners in the supply chain, for example, can use such technology to access and share up-to-date product, customer, stock and delivery information (eg using web-based databases and data tracking systems). Electronic meeting management systems allow virtual meeting participants to talk and listen to each other on teleconference lines, while sharing data and using electronic 'whiteboards' on their desktop PCs. On a more basic level, suppliers may simply offer technical support to production or sales teams, for example, through telephone or online helplines.

Mobile telecommunications

5.10 Mobile telecommunications have exploded onto the social and business scene in recent years, particularly as digital networks have supported more reliable connection and data transmission. Mobile phones allow off-site employees (particularly field sales and transport/delivery personnel) to send and receive telephone messages – and, with the latest devices, also faxes and email.

5.11 Using mobile telecommunications provides numerous benefits.

- A wide range of business activities can be undertaken outside the office or on the move. (This may be particularly helpful for field sales staff, or account managers visiting clients. It is also used for tracking deliveries in transit, and notifying delivery delays from the road.)

- Clients and suppliers have continuous access to key contacts, for improved customer service, without having to leave messages and experience call-back delays.
- Mobile e-commerce is a newer application, with internet access direct to mobile phones. Users can download data from the internet to facilitate conventional commerce (eg locating stockists, consulting timetables, or interrogating product/customer databases prior to meetings). Goods and services can also now be ordered directly over the internet – as discussed below.

6 The internet and e-commerce

The internet

6.1 The internet is a worldwide computer network allowing computers to communicate via telecommunications links. The network can also be accessed from laptop computers, personal digital assistants (such as Palm Pilots) and internet-compatible mobile phones.

6.2 The internet has exploded in the last decade as a business tool, for:

- Promotion: supporting advertising, direct marketing, direct-response advertising, sales promotion, relationship marketing and public relations.
- Market research: using online feedback questionnaires and surveys, and the automatic compiling of browsing/enquiry/transaction histories to build up a picture of actual buying behaviour.
- Direct distribution: of products (through online product ordering, or the downloading of electronic products such as music, video, educational materials and so on) and services (through access to information and contacts).
- Customer service and technical support: through e-mail enquiries, FAQ postings (frequently asked questions), access to database information and help desks, etc.
- Partnership development: through access to extranets, data interchange and collaborative website content (eg joint promotions, cross-selling, or business-to-business forums).

E-commerce

6.3 The term 'e-commerce' (short for electronic commerce) refers to business transactions carried out online via ICT – usually the internet. E-commerce has facilitated direct marketing, linking customers directly with suppliers across the whole value chain. It is a means of automating business transactions and workflows, but it is also a means of improving them.

6.4 Some websites exist only to provide information about products, services or other matters. They might provide contact details for would-be customers to make direct enquiries or orders, or to find a local retail outlet or distributor. A transaction-supporting website, however, can be a 'virtual' retail outlet, warehouse, supermarket or auction room. Customers can perform a range of 'shopping' functions: browse products, download catalogues, put items in 'shopping trolleys', proceed to 'checkout', select delivery options, pay by debit or credit card, track the delivery of their order, and so on.

6.5 E-commerce may not be suitable for all businesses. There are high set-up costs. Some products have selling attributes which are not readily explained or conveyed online. Business buyers, in particular, may require samples for quality/specification checking. Some suppliers may not be ready for the complexities and costs of global distribution and after-sales support.

6.6 If the organisation does not wish to set up its own transaction-based web facility, it may consider:

- Storefronts: getting online retailers/distributors (such as Amazon) to catalogue and sell its products or services through their sites
- Auction sites: putting goods up for bidding, on sites such as eBay. This may be a good way of moving surplus, used or limited-supply items – and securing product promotion. Most auction sites charge a transaction fee, but the supplier is incurring no processing costs of its own. It is also possible to put up a requirement for suppliers to bid for – a reverse auction.

6.7 Perhaps the most obvious way in which the internet has supported the growth of e-commerce and specifically e-procurement (see below) is in providing information in an accessible, up-to-date and voluminous form. By accessing a portal for, say, buying plumbing supplies, the purchaser can view an entire information centre on all types of product from all suppliers who have access to the portal, with prices, specifications, stock levels and delivery times. There are two types of portal.

- Seller's portals – multiple buyers are present who want to buy particular items from suppliers
- Buyer's portals – multiple suppliers offer their products together for the buyer's easy access

6.8 More sophisticated users of e-commerce can engage in electronic value chain trading, which means that information on their entire value chain from customers via partners to suppliers is opened up for collaboration and co-operation on finding new and better ways of doing things.

6.9 For the purchasing function, the internet has also provided other benefits.

- Wider choice of suppliers, including global and small suppliers, via the internet. (Purchasing professionals still have to make strategic and tactical choices; ICT merely provides better-quality information for doing this.)
- Savings in procurement costs, through electronic communication, greater accuracy and electronic transaction processing. In a research project in 1997, management consultants McKinsey noted that the biggest effect of the internet for business overall is the huge saving in transaction and interaction costs – the costs of 'the searching, coordinating and monitoring that people and companies do when they exchange goods, services or ideas'.
- Support for low inventory and efficient stock turnover (as in JIT).
- Improved supply chain relationships and coordination, arising from data-sharing. These in turn facilitate collaboration and improved customer service (by streamlining and integrating supply chain processes).

E-sourcing

6.10 E-sourcing is the process whereby procurement professionals and suppliers use the internet to conduct strategic activities within the procurement cycle, such as: requirements/specification definition; tendering and supplier selection; and contract award and management.

6.11 It may take a number of forms, at different levels of buyer-seller interaction.

- **Electronic (or e-) catalogues**. Suppliers exhibit their products in electronic catalogues, and buyers work with those details (product specifications, prices etc) to purchase materials and services.
- **Bidding**, using electronic RFQs (request for quotation) procedures. RFQs and specifications are posted online or sent to different suppliers, and bids are received and evaluated electronically.
- **E-auctions**, where a seller offers surplus capacity/production and potential buyers bid competitively: prices rise during the auction and the final (open) bid wins.
- **Reverse auctions**, where a *buyer* specifies his needs/demands, and sends an RFQ with a time limit to multiple suppliers. Suppliers submit quotes competitively. Prices may be dropped during the auction and the final (open) bid wins.
- **Market exchanges**: electronic marketplaces where multiple buyers and sellers meet and exchange goods.

6.12 The website of the Office of Government Commerce claims the following benefits for e-sourcing in public-sector procurement.

- Process efficiencies: reducing time and effort spent on tendering and contract management; reduced paperwork; fewer human errors
- Compliance: in the public sector, compliance with the provisions of the Efficiency Review and the National Procurement Strategy for Local Government
- Best practice: encouraging users to adopt best practice and a consistent approach
- Cost savings: reducing the direct costs of preparing, issuing and responding to invitations to tender; more efficient comparability and competition
- Collaboration: making it easier for purchasers to work together on common sourcing projects across different departments and regions: creating 'virtual buying organisations' to increase bargaining power
- Strategic focus: allowing purchasing professionals to focus on value-added and strategic procurement activity (such as supplier screening, supply base development and relationship management), rather than administration

E-procurement

6.13 CIPS defines e-procurement as 'the combined use of information and communication technology through electronic means to enhance external and internal purchasing and supply management processes.'

6.14 As you can see from this definition, a clear distinction is not always made between 'e-sourcing' and 'e-procurement'. Arguably, however, e-procurement addresses the 'purchase-to-pay' stage of the purchasing cycle: the stage from when a purchase has been approved to the receipt of the product, and then (often, but not always) the payment for the product. E-sourcing refers to the earlier stages in the process, when a need is identified and requisitioned, and relationships with suppliers set up. For the full benefits of both methods to be felt, it is important that there is very good communication between the front-line staff who require products and services in order to serve customers and the purchasing staff who use e-procurement to deliver those products and services.

6.15 We discussed some aspects of e-procurement in Section 2 of this chapter.

Chapter summary

- Information technology initially referred to the use of computers, but this has been broadened to take account of a wide range of computerised applications, especially linked to telecommunications: hence the term 'information and communications technology' (ICT) to refer to systems such as the internet.
- IT has increased the speed of communication and information processing; offered wider access to information; facilitated 24/7 global business; supported paperless transactions; and created virtual relationships.
- IT impacts on purchasing and supply in different ways, including streamlining transactions and customer service; reducing human input to expediting; increasing the supplier and customer base; developing supplier and customer relationships; and altering the organisation structure.
- IT systems have been applied with increasing sophistication to integrate information handling not just within the organisation but throughout the supply chain, supported by technologies such as EDI.
- The administrative tasks of purchasing and materials management have been successfully computerised in areas such as stock control and purchase requisition, purchase ordering, expediting, goods receipt and reporting.
- A database is a centralised collection of structured data, organised in such a way that information can be accessed for different applications by different users. Supplier and customer databases supply a wide range of data for transaction processing, decision-making, relationship management and so on.
- The internet is a key tool for promotion, research, direct marketing/distribution of products and services, customer service, technical support and partnership development.
- E-commerce refers to business transactions carried out online via the internet. The organisation may use its website to provide information or to support interactive direct transactions. It may also use 'storefront' sites as distributors, auction sites to administer competitive bidding for products, or seller and buyer portals for seeking information. Because of the high set-up costs and complex demands of global supply, e-commerce may not suit all companies.
- E-purchasing is procurement over the internet, via direct purchasing from suppliers with transaction-supporting websites, or through private exchange (inviting suppliers to bid for supply contracts) or B2B markets (competitive bidding coordinated by third-party software companies or industry consortiums).
- IT and ICT are fast-changing, innovative areas; you need to keep up to date!

Self-test questions

Numbers in brackets refer to the paragraphs where you can check your answers.

1. Explain the general changes brought about in the business world by ICT developments. (1.2)
2. Identify the information systems used at the 'infant', 'awakening', 'developing', 'mature' and 'advanced' stages of the development of the purchasing function. (2.1)
3. What is EDI, and what are its implications for purchasing transactions? (2.6, 2.7)
4. What can EPOS systems be used for, beyond simply recording purchase transactions at the point of sale? (2.8)
5. What is an MkIS? (3.9)
6. How can databases be used to support purchasing decisions? (3.13)
7. Distinguish between an intranet and an extranet. (4.2, 4.3, 4.5, 4.6)
8. What is (a) teleworking and (b) virtual teamworking? (5.3, 5.7)
9. How does the internet contribute to partnership development? (6.2)
10. List four forms e-sourcing might take. (6.11)

Further reading

- The world of IT and e-commerce is constantly changing – and changing fast. Keep up to date with regular browsing, both online and in the quality press and appropriate journals. Check out *Supply Management* on a regular basis. You should also be able to draw on your own experience of e-commerce and e-procurement (where relevant) in the exam.

CHAPTER 16

Mock Exam

THE EXEMPLAR PAPER

The exam paper below was published by CIPS as an illustration of what might be expected under the new syllabus. In the event, the first live exams have proved to be somewhat easier in the style of their questions.

The effect of this is that if you are able to make a good attempt at the paper below you should be very well prepared for the live examination.

Instructions for Candidates:

This examination is in two sections.

Section A has two compulsory questions, worth 25 marks each.

Section B has four questions: answer two. Each question is worth 25 marks.

SECTION A

You are strongly advised to carefully read and analyse the information in the case study before attempting to answer questions 1 and 2.

Bromfield District Council

Bromfield District Council (BDC), an established public sector organisation, achieved a grade of 'good' at its recent Comprehensive Performance Assessment (CPA). The CPA assesses councils against their overall efficiency in supporting services to make improvements, service delivery, benefit fraud and financial health. The organisation employs 2,500 staff across the core activities of housing, planning, transport, schools, council tax, waste disposal and tourism.

In line with the recent Gershon Review, BDC is under pressure to improve performance. This recent Government review aims to make the public sector more efficient, to achieve quality and best value, and to provide a more customer focused approach.

In the last financial year, Bdc achieved the following results in Table 1 below.

Performance indicator	**Actual (%)**	**Target (%)**
Council tax collected	88	90
Household waste to be recycled	80	78
Major planning applications processed within 13 weeks	70	75
Undisputed invoices paid within 30 days	85	90

Table I *(source: fictitious data prepared for assessment purposes only)*

The procurement department has grown in the last decade from five to 20 staff, in a mixture of roles including purchasing assistants, buyers, e-commerce assistant, e-commerce manager, IT champion and business analyst. All staff report directly to the procurement manager.

The procurement manager, Harry White, has been headhunted by another organisation, and is leaving in the next two weeks. He has been with the Council for nearly 20 years, is MCIPS qualified, and has steered the procurement department through Phase One of the new 'BDC online' system. Although very astute technically, with good ideas, Harry is a systems and procedures person, and lacks softer people skills.

'BDC online', affectionately known as 'Customquick', was introduced firstly to achieve better prices from suppliers, through electronic tendering and a more transparent process, to tighten up internal controls (with e-purchase orders and e-invoicing) and provide better information to managers for forecasting purposes.

The second phase of the programme is the implementation of the new customer facing platform that will enable customers to access services via an e-catalogue, pay bills online, and contact the customer services team via email.

Phase One caused many problems internally, not just for the procurement department, but across the whole organisation. More experienced staff such as Tom Bolton, senior buyer, met the changes with an air of hesitancy and reluctance. As he strongly explained to the procurement manager one Monday morning before the launch:

'I can see the benefits for the organisation but I have worked in purchasing and supply for over 15 years. How do I fit in the picture? Is this new system going to take away my job? What about all the experience and knowledge I have built up? It will all go to waste!'

Younger members of staff were being recruited to work on the new project and take it forward. Kirsty Craven, aged 19, was recruited through a local recruitment agency. She has purchasing experience and a Certificate in Purchasing and Supply. She was one of the new purchasing assistants, and following a two-week training programme was playing her part (along with other new members of the team) in rationalising the purchasing operation.

The existing procurement manager had led the review of existing procurement processes, which had included an analysis of spending patterns, a vendor analysis, streamlining processes and a review of roles and responsibilities within the department.

At the recent away-day, which had included the procurement department and representatives from customer service, administrative support, payments and human resources, the new procurement manager (who had been invited along to meet the team) had managed to get a real feel for the atmospheres and morale across the organisation.

Jan Bridges, receptionist, has been with the organisation for five years. She worked full time and was worried whether her hours would be cut, with the hold on recruitment at the moment and increased use of agency staff.

As she explained: 'If customers can pay online and get queries answered by email, why will they need to come into town to the council offices?'

Bret Hammell worked in the post room and had already noticed a reduction in the amount of mail he was distributing to other departments. He wondered what the impact would be with the implementation of Phase Two. He cited a recent incident where staff members were bickering and almost ended up fighting about who would be made redundant first.

Nobody whom the new procurement manager met across the organisation really seemed clear as to what the long-term plans were. Most people had been briefed as to what the changes were, but were unsure how they would affect them personally.

Already there had been a number of concerns aired by existing suppliers: a photocopying firm had had five machines returned at the end of the leasing period, and a local paper supplier had started to notice a reduction in the amount of paper ordered by BDC. An external marketing organisation had been informed that its services (producing promotional literature) would no longer be required.

Customers had been informed of the changes that were about to take place. A briefing had been held at the council offices for ratepayers to air their views, although it was badly attended. Posters had been placed at the main council buildings and advertisements had been placed in the local newspaper. Unfortunately, owing to IT problems in rolling out the system, the lead time to inform the public had been only two months instead of the intended four months.

The information in this case study is purely fictitious and has been prepared for assessment purposes only.

Any resemblance to any organisation or person is purely coincidental.

QUESTIONS

Questions 1 and 2 relate to the case study and should be answered in the context of the information provided.

Question 1

As the new procurement manager, write an informal report to the senior management team of the council, which will:

(a) Summarise the lessons learned from Phase One of the new BDC 'online system'. **(10 marks)**

(b) Make proposals for the successful implementation of Phase Two of the BDC online system to include considerations of: planning; staffing; communication; benefits to the organisation; recommendations and a proposed action plan (with timescales and resource implications) **(15 marks)**

Question 2

(a) Evaluate the immediate staffing issues relating to the implementation of the BDC online system within the procurement department and wider organisation, making reference to concepts and theories of organisational behaviour and group and team dynamics. **(15 marks)**

(b) Discuss the leadership style(s) you could adopt to introduce the Phase Two changes successfully in the BDC procurement department. **(10 marks)**

SECTION B

Answer **TWO** questions from section B.

You are strongly advised to carefully read all the questions in section B before selecting **TWO** questions to answer.

Question 3

Argue the case that the changes in employment and equal opportunities legislation have had a positive influence on the managing of the purchasing function. Illustrate your answer with reference to specific legislation. **(25 marks)**

Question 4

Evaluate the structure, culture and values of an organisation with which you are familiar. **(25 marks)**

Question 5

Formulate a convincing business case to be submitted to the human resources manager, of an organisation with which you are familiar, to improve the recruitment, retention and development of staff within the procurement function. **(25 marks)**

Question 6

Prepare briefing notes for the senior management team of an organisation with which you are familiar, outlining how an effective procurement department can demonstrate its value within a modern organisation.

(15 marks)

CHAPTER 17

MOCK EXAM: SUGGESTED SOLUTIONS

THE EXEMPLAR PAPER

Some general observations

Make sure that you have read the 'Instructions for Candidates' section at the front of the Mock Exam, in order to be quite clear as to what is required.

In the first version of this specimen or 'Exemplar' paper published by CIPS, the examiner also gave recommendations as to how much time you need to spend on each section of the exam, as follows.

- **Section A**: 'You are strongly advised to spend approximately 30 minutes reading the case study and questions... It is recommended that you spend 35 minutes answering each question from section A.'
- **Section B**: 'You are strongly advised to spend 10 minutes carefully reading the questions in section B before selecting two questions to answer. It is recommended that you spend approximately 35 minutes answering each question.'

If you find this exam particularly challenging, be reassured: (a) you are not alone and (b) the first 'live' exams under the new syllabus have been much clearer and more straightforward in their requirements! If you can put together answers for this Mock Exam, you can consider yourself well-prepared and well on top of exam technique. (Please bear in mind that our solutions are lengthier than you would attempt in an exam, in order to cover the wide range of points that might be included.)

SUGGESTED SOLUTIONS

SECTION A

Solution 1

Although the question asks clearly for an informal report, the Answer Guidance provided by CIPS states that candidates were expected to use a standard short report format (with terms of reference, short introduction, findings, conclusions and recommendations): worth bearing in mind for future exams. This creates the significant challenge of making the introductory sections meaningful (not just repeating case study material) – and not taking too much time over them.

You are advised to spend about 30 minutes reading the case study and questions, and digesting the information. Use this time to prepare brief answer plans: the examiner suggests that you either highlight areas to cover within the case study, or draw up a short plan in your answer booklet. You should then be able to 'tick off' each point as you cover it in your answer.

Of your 35 minutes' answer time for this question, you are advised to spend 5 minutes on the report format (earning about 3 marks), 10 minutes on part A of the question (about 7 marks) and 20 minutes on part B (15 marks). This is a useful habit of mind to get into: allocate your time according to the marks available.

This is basically a question about change: don't get pre-occupied by technical aspects of the online system. 'Candidates who demonstrate a good understanding of the practical issues of implementing change, highlighted from the case study, and realistic plans to manage the change process will gain the best marks.'

We have tried to cover a wide 'spread' of the potential issues that may be included: our answer is therefore likely to be rather longer than you would attempt in an exam. Just check that you have 7 and 15 marks' worth (respectively) for each question part.

The examiner states that 'ideally', candidates would produce an action plan with costs and timescales – but we do not think the case study gives sufficient (or sufficiently clear) information about what is intended, or where the implementation programme is currently 'up to'. We have therefore discussed time and resource requirements in more general terms.

REPORT ON IMPLEMENTATION OF THE BDC ONLINE SYSTEM

[Today's date]

1. Terms of reference

This report was prepared by Your Name, Procurement Manager, for the attention of the Senior Management Team of Bromfield District Council. It is designed:

- To summarise the lessons learned from Phase One of the implementation of the Council's new 'BDC online' system, and
- To make proposals (including a draft action plan) for the successful implementation of Phase Two.

The report focuses on issues of change management, rather than operational and technical issues arising from the design and functioning of the online system itself, which should be reviewed separately.

2. Introduction

Council has recently completed implementation of Phase One of the new 'BDC online' ('Customquick') system, an integrated procurement platform. Prior to implementation of Phase Two, the customer facing platform, it is considered advisable to review, evaluate and learn from the issues raised in Phase One.

3. Lessons from Phase One

A number of operational and employee morale problems have been attributed to the way in which Phase One was implemented, both in the procurement department and across the whole Council organisation. Key lessons from review of the change management process include the following.

(a) Briefings on the nature of the changes, and their benefits for BDC, have been effective. However, there is widespread uncertainty in two key areas: what the Council's long term plans are, and how changes are likely to affect specific individuals and teams within the organisation.

(b) Lack of communication and managerial empathy on these matters has led to a number of dysfunctional effects, including:

- Lack of commitment (expressed as hesitancy and reluctance) towards changes – particularly in some key, experienced staff who might otherwise be expected to drive and champion change
- Low staff morale, arising from uncertainty about job security (arising in turn from fears of de-skilling, downsizing and redundancy of automated roles). In some cases, this may be contributing to problems in retaining key staff (such as the current Procurement Manager, Harry White).
- Proliferation of inaccurate information and speculation via the 'rumour mill' or grapevine, in the absence of clear and credible information from official channels.
- Incidents of interpersonal conflict, arising from perceived 'competition' for survival in the event of staff downsizing.

(c) There appears to have been a similar lack of intentional communication within supply network stakeholders. Lack of information about future plans has already caused concern among suppliers. Meanwhile, the ratepayer briefing, to address potential customer concerns, was poorly advertised (using limited media and an inadequate lead time), encouraging poor attendance.

(d) Some combination of all the above factors, in addition to 'teething troubles' with the implementation of the e-procurement platform itself, may be responsible for observed short-falls in productivity (as evidenced by failure to meet three out of the four performance targets for the last financial year).

(e) On the positive side, it was felt that the management 'away day' was a positive initiative, allowing cross-functional information-sharing and a barometer of issues and morale across the organisation. Such initiatives may support greater clarity and coherence of change management messages, and greater managerial willingness to share information with stakeholders.

4. Recommendations for Phase Two

The following recommendations address key areas for carrying the changes forward into Phase Two, bearing in mind the lessons identified above.

4.1 Planning

It is recommended that a clear project management orientation be adopted for change management at Phase Two, to be co-ordinated (in a programme management structure) with the project management of the IT system implementation. Issues for consideration in change project planning include:

- **Roles and responsibilities**. Clear roles and accountabilities should be allocated for overall project management, and for communication with target stakeholder audiences (staff, suppliers, customers).

  Change champions should be co-opted within key user departments affected by Phase Two. A cross-functional Change Drivers taskforce might be used as a mechanism for ideas-sharing and knowledge-sharing between these champions, for example, so that a coherent message can be communicated to stakeholders.

  Clear reporting lines should be established, together with a structure of end-stage assessments, milestone reviews and feedback meetings to monitor and address productivity, schedule and cost variances as they occur.

- **Resource requirements**. In addition to the budget for the system itself (hardware/software development, consultancy, contingency funds and so on), the resource implications of change management should also be considered. These may include: staff time for training/consultation activities; the time of trainers and project managers; costs of external training provision and resources (where required); facilities for meetings and briefings; and advertising/communication costs (particularly to external customer audiences).

- **Timescales**. A project management orientation will aid in the setting of timescales for communication and implementation, establishing stages and milestones. Critical path analysis could provide an overall timeline for the complex, interdependent activities required. Timescales for implementation must be realistic, particularly since remedial action must now be taken to consult and inform key stakeholders in advance of the roll-out of Phase Two.

4.2 Staffing implications

A number of issues must be addressed, including:

- **Skills audit and training needs analysis** should be carried out in each user department, where this information does not currently exist.

- **Staff training and development** to develop required competencies, along with the confidence which will be essential in rebuilding staff morale and reducing resistance. In addition to skills in the use of the new technology, Phase Two will bring changes in the way customer services are delivered: a blended learning approach (eg programmed e-learning, briefing, job instruction and individual/group coaching, say) may be required to cover the range of technical, procedural and cultural requirements.

The Council's ethical employment policy suggests that skill gaps be met where possible through retraining of existing staff. This will also be helpful in retaining the knowledge base of long-serving staff, who currently fear that their experience will 'go to waste' as a result of the new system.

- **Performance management**, to ensure the effective consolidation and application of learning, to solve emerging performance problems and to plan ongoing development needs.

  Initial post-implementation performance may require close supervision, monitoring and/or coaching. Appropriate incentives and rewards (including acknowledgement and what Kotter calls 'the celebration of small wins') should be used to motivate employees through the learning curve.

4.3 Communication

Gaining stakeholder 'buy-in' is an essential part of any change programme, and many of the problems identified in Section 3 of this report can be attributed to inadequate stakeholder communication. The following measures are therefore strongly recommended.

- An immediate programme of **employee communication**, at all levels, should be drawn up, to allow staff concerns to be aired and addressed – and misconceptions and rumours countered. BDC's vision and long-term plans should be clearly articulated at a general staff meeting, by the senior management team and change project manager. The implications of the change for jobs and skills should also be set out, and questions taken. Key points should be published on the BDC intranet, for perusal and discussion.

  Follow-up departmental meetings should discuss the implications of the changes for individual departments. This may highlight individuals with particular concerns (or areas of particular resistance) which can be followed up in one-on-one discussions with mentors or line managers. Lack of individual direction and reassurance has been a problem so far, and must be addressed as a matter of urgency.

  Whatever the mechanisms of this process (which may also include intranet discussion boards, suggestion schemes and so on), its intention should clearly be to elicit – and demonstrate genuine consideration of – the concerns, questions, ideas and feedback of staff. The benefits of the changes to the Council and its stakeholders can then be more credibly promoted, as the basis for 'buy-in' and commitment.

- A similar programme of **external stakeholder communication** should be implemented for the supply network and customer/community, using appropriate media. It is particularly recommended (budgetary constraints permitting) that an information leaflet should be sent to all ratepayers, informing them in detail of the forthcoming changes to the delivery of Council services, and the benefits to them.

5. Conclusion

The implementation of the 'BDC online' system is intended to benefit the Council in assisting it to create efficiencies and improve performance, in line with the Gershon and Lyons recommendations. It is also designed to achieve best value for customers – and to increase the transparency of procurement processes, to the benefit of suppliers.

All stakeholders therefore have a potential interest in the successful implementation of the system. It is hoped that their acceptance and indeed commitment can therefore be secured, given appropriate change management leadership.

Solution 2

The CIPS Marking Scheme notes that the topic of this question is touched upon in Question 1, but that 'this question enables the candidate to consider in more detail the group dynamics and organisational implications of change for staff'. Make sure, however, that you don't cover the same ground twice: focus on outlining key theories and concepts and applying them to the problems faced by staff in the case study.

No format is specified, so you can use an essay-type style. Don't waste time on detailed report format. On the other hand, don't be tempted to write in 'note' or bullet-point form: this is still an 'extended written answer' question.

In part (a), you may use a range of theories of organisational behaviour and team dynamics in your answer, including: Belbin (team roles), Tuckman (team development), Maslow, Herzberg or Vroom (team motivation), Lewin or Kotter (change models). The Marking Scheme allocates 5 marks to highlighted problems; 5 marks to links to relevant theories and concepts; and 5 marks for recommendations (although these are not explicitly required by the question).

Organising our answer more broadly (for the purposes of your revision), we have provided 5 issues for discussion. If you were to do this, you would aim for 3 marks per issue: 1 for the problem, 1 for the relevant theory and 1 for a recommendation. Again, however, we've put more in our answer than you would be able to do in the time available, to cover all the bases for you.

In part (b), you may use a range of leadership style models, including: Hersey and Blanchard, Blake and Mouton or the Ashridge model: make sure that you outline the model concisely and correctly. There is no 'right' style, as long as you explain why you recommend a particular leadership style (or the ability to adapt styles) for the situation at BDC.

(a) Immediate staffing issues

Five major 'people management' issues can be identified in the situation at BDC.

Loss of motivation and morale

There is a clear loss of motivation and morale around the implementation of the online system, expressed in reluctance to change, expressed fears and the proliferation of dysfunctional rumours, spilling over into interpersonal conflict and reduced productivity.

Frederick Herzberg's two-factor theory of motivation can be used to explain this, as job security is identified in his model as a 'hygiene' or 'environmental' factor. If not adequately managed (or if subject to negative perception by employees), hygiene factors have the capacity to cause job dissatisfaction and loss of morale.

Herzberg argued that positive morale and motivation comes only from 'motivator factors' in the job itself. One approach for BDC managers to address the problem would therefore be to add motivator factors in the work – and in the change process: for example, by involving employees in the decisions that will affect them; by removing unnecessary supervision and controls as the learning curve is overcome; and by emphasising opportunities for training, development, new challenges/responsibilities and interest as a result of the change.

Resistance to change

Fear of change, and a resulting 'hesitancy' and 'reluctance' (lack of commitment) to change, is a key problem for BDC at this stage.

A number of models can be used to explain individual/group response to change. The coping cycle and transition curve, for example, show that people undergoing a period of transition go through highs and lows of emotional energy and competence development, as they respond to the 'loss' of the *status quo* and the threat of new challenges. Using this model, BDC managers may seek to support and facilitate staff members through the stages of grieving, towards acceptance.

Kurt Lewin's three-step model of change likewise illustrates how people become 'frozen' in patterns of behaviour, values and expectations, which become restraining forces resisting change. Using this model, BDC managers should seek to 'unfreeze' existing patterns by 'selling' and motivating the change, addressing sources of resistance, involving staff in change decisions, breaking up coalitions and so on; then implement change; and finally, 'refreeze' the new patterns, through coaching, positive reinforcement, new criteria for performance appraisal and so on.

Team roles, differences and conflict

BDC is facing loss of cohesion in its teams, due to a number of factors: uncertainty as to what roles members will fill in the new system ('how do I fit in the picture?'); increased team diversity and power shifts (eg through the recruitment of younger members); and the spilling over of fear and uncertainty into interpersonal hostility.

One model relevant to this issue is Belbin's model of team roles, which suggests the need for a mix and balance of process roles in a functioning team. This includes team maintenance roles (inspiring, conflict smoothing, encouraging) as well as task roles (co-ordination, ideas generation, follow-through).

At BDC, it may be that change has disrupted people's sense of which roles they occupy (as in Tom Bolton's case), or unbalanced/unfocused the team, so that maintenance roles are not being adequately fulfilled. Unit managers should therefore use team-building exercises (such as leaderless discussion groups and scenarios, or away days) to identify roles for which individual team members are naturally suited, and to encourage more balanced team dynamics.

Team re-formation

One particular team issue facing BDC is the re-organisation of work around the new technology, which may create 'new' team structures and membership. (There may also be the need for temporary project teams to plan and implement the changes.)

Part of the loss of morale in the current team may be explained by Tuckman and Jensen's model of team formation and development. The current team is going through the stages of 'mourning' and 'adjourning' as it prepares to disband and change: members are disengaging from the task and the group. Newly-formed teams will effectively 'start again' at the stages of 'forming' (getting to know each other), 'storming' (testing boundaries and roles with conflict) and 'norming' (establishing shared values and methods) prior to 'performing'.

Team leaders will need to be aware of these dynamics and facilitate their teams through the stages to re-establish effective functioning and performance. Team events and discussions may be used to accelerate forming; clear and open communication to facilitate constructive 'storming'; and modelling/expressing of values and expectations to facilitate 'norming', for example.

The need for cultural change

Changes in technology (and customer service delivery) have major implications for the values and culture of the organisation as a whole. BDC faces the challenge of creating a climate in which change is embraced as progress, and customer service becomes a core value – rather than a source of disruption.

One influential model of organisational culture is the 'cultural web' (Johnson and Scholes), which describes how 'the taken-for-granted assumptions, or paradigm, of an organisation' is bound up with its 'behavioural manifestations', including: stories, rituals and routines, symbols, power structures, organisational structures and control systems.

The challenge for BDC is to leverage key aspects, to bring all aspects into line. Alongside the implementation of new systems, managers need to model and express core values about progress; establish powerful symbols and stories to celebrate successful use of the technology; co-opt influential IT champions; create results/customer-focused (horizontal) team structures; and so on.

(b) Leading phase two changes

Leadership style models can generally be placed on a continuum from wholly task-centred, leader-driven, authoritarian styles (clusters of leadership behaviour) at one extreme, to wholly people-centred, subordinate-driven, democratic styles at the other. The essence of **contingency** approaches to style is that 'Using only one leadership style is a bit like a stopped clock: it will be right twice a day, but the rest of the time it will be inaccurate to varying degrees. Leaders need to interact with their team in different ways in different situations.' (Gillen).

Leading the Phase Two implementation in the procurement department at BDC is likely to place a variety of demands on the team and on the leader, which suggests a contingency approach.

Hersey and Blanchard's situational model, for example, argues that different leadership styles will be effective at different stages of employee 'readiness': different degrees of competence, willingness and confidence to complete the task successfully. The introduction of the new online system is likely to cast the team into a state of comparatively low readiness (in terms of both competence and morale). Such a team may require more direction to secure adequate task performance and clarity about what is required, in the steep part of the learning curve: this is likely to be BDC's priority, especially given a short period of time in which to have the system running effectively. Hersey and Blanchard recommend a 'telling' style, relatively high in task behaviour (guidance) and relatively low in relationship (supportive) behaviour: providing specific instructions and closely supervising performance.

However, the previous Procurement Manager was acknowledged as weak on 'people skills', and the resulting lack of empathy, communication and involvement has contributed to the morale problems of Phase One. A move to a more supportive, participative and/or consultative approach may help to reduce the sense of helplessness and insecurity in the change situation.

Hersey and Blanchard's model allows for such a shift in style over time. As the team's competence increases, it will move towards a moderate-high state of readiness: a 'participating' style will be effective in order to build morale and confidence. This consists of sharing ideas and facilitating the team in taking increased responsibility for decision-making.

Such a situation-appropriate shift will be gradual and intentional, avoiding the pitfall (identified in earlier style research) of inconsistency, which is highly stressful for team members.

More information will be required by individual team leaders, however. The appropriate leadership style may vary not only through the change and team development process, but according to the leadership context (Handy): the amount of power the leader has; the extent to which staff input to decisions is necessary or valuable; the amount of time available to introduce a particular phase of the change; the prevailing management culture at BDC; and other factors.

SECTION B

Solution 3

You are given flexibility in the format of your answer, but in the absence of specific requirements, an essay style is expected. (Don't waste time on report or e-mail format, for which you won't earn any marks...)

The challenge here is to balance the requirements of the question. You will need to demonstrate your awareness of specific employment and equal opportunities legislation – but the main thrust of your answer should be to show how such legislation has positively influenced management of the purchasing function. We have approached this by taking literally the instruction given in the question: 'Illustrate [the argument] with reference to specific legislation.'

Note that there are many ways you could interpret 'positive influence on the management of the purchasing function': from whose point of view? We have covered a number of angles, to show how a relatively unstructured question can be 'milked' for 25 marks.

The 'positive influence' of employment and equal opportunities legislation on the management of the purchasing function can be seen from a number of points of view: that of management (how has legislation made the task easier?); the organisation (how has it improved performance?); and the employee (how has it improved the quality of working life?).

Several arguments may be cited for the positive influence of such legislation, from each of these viewpoints.

(a) **It enhances the ability of the organisation to attract and retain quality, skilled staff.**

The various Acts (and supporting regulations) covering equality of employment opportunity, for example, ensure that organisations recruit both from a wider labour pool and from a more diverse labour pool: including women, racial and religious minorities, the disabled, and older/younger workers. (The most recent legislative changes include amendments to the Sex Discrimination and Race Relations Acts, and Employment Equality Regulations covering sexual orientation, religion and belief, and age.) Access to a wider labour pool helps to overcome local and sectoral skill shortages, and to 'refresh' the culture and skills of the organisation.

Meanwhile, equality of opportunity in areas such as pay (Equal Pay Act and amendments), training and promotion, and protection from discrimination and harassment at work, may contribute to the retention of skilled staff.

(b) **It enhances the appeal of the organisation and its brands to an increasingly diverse consumer base.**

One of the key arguments for diversity in employment is that it makes an organisation more representative of the general population and/or the market sectors to which it supplies goods and services. A diverse staff (as supported by equal opportunity legislation), is more likely to generate products and services of appeal to diverse markets, and to present itself positively within a diverse society. Meanwhile, the legislation specifically supports exceptions which can be objectively justified on business grounds (such as 'genuine occupational qualifications' in sex/race discrimination law).

(c) **It supports fairness and justice in the workplace.**

Equality of opportunity and diversity legislation ensures that access to opportunity is fairly available to all. Other employment legislation likewise supports the rights of individuals and provides basic protection against exploitation by employers. This includes the right: to engage (or not to engage) in trade union activity and lawful industrial action (Employment Relations Acts); to have individual grievances and disciplinary actions fairly investigated (Employment Act); to be protected from unfair dismissal and selection for redundancy (Employment Rights Act, TUPE Regulations); and so on.

Note that enhanced rights for employees are also intended to be beneficial for management and organisations: consultation with employee representatives on issues of concern, for example, can facilitate change management and foster innovation and problem-solving.

(d) **It provides minimum standards of protection for all parties in the workplace.**

This most obviously applies to Health and Safety Legislation (including ongoing regulations under the Health and Safety at Work Act, the banning of smoking in public places and so on). This in itself provides benefits not just for employees (in terms of reduced risk), but also for managers and employers: reduced costs of illness, accident, lost production and insurance; enhanced employee morale and retention etc.

It also provides legal protections for the rights and benefits of both sides of the employment relationship: legislation enables managers and employers to defend against claims of discrimination, unfair dismissal etc, as well as enabling employees to make such claims.

(e) **It enables individuals (including managers) to develop work/life balance.**

This is partly an equal opportunities issue, since it enables women to balance family responsibilities with work. However, it has also been a focus of UK government policy in recent years, to support family-friendly practices, maternal/paternal leave, and requests for flexible working (Employment Act 2002)

(f) **It creates transparency within organisations, in the interest of stakeholders and the general public.**

One example is the EU Procurement Directives, ensuring transparency of tendering criteria and processes in public sector purchasing: this is designed to ensure both fairness and efficiency in procurement practices.

Another example is legislation giving members of the public the right to access information held by public authorities (Freedom of Information Act) and protecting data subjects from abuse of data held about them (Data Protection Act).

(g) **It supports managerial decision-making, policy development and compliance.**

Stakeholder consultation, legislative provisions and related Codes of Practice give purchasing managers clear guidelines for good practice within the employment relationship.

Having made this case, however, it is important to acknowledge the counter-arguments of: the costs and administrative burden of compliance (increased bureaucracy, legal advice); the cost of increased worker rights and entitlements; loss of managerial prerogative (managers' right to manage), particularly in crisis situations; changes to managerial and organisation culture as a result of diversity; potential for 'over-sensitive' claims and conflicts; and so on. UK business has long favoured voluntary self-regulation over legislation, but as the recent introduction of age discrimination and sexual harassment provisions show, legislation is sometimes necessary to enforce good practice.

Solution 4

It is difficult to provide a 'suggested answer' to a question which gives such wide scope, given the brief to evaluate a named organisation of your choice. We have selected an organisation that provides an interesting mix of issues: note that the instruction to 'evaluate' means discuss positives/benefits and negatives/drawbacks. (According to the Marking Scheme, 4 marks were available for also recommending improvements, although this was not explicitly asked for.)

Describing the organisation's structure should allow you to define terms such as tall/flat, span of control, departmentation, federal/network structure and so on: 6 marks were available for use of theories/concepts. You could then evaluate aspects such as decision making, empowerment, control, communication, co-ordination and so on.

Describing culture should likewise allow you to discuss a range of aspects (using McKinsey's 7S or Johnson and Scholes' cultural web as a framework, if you wish), and issues including organisational learning, innovation, risk-aversion, mission and values and so on.

Bear in mind that our answer is only indicative – and, again, that our answer is longer than you might attempt, to try and cover more ground for your revision.

Structure, culture and values at JFL Corporation Ltd

Background

JFL Corporation is a group of companies, based in Australia, operating in the field of property development and investment. The flagship business is Custodian Investments, which acquires sites and constructs investment housing on behalf of clients looking to build wealth through residential real estate. Other companies in the group include a mortgage/finance brokerage (LoanInvest), a project management service (Custodian Care), an education/publishing company (JFL Media), and a charitable foundation (Toogoolawa).

The group was founded in 1989 by John Fitzgerald Lewis, a successful entrepreneur and philanthropist: as CEO, he still remains the focus of the group's brand, corporate identity, media activities and business development.

Structure

At the **group level**, JFL is a federation of businesses linked by the personal direction and control of John Lewis. Such a structure allows each business to specialise and establish a brand in its own field, while also 'pooling' expertise to make a menu of complementary services available to clients (adding customer value and extending the brand) and benefiting from identification with the strongly branded figure of John Lewis himself (as with Richard Branson at the Virgin group).

There is a potential drawback to such a structure, in the need to co-ordinate activities and messages across the federation. However, this is facilitated at JFL both by strong centralised leadership and by the co-ordinating hub of centralised Head Office functions (see below). Senior managers of all group companies are located at Head Office and meet regularly to maintain alignment and share ideas and contacts. All customer communications cross-sell the services of 'sister' companies, and the full 'suite' of services is promoted as a coherent offering.

Within its core business of property development and investment services, JFL expresses itself as two different 'layers' of structure.

(a) The **Head Office** structure centralises the operational functions involved in the core business, and also group-wide services, including HR and Procurement (under Business Services) and group Marketing.

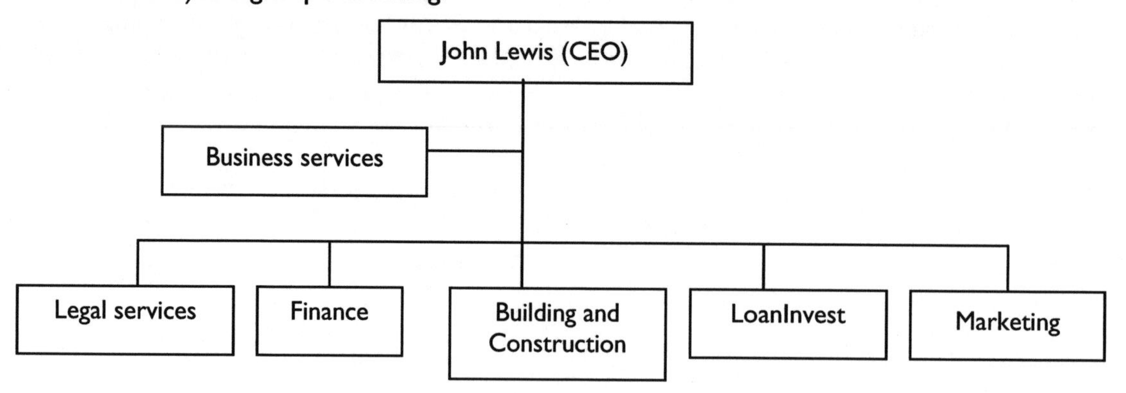

This focus on centralisation reinforces the brand leadership of John Lewis, and supports consistency (for example in marketing messages), compliance (through centralised legal counsel) and economies of scale (eg in procurement).

The head office staff is not large: the average span of control (the number of individuals reporting to a given manager) is three, and there are few layers, creating a relatively 'flat' organisation structure. This shortens channels of communication and decision-making, facilitating flexible response to client needs and swiftly-changing environmental factors in the building industry. It is noticeable, however, that John Lewis himself has a far wider span of control, and this may be of concern as the business continues to grow.

(b) The **Sales Structure**, in contrast, is devolved to the different regions in which JFL operates, allowing regional sales offices to interact directly with their local markets and client base. Each regional office has its own basic administrative services, financial adviser and sales consultants, reporting to a State Manager. All State Managers report directly to John Lewis.

This devolved structure allows units to be physically close to clients and to respond flexibly to local market variations. Units are small and flexible, able to vary their staffing and structure in response to local demands: some units, for example, have in-house telemarketing teams; others form mini-networks, as required, with a flexible group of local legal and financial advisers.

The challenge for such a devolved structure is to maintain brand consistency and co-ordination. Again, this is facilitated through the central leadership of John Lewis. It is also supported by continuous information-sharing (eg on product availability, via a centralised database and intranet), regular inter-personal communication (eg via teleconferencing and email) and six-monthly Sales Conferences.

There is potential for co-ordination to be developed further, by improving central data (mission statement, Operations Manual) and working towards fully integrated information systems.

Culture and values

Organisation culture has been defined as 'a pattern of beliefs and expectations shared by the organisation's members, and which produce norms which powerfully shape the behaviour of individuals and groups in the organisation' (Schwartz and Davies). Johnson and Scholes describe the 'cultural web' as an interlocking set of aspects: the paradigm (basic assumptions) of the organisation, and its behavioural manifestations in stories, symbols, rituals and routines, power structures, control systems and organisational structures.

The culture of JFL is powerfully shaped by, and identified with, the personality and values of its founder and leader, John Lewis. Lewis set out deliberately to create a values-based organisation, summarised in the corporate philosophy as:

'Purpose:	To create wealth
	To serve humanity
Integrity:	To accept responsibility
Truth:	To keep questioning.'

The concept and symbols of 'Custodianship' are key to the corporate identity: expressed in branding, slogans, artefacts (statues, logos) and so on. The philanthropic motive is built into all activities: percentage of proceeds going to charitable programmes, giving clients and staff opportunities for voluntary service and so on.

This strong cluster of guiding values is heavily communicated, widely shared and highly influential on staff (and client) behaviour: a classic example of what Deal and Kennedy identified as 'strong culture'. It has the beneficial effect claimed for strong culture of uniting the organisation, creating a strong coherent identity, and staff/client commitment and loyalty.

However, there is also a weakness in the culture's dependency on John Lewis. The organisation's guiding paradigm, and its behavioural manifestations, centre on Lewis's personal values, history and example. While this supports strong branding, it is arguably a limitation on the organisation's ability to learn and innovate beyond the areas of Lewis's interest and expertise. It also creates a major risk of cultural disintegration on the loss or retirement of Lewis.

Harrison developed a model (later popularised by Handy) of organisation structure/culture types. JFL corresponds closely to the 'Power culture' model, focused on the central control and direction of a dominant figure. This suits small, entrepreneurial organisations in complex and fast-changing environments – but becomes less suitable as the organisation grows: there is a greater need for formalisation, delegation and non-personal mechanisms of co-ordination in order to manage complexity. JFL Corporation may need to move towards a Task culture model (already foreshadowed in its elements of a networked, project-based approach), in which John Lewis de-personalises his leadership.

Solution 5

The requirement for your case 'to be submitted to the HR manager' is sufficient to indicate a professional business-context format for your answer: a short report, review document or briefing notes would be acceptable.

The question is a little hard to read, and you might almost miss the topic keyword: 'improve'. You are being asked to argue your case for the improvement of HR policy and practice within a procurement function.

The Answer Guidance suggests that the examiner had in mind a systematic review of existing HR processes in the procurement function of a named organisation, from recruitment to development, and recommendations for how these could be improved, with consideration of costs, resources and realistic time-frames.

We have offered a slightly more 'generic' answer, in order to raise a range of relevant points that you might have included in your (more specific) answer. In the time available (and in the context of your named organisation) you might have identified fewer issues, and gone into them in more depth, with more specific consideration of costs, time and physical resources required to action your recommended improvements.

MEMORANDUM

From: Your Name, Procurement Manager
To: The Human Resources Manager
Re: Recruitment, Retention and Development in the Procurement Function
Date: [Today's date]

1. Background

Following our recent discussion, I submit a review of current HR processes in the Procurement Department, together with my recommendations of opportunities for their improvement.

2. Recruitment

As you are aware, Human Resource and recruitment planning are crucial to the long-term effectiveness of the procurement function, in order to ensure the availability of the right quantity of the right skills at the right price and at the right time to meet ongoing operational requirements. As with any other resource, the flow of people into and through the function (and the organisation as a whole) must be planned and controlled so as to meet requirements efficiently and effectively. This is a particular issue in procurement at this time, as the role of the function becomes more strategically integrated, and as skill requirements change to embrace e-procurement, supply chain management and other developing areas.

Having reviewed current recruitment practices, the following areas may require attention.

(a) Competencies and skills required by the Procurement team are inadequately defined: **job/person specifications** are outdated and inflexible, and do not reflect the requirements of the role. It is recommended that they be revised and updated (and thereafter reviewed on a regular basis): a competence framework or role definition approach may be considered. This would help to increase the accuracy and cost efficiency of recruitment and selection decisions: it would also enable Procurement roles and criteria to be defined more directly in terms of business objectives and target outcomes.

(b) **Vacancies** are currently filled on an *ad hoc* basis, without reference to a tactical recruitment or HR plan. This can lead to costly over-staffing or inefficient staff deployment, where the requirements of a position no longer exist. It is recommended that a system of vacancy review be implemented (with input from the outgoing member of staff and team leader), resulting in more intentional job requisitions to trigger recruitment or role re-definition.

(c) The **recruitment process** as a whole is carried out on an *ad hoc* basis by section heads. This not only leads to inefficiencies, but carries compliance risk if practices are potentially unfair to candidates. It is recommended that the process be standardised and documented (as policy, codes of practice and procedures) for consistency and efficiency.

(d) **Recruitment advertising** attracts unnecessary costs, and is inefficient in pre-selecting target audiences, because of lack of targeting of media and messages. It is recommended that the HR function consult with department managers to compile agreed definitions of target audiences, and a shortlist of approved media. (There may be additional economies of scale in consolidating media purchases for this purpose.)

(e) **Selection processes** are currently confined to interviewing, for which unit heads are inadequately trained. This materially reduces the effectiveness of selection and incurs risk/costs of having to manage or terminate unsuitable recruits – and of high turnover of recruits (with re-recruitment and loss-of-productivity costs). It is recommended that a wider menu of selection techniques be considered, including selection testing, careful reference checking and perhaps group assessment for senior procurement positions. As a matter of urgency, briefing, coaching and monitoring of selection interviewers should be put in place.

3. Retention

As you are aware, *People Management* has recently highlighted local and sectoral skill shortages in the UK, creating a heightened need to retain quality staff. The specific nature of our procurement requirements places a high premium on the experience and knowledge of our staff, and the contacts and relationships they have built up within the supply network. Retention of valued staff is therefore a matter of risk management, and preserving the human capital of the business.

(a) **Financial rewards** are currently in line with market rates and perceived to be fair (owing to systematic job evaluation). However, greater attention could be given to higher-order motivating factors (as defined by Frederick Herzberg), to increase job satisfaction and loyalty. This could be accomplished at little financial cost, by encouraging (and if necessary, coaching) managers and team leaders to adapt their leadership styles: soliciting feedback, ideas and suggestions from staff members; giving recognition and praise for achievement; coaching and facilitating on-the-job learning and challenge. This would have further benefits in harnessing staff commitment, ideas and initiative for value-added procurement.

(b) More attention should be given to the systematic and ongoing **induction** of new staff, both to accelerate the learning curve to full contribution *and* to avoid 'induction crisis' whereby new recruits leave because of poor adjustment. Standardised initial induction procedures should be supplemented by support for individual learning needs analysis, beginning an ongoing cycle of appraisal and development planning.

4. Staff development

Again, you will be aware that the modern approach to HR development is described as 'the process of achieving outstanding organisational performance through empowering people to achieve and give of their best'. Systematic, needs-targeted training and development activities benefit the organisation in a number of ways: enhancing job performance, commitment and contribution; enhancing the value of the organisation's human assets; supporting greater workforce versatility and flexibility, for more efficient labour utilisation; reducing the need for supervision, freeing management for more value-adding roles; enhancing our employer brand to attract and retain quality staff; and providing a foundation for continuous learning and improvement, the key to our competitive advantage.

Specific opportunities for improvement have been identified in the following areas.

(a) All training activity should be based on **learning needs analysis** (rather than self-nomination for available courses). A systematic training plan should be drawn up for procurement units, based on the latest developments in procurement and in our specific supply markets: learning objectives should be directly integrated with business performance indicators, to ensure measurable performance benefits from application of learning. This also helps to leverage the existing training budget: not more training, but better targeted training for added value.

(b) Individual **performance appraisal** should be clearly based on learning and improvement needs (rather than merely performance/reward review). Appraisers may need to be briefed (and possibly retrained) to take a more forward-looking, developmental approach (such as performance management). Appraisal policies/procedures may need to be adapted accordingly, and this will also require time and resources to educate staff, if the new approach is to be understood and accepted. It is further recommended that 360-degree appraisal be introduced for procurement staff: while costly to administer and develop in the first instance, it offers long-term business benefits through linking development more closely to unit and business objectives (including performance feedback from suppliers and outsource partners, for example).

(c) Further developmental benefits could be obtained, without significant added cost, by co-opting section heads and team leaders to **support** coaching, mentoring, self-managed learning and continued professional development (for CIPS-qualified staff). The aim is to create a 'learning climate' in which continuous learning and improvement is undertaken to improve customer value and distinctive competencies, supporting competitive advantage.

5. Conclusion

These are just some of the key areas in which HR practices could be improved in the procurement function. Some require significant input, time and resources from the HR function and line managers: for example, the redefinition of roles or the redesign of the appraisal system. Other measures could be implemented, as suggested, with comparatively little cost other than managerial time and input: these represent investments with a potentially short payback period. In either case, procurement staff are regarded as a key resource which could be better leveraged for significant added value and performance gains.

Solution 6

The format of your answer is specified here as 'briefing notes': you should use a recognisable format, suitable for use as the basis of a briefing, presentation or discussion with senior managers. The CIPS Answer Guidance notes that: 'Although this does not have to be as fluent as a report or essay, it should be comprehensive... Bullet points or headings can be used, but need to be expanded on, to ensure that the examiner understands your points fully.'

Again, the question is not altogether easy to interpret, because of the word: 'demonstrate'. This is not just a question about how procurement adds value to a business, but about how it demonstrates its value within an organisation in a way that is meaningful and convincing to senior organisational stakeholders and decision-makers.

This distinction is not easy to capture, but it helps if you consider your audience: perhaps managers from marketing, finance, IT, HR, operations and administration. Try and cite the benefits of an efficient procurement function for each of these internal stakeholders (and perhaps also for the value linkages between them): this ensures that you are 'selling' benefits that are relevant to your target audience – and showing an awareness of how securing support and buy-in works in organisations. You might also try to anticipate your response to questions, arguments or criticisms which might be raised at the briefing.

Note that for the purposes of coverage, we have again provided a 'generic' answer: your briefing should be set in the context of a named organisation, so ensure that you refer to some specific examples to illustrate your points).

Delivering procurement value

1. Context

Business objectives

[Summary of key strategic/competitive objectives of the specific business you have chosen]

The role of an effective procurement function is to support the achievement of business objectives by securing customer value and competitive advantage.

Relationships

An effective, modern procurement function aims to develop towards:

- Strategic alignment, systems integration and synergistic collaborative relationships with internal stakeholders and customers
- Mutually beneficial relationships and value-adding systems integration within a carefully selected supply network
- Mutually beneficial relationships with external stakeholders, in line with corporate sustainability and social responsibility values.

2. Benefits of an efficient, modern recruitment function

- Supporting **efficiency** objectives

  Example: reducing non-value-adding (waste) activities within internal processes and throughout the supply chain (eg by reducing unnecessary handling, inventory, waiting and processing; leveraging technology applications to streamline business and procurement processes; rationalising the supply base and purchasing organisation (eg through centralisation)

- Supporting **cost reduction and control**

  Example: contributing supply market expertise to make/do or buy and capital investment decisions; applying value analysis and engineering; developing sourcing strategies, systems and negotiating expertise to reduce materials, transaction and inventory costs

- Supporting **innovation** objectives

  Example: reducing cycle times, building market-responsive (agile) supply chains, facilitating early supplier involvement in specification, managing inventory to enable response to unpredictable demand

- Supporting corporate **quality objectives**

  Example: early supplier involvement, supplier selection and development, collaborative quality management and continuous improvement initiatives, ongoing supplier relationship management and motivation, consultation on materials specification, benchmarking

- Supporting **marketing** objectives

  Example: enhancing product quality, supporting customisation and responsiveness to customer requirements (developing supply network agility), supporting e-commerce applications (with e-marketing potential) – plus knock-on benefits for customer loyalty and sales revenue

- Supporting **operational planning** through improved service/delivery performance and better capacity utilisation

  Example: via integrated materials/resource planning, supplier relationship and contract management, expediting: 'the right materials in the right quantity at the right place at the right time at the right price'

- Improving the quality and integration of **information** available for management reporting, operational/administrative planning and control, supplier and customer relationship management, and wider stakeholder communication (as a boundary-spanning function)

  Example: via automation, systems integration, business process focus, information-gathering from network contacts and systems, collaboration in IT procurement

- Supporting **CSR, ethical and environmental** objectives

  Example: ethical monitoring and development of suppliers; management of reverse logistics and compliance (eg re recycling); 'green' materials specifications; professional ethics in procurement/trading; sustainable procurement; fair/transparent tendering processes

- Supporting the development of **distinctive (core) competencies** for competitive advantage

  Example: developing supply market expertise, developing preferential/exclusive supply/distribution relationships for key commodities (creating barriers to competitor entry). (NB: recognition that strategic competition is now between supply chains, not just firms.)

3. Questions and challenges

- **'P and S is too systems/process driven'**

  With increased collaboration and strategic integration: shift focus towards business process, aiming for total value system gains. Procurement performance measures increasingly matched to business KPIs.

- **'Separate "silo" mentality'**

  Increased strategic/systems integration, cross-functional project management orientation, CLAN-style structural collaboration with user departments, line manager recognition of procurement value: break down functional (and organisational) barriers

- **'Focus on cost reduction/control at the expense of quality/delivery'**

  Some genuine trade-off between CQT (Cost, quality, time) objectives. BUT (a) collaboration and internal service/quality agreements with line stakeholders; (b) shift of focus to added value (not just cost reduction); and (c) sometimes positive synergy, not negative (eg reducing defects/inspections also reduces costs).

- **'Lack of flexibility for marketing/operational requirements'** (eg lack of buffer stock for lean inventory v rush orders; standardisation for economies of scale v customisation)

  Flexibility can be built into strategies/processes – with greater strategic alignment, communication/co-operation, feedback etc.

- **How exactly does procurement contribute to bottom line profit?**

  Eg through reduction and control of total costs; support for quality and customer service (increased sales revenue); management of supply network relationships to maximise share of value gains.

Subject Index